THE KEY
TO THE
ASIAN MIRACLE

THE KEY
TO THE
ASIAN MIRACLE

Making Shared Growth Credible

Jose Edgardo Campos
Hilton L. Root

The Brookings Institution
Washington, D.C.

About Brookings

The Brookings Institution is a private nonprofit organization devoted to research, education, and publication on important issues of domestic and foreign policy. Its principal purpose is to bring knowledge to bear on current and emerging policy problems. The Institution was founded on December 8, 1927, to merge the activities of the Institute for Government Research, founded in 1916, the Institute of Economics, founded in 1922, and the Robert Brookings Graduate School of Economics, founded in 1924.

The Institution maintains a position of neutrality on issues of public policy. Interpretations or conclusions in Brookings publications should be understood to be solely those of the authors.

Copyright © 1996

THE BROOKINGS INSTITUTION

1775 Massachusetts Avenue, N.W., Washington, D.C. 20036

Library of Congress Cataloging-in-Publication data
Campos, José Edgardo
     The key to the Asian miracle: making shared growth
credible / Jose Edgardo Campos, Hilton Root.
          p.   cm.
Includes bibliographical references and index.
ISBN 0-8157-1360-6 (cloth : alk. paper)
     1. East Asia—Economic policy—Decision making.   2. Asia,
Southeastern—Economic policy—Decision making.   3. East Asia—
Economic conditions.   4. Asia, Southeastern—Economic conditions.
I. Root, Hilton L.   II. Title.
HC460.5.C26   1996
338.95—dc20
                                                              96-428
                                                                CIP

9 8 7 6 5 4 3 2 1

The paper used in this publication meets the minimum
requirements of the American National Standard for
Information Sciences—Permanence of Paper for Printed Library
Materials, ANSI Z39.48-1984

Typeset in Palatino

Composition by Monotype Composition Company, Inc.
Baltimore, Maryland

Printed by R. R. Donnelley and Sons, Co.
Harrisonburg, Virginia

To our parents:
Marita, Peping, Rosaline, Stanley

Preface

THREE explorers, Ken, Doug, and Rebecca, reached a planet that resembled earth only to find themselves trapped in a broad crater, twenty feet deep and six feet wide. The soil in the crater was rich enough for small wild plants bearing edible berries to grow during the spring and summer. But the cold months had just arrived, and although the explorers had enough clothing to keep warm, they had saved barely enough berries to last a few days. Thus death by starvation awaited them if they failed to climb out.

To solve their problem, Rebecca, an applied neoclassical economist, suggested that Ken stand on Doug's shoulders and she on Ken's. Doug was the tallest of the three, and Rebecca was the shortest. Their combined height would enable Rebecca to reach the shoulder of the crater and climb out.

Ken, an economic theorist, argued that the plan was flawed. He asked what would prevent Rebecca from simply abandoning the remaining two once she got out. Hence, he opposed the solution. Doug, an institutional economist, concurred with Ken but then countered with a variant. He agreed to be the bottom person and thus the last one out. But then he required both Rebecca and Ken to surrender their clothes to him. That way, he argued, they would have to pull him out, because without clothes they could not survive more than a few hours in the cold. Rebecca and Ken recognized the validity of Doug's argument. Without clothes the two explorers who went first had an incentive to pull the third one out. The solution to the problem required an agreement or bargain among all three parties.

The task of climbing out of poverty and underdevelopment is similar to the dilemma of the three explorers. The appropriate policies are well known, but mechanisms must be designed to gain the support of those parties whose cooperation is necessary for the policies to work. Rebecca's solution for getting the three out of the crater was ideal. But making it work required a mechanism—surrendering the clothes to the bottom person—that guaranteed all three a reasonable chance to escape. Each individual had to believe that the solution could be successfully implemented, which implied that each one would share in the benefits.

Like Rebecca's solution, the successful East Asian rulers designed special institutions to address a general feature of most development policies—the benefits generally accrue in later periods while the costs are incurred earlier. The nonsimultaneity of benefits and costs makes the potential gains from a new policy or policy change largely promissory. East Asia's high performers developed institutions to make policies credible to the polity. Their leaders understood that policies would not work unless individuals and groups believed that the policies could be sustained and that they would enjoy some of the benefits.

In the hope of providing concrete lessons for the rest of the developing world, this book explores the rationality of the structure and performance of characteristic institutions found among the high-performing East Asian economies. These institutions helped solve coordination problems that would have otherwise disrupted the implementation of growth promoting policies. Although these institutions might not be directly transferable to other countries, understanding how and why they work can guide others as they address the same problems and develop similar mechanisms to solve them.

This analysis of East Asia's high-performing economies is the product of a dialogue on institutions and economic change that began more than ten years ago when we first published an article on peasant politics in *Rationality and Society*. We would like to acknowledge the Mellon-sponsored seminar, Historical Data and Theories of Rational Choice, which we convened as professors at the University of Pennsylvania. Many of the scholars whose work influenced the direction of this study and the revival of political economy more generally passed through the seminar: Alice Amsden, Robert Bates, Stephan Haggard, Leo Hurwicz, Margaret Levi, Kenneth Shepsle, Robert Wade, and Barry Weingast, to name a few.

Over the years exposure to the ideas of leading scholars of public choice and political economy has allowed us to enrich our understanding of the role of institutions in sustaining economic growth. Oliver Williamson's work on contracting problems, Douglas North's theory of the predatory state, Mancur Olson's logic of collective action, and James Coleman's applications of rational choice theory to analyses of the microfoundations of macro social behavior helped us draw connections among the historical, political, and economic phenomena that have characterized the experience of East Asia's high performers.

This book has benefited from the support of numerous individuals and institutions. Arup Banerji, Gary Becker, Bob Boase, Bidhya Bowora-thana, Oh-Hyun Chang, Siow Yue Chia, Ajay Chhibber, Scott Chris-tensen, James Coleman, Larry Diamond, Ramon Ereneta, Jose Gari-baldi, Avner Grief, Bob Hahn, Farrukh Iqbal, Estelle James, Erik Jensen, Phil Keefer, Kathleen Lauder, Araceli de Leon, Brian Levy, Christopher MacCormac, Lawrence MacDonald, Kenji Matsuyama, Bill McCleary, Bruce Bueno de Mesquita, Thomas Metzger, Ramon Meyers, James D. Morrow, Shoji Nishimoto, Minlin Pei, Jon Quah, Henry Rowen, Dick Sabot, Karti Sandilya, Masaki Shiratori, Hadi Soesastro, Arnold Sowa, David Steedman, Joseph Tan, Prijono Tjiptoherijanto, George Tsebelis, Bruce Tolentino, Barry Weingast, Ronald Wintrobe, and Gavin Wright gave time and effort to this project. John Page and Nancy Birdsall provided the impetus to begin work on the manuscript. Hadi Esfahani and Don Lien provided assistance and advice on some technical issues. Rebecca Hife and Jay Gonzalez collected and collated the data and prepared the tables and figures, while Polly Means, Joyce Cerwin, and Daniele Evans provided valuable logistical support throughout the project. Hannah Moore edited our original technical manuscript.

At Brookings Nancy Davidson and Bob Faherty made the final phase of placing the manuscript with the Brookings Institution a delight. Theresa Walker edited the final manuscript, Alan Johnson verified it, and Julia Petrarkis prepared the index.

Research and writing inevitably demand sacrifices from loved ones. To Ed Campos's children—Mylin, Mychal, Chit, and Eric—and to our spouses—Rica and Nancy—many thanks.

We gratefully acknowledge the support of the Policy Research De-partment of the World Bank and the Overseas Economic Cooperation Fund of Japan, the Hoover Institution National Fellows Program, the Earhart Foundation, the Institute for Policy Reform (IPR), and the Agency for International Development (AID) Cooperative Agreement no. PDC-0095-A-00-1126-00 for their support.

Views expressed in this book are ours alone and not necessarily those of the Brookings Institution or any of the above-mentioned supporting institutions.

Jose Edgardo Campos
Hilton L. Root

Contents

Figures

One

East Asia's Road to High Growth

A MONG THE few countries that have overcome underdevelopment, eight East Asian economies—Japan, the Republic of Korea, Taiwan, Hong Kong, Singapore, Thailand, Malaysia, and Indonesia—stand out because of their unusually rapid growth. Their dramatic success is frequently attributed to the adoption of appropriate economic policies. But their policies would not have worked unless each country's populace believed that the policies could be sustained and by implication that some of the benefits would be available to all.

Introduction

Regime leaders in the high-performing Asian economies (HPAEs) understood that the challenge of economic growth required the coordination of expectations of different sectors of the population. They responded to this challenge by collaborating on the design of institutions that spread the benefits of growth-enhancing policies widely, made the reversibility of the policies costly, and consequently, gave individuals and firms confidence that they would share the growth dividend.[1] This assurance, in turn, mitigated opposition to the policies and created a sociopolitical environment conducive to sustaining economic growth. Divisive methods for growth that would have favored one group over another would have undermined the cooperation needed to politically sustain rational economic policies.

The solution, embodied in the principle of *shared growth*, incorporated

1. The question of whether the policies that the East Asian high performers adopted were conducive to stimulating economic growth is not discussed here. See the World Bank (1993a); Oshima (1993); Wade (1990); Amsden (1989); Hughes (1988).

1

two themes. First, the business community was courted to build a dynamic industrial base. Second, the wider population was given opportunities to reap long-term, lasting benefits from the resulting economic expansion. The benefits to the regime of enforcing this bargain have been considerable.

Sharing gave the less fortunate a stake in the economy, thereby discouraging disruptive activities and diminishing the risk of regime failure. It also enabled the regimes to concentrate on promoting rational economic policies by reducing the need to constantly contend with issues of redistribution: when everyone starts out under less disparate conditions, there will be less concern with choosing policies strictly for their distributional consequences. Growth-promoting policies were made more durable over the long term and more credible to the business community. Shared growth resulted in broad support for the regimes. The regimes, then, could avoid standard interest group pressures to provide special privileges and thus could mitigate capture by narrow interests.[2] A virtuous circle was ultimately affirmed: investment increased, spurring growth and higher real incomes, which reinforced the credibility of the regime, further stimulating investment and economic expansion. If the commitment to sharing faltered, the regimes, in need of support, might have had to respond to the demands of interest groups for advantages, or worse, insurgent movements might have gained support. A vicious circle of decay could have materialized instead.

A geopolitical environment characterized by the high risk of insurrection explains the urgency of finding a cooperative solution to economic growth in East Asia. With Maoist China, and to some extent the former Soviet Union at its back door, rulers in the high-performing Asian economies could not afford to ignore the dangers of unrest leading to insurgency among the less fortunate members of the population. The Korean War, the war in Vietnam, and the widespread appeal of militant

2. For example, broad-based social support allowed the governments of the Republic of Korea and Japan to ignore radical labor union demands without the risk of regime failure. By appealing to a broad constituency, the goal of growth enhancement dominated the selection of economic policies. As long as the benefits of that growth were perceived to be widely distributed, the government could resist buying the support of organized labor with privileges that could restrain overall productivity. Concessions to radical segments of labor could be resisted by offering the benefits of growth to the working population (broadly defined).

socialism highlighted the importance of finding a solution to the region's economic backwardness, from which everyone could benefit.

The ability of a regime to stay in power depends in large part on its legitimacy. If it is to remain in power, a regime must be able to justify why it should rule and not others. Leaders in East Asia's high performers chose to do so by promoting economic growth and having the proceeds of growth filter down to the general population. Broadly similar historical circumstances led each regime to pursue shared growth as a strategy for legitimating its rule. The threat of communist takeover, made credible by a successful peasant-based communist revolution in China, induced regime leaders to pay close attention to the needs of the rural poor and the working class. The leaders recognized the importance to their survival of improving the living standards of the less well-off. But they also recognized that they could not do so without expanding the economy since their countries were very poor. They had to stimulate investment and thus address the concerns of the business community.

In Japan, Korea, Thailand, Singapore, Malaysia, and to a lesser extent Hong Kong, committees, often referred to as deliberation councils, are composed of representatives from private industry, the government, academia, and in some cases, the press, consumer groups, and labor. They have facilitated communication between the private and public sectors by offering inputs into the policy process while at the same time providing ownership of policy outcomes.

The councils have been effective partly because of the export orientation promoted by national leaders, particularly in the northern tier countries. This relatively objective measure of economic performance allowed governments to establish contests with rules known to all. To gain access to cheap credit, firms had to increase their market share in the world economy, a yardstick that could not be politically manipulated. Firms could increase their rating only by increasing exports, allowing the private sector to obtain credit on objective criteria rather than by corruption or favoritism.

By giving bargaining power to constituent groups in exchange for information needed to formulate rational economic policies, East Asian rulers reduced the inefficiency of limited communication about policy performance. That failing typically hinders development and ensures the survival of ineffective policies in much of the developing world. Being allowed to share in the growth surplus induced private business to reveal private information. The arrangement adhered because of the government's implicit commitment to growth. Business sector leaders recognized that regime leadership needed growth to acquire stability. Consequently, the risk of confiscation or ex post expropriation of private sector assets was reduced. Firms could keep the economic profits while leadership gained the political benefits of rapid growth.

Leaders must convince the general population that it will benefit from market-oriented policies. Failure to do so can have several undesirable consequences. Professionals and intellectuals may emigrate, depriving the country of their knowledge and skills. Others, despairing of finding a job in the formal economy, may focus on the less efficient informal sector or, worse, engage in criminal or subversive activities. In these ways, the economy loses valuable human resources. Growth falters, undermining the basis for leadership's legitimacy.

In East Asia's high performers, many wealth-sharing mechanisms were designed to incorporate the wider population into the growth process. Some countries undertook radical land reform, supported by institutions that fostered the prosperity of small- and medium-sized farms. The methods contrasted sharply with the practice in much of the developing world, where governments subsidized urban well-being at the expense of agriculture. In the cities, small- and medium-sized enterprises were also given special support. Seed money from the government funded worker cooperatives. These and other mechanisms gave urban workers opportunities for upward mobility and a stake in the continued success of the economy.

When regime legitimacy depends on keeping promises to share growth, leadership must avoid the logic of allocating public responsibilities to building a political clientele. This requires as a first step signaling commitment to long-term growth in order to persuade public servants that they can reap long-term rewards for continuous good performance. Thus public servants will also be encouraged to use their specialized information and skills to serve the national interest. Once leadership effectively demonstrates its commitment to growth, appropriate incentives increase the likelihood that policies will be implemented effectively. For instance, instead of allocating the spoils of office as booty in exchange for political support, a typical outcome in many developing countries, East Asian leaders built rewards for good performance into the system. They introduced merit-based recruitment and promotion grounded in tough civil service examinations, well-defined career paths for civil servants, and 'one-way street' retirement schemes, all of which contributed to making a bureaucratic career attractive. Although they established the rules, leaders gave the economic bureaucracy the responsibility and authority to enforce them. And to make officials accountable, the government introduced relatively low-cost means of monitoring their performance. In most of the high performers, the same mechanisms designed to win the consent and cooperation of business groups, the deliberation councils, were used to strike a delicate balance between agency independence and bureaucratic accountability. In the less-advanced high performers, Indonesia and Thailand in particular, constitutionally imposed budgetary controls were introduced to give some protection from political pressure to government agencies responsible for formulating and managing macroeconomic policies. These same measures made agencies accountable for maintaining macroeconomic policies.

Because East Asia was a principal battleground of the cold war, economic failure could potentially jeopardize national sovereignty. Because economic failure could threaten all of the established national interests, leadership was willing to give economic bureaucrats room to maneuver, relatively free of political interference. In contrast, rulers in many other developing countries did not worry very much that economic failure would result in conquest or peasant revolution. As a result, creating a politically neutral sphere for economic bureaucrats to operate was a less urgent goal. By the same token, internal sanctions within the bureaucracy have rarely been imposed for failed policies or policymakers. Such sanctions have not been imposed because the bureaucracy was created to consolidate the rulers' political following. Economic success has mattered less than paying off a coalition to justify some strongman's seizure of power.

A circle of negative policy outcomes results when regimes build their legitimacy by appealing to narrow groups. Such regimes then become the target of other narrow, but excluded, coalitions. This undermines stability. Uncertain about the future, insiders try to gain as much as they can from government office while it is their turn. In this environment, rulers have neither an incentive nor the time to develop a rule-based bureaucracy. Instead, bureaucratic appointments are disbursed to develop a political clientele enriched by corruption and favoritism.

When leaders offer access to fees and bribes as a reward to followers, they do not develop institutions to oversee performance. The benefits gained by regime insiders impose costs on everyone else. To escape, business flees to the informal sector, depriving the regime of a fiscal base, which further increases regime dependence on narrow support from privileged insiders. This inevitably leads to political crises.

The experience of Asia's high performers suggests that by establishing a different pattern of political incentives, government can generate a virtuous circle of policy outcomes. There the various occupational and social subsets of the population benefited by playing according to rules set by the regime. Business stayed largely within the formal sector, greater investment and trade occurred, increasing the resource pool for the state to reward its officials. The key was inducing citizens and government alike to accept smaller returns in the short run in exchange for larger ones over the long term. Once this equilibrium was established, both the population and the officials of the government could identify the state with interests that transcended the individual.

The history of economic development has been one of increasing social inequality during periods of high growth. The East Asian exception to that pattern is rich in implications for both economic history and economic policy. The rise of industrial Asia suggests that the key to uninterrupted growth rests on the regime's ability to reward groups that sacrifice today for greater future gains. This willingness reflects the expectations of constituents concerning the regime's political and institutional capability and durability. Making the promise of shared growth credible allowed East Asian leaders to alter the risk-reward calculations that motivate economic behavior, so that the compensation for taking smaller benefits in the present was greater gains over time.

Yet, when linking the role of East Asian political institutions to the promotion of economic development, many observers link East Asian success to the concentration of power in the central state and tout the regime's authoritarian character as a virtue. Obviously something is amiss in an analysis of the role of political institutions that fails to distinguish the political logic of East Asian success from the economic failures of autocracies throughout the world.[3]

The role of a "strong authoritarian state" in facilitating this bargain needs to be reconsidered. Hard dictatorial regimes in which policymakers act independently of constituent oversight have rarely generated

3. This view is often reinforced by the standard indexes of political freedom, which correlate the political institutions of the high-performing states in East Asia with known kleptocracies in which rulers act as roving bandits plundering their own populations.

sustained economic growth. An inherent contradiction exists among authoritarianism, investment, and growth. Being above the law, authoritarian regimes can use their power to expropriate the wealth of citizens. This prompts investors to take their investments and expertise elsewhere or to limit investments to short-term projects. Economic growth has been durable in East Asia, as contrasted with autocratic regimes throughout the developing world, precisely because leadership established institutions, rules, and procedures that limited government discretion over economic policy.

One element not captured in the standard analysis is that a change in leadership in most autocracies can reverse the course of development. Typically, the fall of an autocrat results in the radical redistribution of property rights and even the execution of regime leaders and followers. Hence, private sector actors perceive the institutional or policy environment in autocratic regimes to be unpredictable. By contrast, the threat of confiscation and radical redistribution of wealth has not deterred investment in East Asia. The policy environment in the East Asian high performers, even those such as Thailand experiencing frequent coups and political instability, are viewed by multinational business leaders as relatively stable and predictable compared with those in other developing areas. This means we must look to political indicators other than regime type to predict investment in both human and physical capital.[4]

Rapid Growth, Reduced Poverty, and Improved Income Distribution

As already mentioned, rapid growth is generally associated with high levels of inequality, at least in its early phase. First, to generate the high savings rate that is a prerequisite of rapid growth, income, it is assumed, must be concentrated in the hands of the relatively rich, whose marginal propensity to save is relatively high.[5] Second, Simon Kuznets has suggested that as the labor force shifts from low-productivity sectors to high-productivity sectors, aggregate inequality initially increases substantially, decreasing only later.[6] Contrary to this conven-

4. See Barro (1991); Alesina and Perotti (1992); Levine and Renelt (1992); Brunetti and Weder (1993).

5. More savings means more funds available for domestic investment.

6. Kuznets (1955).

tional wisdom, in East Asia rapid economic growth has been associated with relatively *low* and *declining* levels of income inequality.[7]

Analysis of the high-performing Asian economies has focused on their rapid growth over the past twenty-five years.[8]. Isolated studies on the distributive qualities of growth in a few of these countries exist, but not of the growth-equity nexus for the group as a whole.[9] The indicators show that the Asian high performers have been unusually successful in distributing the benefits of growth widely.

Growth and Income Distribution: Cross-Country Evidence

The Gini coefficient is the most widely known measure of income distribution. The lower the coefficient, the lower the income inequality. Though its interpretation is straightforward, because of differences in income definitions and survey methodologies across countries, it may not be well suited for cross-country comparisons. Nevertheless, it suggests the relative standings of countries, especially if differences among countries are large. Based on the index, each of the HPAEs has done reasonably well: their indexes are lower than the average across all countries for which the index is available (table 1-1). Japan, Taiwan, and Indonesia have outperformed every other country.

When the Gini coefficients and the average per capita growth rate are used jointly as performance measures, the HPAEs (minus Japan) dominate other middle-income countries for which the index is available (1970–90).[10] A scatter plot is depicted in figure 1-1. By construction, countries closer to the southeast corner of the diagram perform better. The HPAEs fall within a small area of the southeast corner: their average GDP per capita growth rates are significantly above the average (indicated by the vertical line) for the sample; their Gini coefficients are below the average for the sample (indicated by the horizontal line).

The HPAEs' performance improved over time. In the 1970s Malaysia, Thailand, and Indonesia saw their per capita GDP growth rates in-

7. Improved equity is not unique to East Asia. What is unique is the combination of rapid growth with modest (and, in a few high performers, dramatic) improvements in equity and reduction in absolute poverty.

8. See, for instance, Balassa (1988); Lau and Kim (1992); Hughes (1988).

9. See Fei, Ranis, and Kuo (1979) for an economic analysis of Taiwan's approach to growth with distribution and Adelman and Robinson (1978) for Korea.

10. Japan is excluded since it was at the tail end of its rapid growth phase during the late 1960s and early 1970s.

TABLE 1-1. *Gini Index, Period Averages, 1965–90*[a]

Region	1965–70	1971–80	1981–90
High-performing Asian economies (HPAEs)			
Korea	0.34	0.38	0.33
Taiwan	0.32	0.36	0.30
Singapore	0.50	0.45	0.41
Indonesia	0.40	0.41	0.30
Thailand[b]	0.44	0.38	0.46
Malaysia	0.50	0.48	0.42
Hong Kong	0.49	0.42	0.39
Japan	.31 (1965)	.28 (1979)	. . .
Average	0.41	0.39	0.36
Others			
India	0.40	0.41	. . .
Pakistan	0.37	. . .	. . .
Nepal	. . .	0.53	. . .
Bangladesh	. . .	0.37	. . .
Sri Lanka	0.41	0.35	. . .
Philippines	0.48	0.45	0.39
Argentina	0.43	0.41	0.43
Brazil	0.57	0.60	0.60
Colombia	0.56	0.58	0.51
Chile	0.50	0.53	0.53
Mexico	0.58	0.52	0.53
Peru	0.59	0.57	0.40
Venezuela	0.52	0.53	0.44
Gabon	0.65	. . .	. . .
Sudan	0.44	. . .	. . .
Zambia	0.49	0.53	. . .
Kenya	. . .	0.59	. . .
Average	0.50	0.50	0.48

Sources: World Bank, Economic and Social database, Washington; for Latin America, Psacharopoulos and others (1992).

a. Average across all available index values for the period.

b. Oshima's (1993) estimates indicate that the average for 1981–90 may be around .43, and the average for 1965–70, .43.

crease. Except for Thailand, distribution improved for all the HPAEs over the three decades. Thailand's distribution improved from the 1960s to the 1970s, declining in the 1980s.[11] Average per capita GDP

11. The government has become concerned about the deterioration in income distribution during the 1980s and has made it a priority issue for the 1990s. The Seventh Five-Year Plan (1993–98) actively addresses distribution and poverty issues.

FIGURE 1-1. *Gini Coefficient and GDP per Capita Growth Rate,*
Annual Average, 1970–90

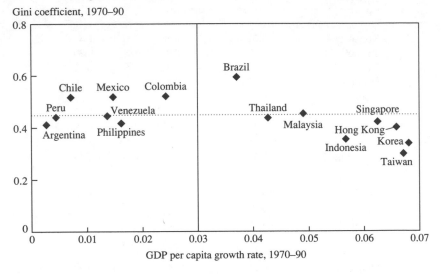

Source: World Bank, East Asia Miracle database, 1994.

growth rates declined slightly for all countries during the 1980s, partly
because of the oil crisis.

Another measure of income distribution is the ratio of the income
share of the top income quintile to the income share of the bottom income quintile. Because it gives a better idea of the dispersion of the distribution, it is sometimes preferred to the Gini coefficient. Table 1-2
compares East Asian and other developing countries in economic
growth during the period 1960–85 and the ratio of the shares of the
top to bottom income quintiles for selected years. On average, the East
Asian countries have grown faster and had a far more equal distribution
of income than other developing countries. When the East Asian countries are divided into a fast-growing and a slow-growing group, the
distribution of income is, again, substantially more equal in the fast-
growing group.

The HPAEs' unusually strong association between rapid growth and
equity is also supported by a ranking of forty countries in terms of the
ratio and per capita real GDP growth. The ranking is based on the
Borda method, which allows for ranking under multiple criteria.[12] A

12. See Sen (1973, 1981) for an explanation of the merits of the Borda method.

TABLE 1-2. *Ratio of Top to Bottom Quintile and per Capita Growth Rate, Selected Years, 1976–88*

Country	GNP per capita growth (per year) 1965–90	Year	Income share of bottom 20 percent of households	Income share of highest 20 percent of households	Ratio of top 20 percent to bottom 20 percent
East Asia, fast growers					
Korea	7.1	1976	5.7	45.3	8.0
Hong Kong	6.2	1980	5.4	47.0	8.7
Japan	4.1	1969	7.9	41.0	5.2
		1979	8.7	37.5	4.3
Taiwan	6.7	1976	9.5	35.0	3.7
		1985	8.4	37.6	4.5
Singapore	6.5	1982–83	5.1	48.9	9.6
Unweighted average	6.1		6.7	43.3	7.0
East Asia, slow growers					
Indonesia	4.5	1976	6.6	49.4	7.4
		1987[a]	8.8	41.3	4.7
Philippines	1.3	1970–71	3.7	53.9	14.6
		1985[b]	5.5	48.0	8.7
Thailand	4.4	1987	6.0	51.0	8.5
Malaysia	4.0	1973	3.5	56.1	16.0
		1987[c]	4.6	51.2	11.1
Unweighted average	3.6		6.1	47.5	8.3
Latin America					
Brazil	3.3	1972	2.0	66.6	33.3
		1983	2.4	62.6	26.0
Mexico	2.8	1984	4.1	55.9	13.6
Peru	−0.2	1972	1.9	61.0	32.1
		1985–86[b]	4.4	51.9	11.8
Venezuela	−1.0	1970	3.0	54.0	18.0
		1987[c]	4.7	50.6	10.8
Costa Rica	1.4	1971	3.3	54.8	16.6
		1986[a]	3.3	54.5	16.5
Colombia	2.3	1988[c]	4.0	53.0	13.3
Unweighted average	1.4		3.6	55.1	16.4
Africa					
Kenya	1.9	1987	3.0	62.0	20.6
Ghana	−1.4	1988–89[a]	7.1	43.7	6.2
Ivory Coast	0.5	1986–87[a]	5.0	52.7	10.5
Botswana		1985–86	2.5	59.0	20.0
Unweighted average	0.3		4.3	54.0	15.0

TABLE 1-2. *(continued)*

Country	GNP per capita growth (per year) 1965–90	Year	Income share of bottom 20 percent of households	Income share of highest 20 percent of households	Ratio of top 20 percent to bottom 20 percent
South Asia					
Pakistan	2.5	1984–85[b]	7.8	45.6	5.9
		1964–65	6.7	48.9	7.2
		1975–76	7.0	49.4	7.0
India	1.9	1983[a]	8.1	41.4	5.1
Unweighted average	2.2		8.0	43.5	5.5

Sources: World Bank, *World Development Report* (Washington, various years); World Bank (1993b); Taiwan, *Statistical Yearbook, 1987.*
a. Per capita expenditure.
b. Household expenditure.
c. Per capita income. Unweighted average uses latest year available.

country is assigned a score for each criterion; the score corresponds to the country's rank according to the criterion. The scores for each criterion are then added up to obtain each country's Borda score or index. Countries are then ranked in inverse order to their Borda scores, so that lower scores signify higher ranks.[13]

The results of this ranking are shown in table 1-3. The ratios for each of the countries are not taken from the same year, nor do they represent averages over the period. Data are insufficient and do not permit such calculations. For each period the latest available data in each period were used. Except for Malaysia, all of the HPAEs ranked in the top ten, and five top the list. Malaysia is included in the top fifteen; note however its significant rise in rank from the first period to the second. The implication is clear. For the HPAEs, rapid growth and low inequality are shared virtues.

The Welfare of Low-Income Households: Growth and Poverty

Though economic growth need not necessarily reduce poverty, the experience of the HPAEs suggests that growth can alleviate poverty. An important feature of the HPAEs' performance is their relative success in

13. For a similar approach, see Reidel (1988).

TABLE 1-3. *Rank Based on Income Distribution and Growth in Real per Capita GDP*

Country	1965–75		1976–90		1965–90	
	Borda index	Rank	Borda index	Rank	Borda index	Rank
HPAEs						
Korea	16	3	20	5	16	3
Taiwan	13	2	6	1	7	1
Singapore	16	3	29	9	24	6
Indonesia	27	6	11	2	17	4
Thailand	40	11	28	8	30	7
Malaysia	45	16	34	12	41	15
Hong Kong	30	7	20	5	26	6
Japan	9	1	13	3	9	2
Other Asia						
Bangladesh	45	16	34	12	38	12
India	51	20	28	8	38	12
Nepal	54	23	54	22	55	21
Pakistan	41	12	22	6	32	9
Sri Lanka	43	14	35	13	39	13
Philippines	50	19	49	19	45	17
Latin America						
Argentina	52	21	64	25	63	25
Bolivia	46	17	70	28	63	25
Brazil	45	16	59	23	50	19
Colombia	58	25	51	20	52	20
Chile	71	29	48	18	55	21
Mexico	45	16	66	27	60	22
Peru	65	28	64	25	69	27
Venezuela	42	13	61	24	55	21
Sub-Saharan Africa						
Botswana	42	13	43	17	40	14
Côte d'Ivoire	27	6	72	29	62	24
Gabon	37	8	53	21	43	16
Ghana	77	30	49	19	68	26
Kenya	44	15	65	26	61	23
Malawi	16	3	40	16	31	8
Mauritania	60	26	35	13	49	18
Mauritius	53	22	33	11	34	10
Sudan	64	27	59	23	63	25
Zambia	55	24	80	30	80	28

TABLE 1-3. *(continued)*

Country	1965–75		1976–90		1965–90	
	Borda index	Rank	Borda index	Rank	Borda index	Rank
OECD						
Australia	37	8	37	15	36	11
Austria	16	3	19	4	17	4
Belgium	21	4	36	14	23	5
France	37	8	29	9	31	8
Italy	38	9	24	7	24	6
Spain	24	5	37	15	24	6
Switzerland	49	18	33	11	39	13
UK	39	10	30	10	31	8

Sources: Data for top 20 percent to bottom 20 percent come from World Bank, Social Indicators of Development and the Economic and Social database, Washington. Data for per capita GDP are also from World Bank, Economic and Social database.

raising the incomes of the poor. The per capita income of the poorest fifth of the population is higher in East Asian economies with low inequality than in other economies with the same level of average income but higher inequality. Table 1-4 pairs East Asian countries with other developing countries with very similar levels of average per capita income but much higher levels of income inequality. In the non-HPAEs, the poor have considerably lower absolute incomes. For example, in 1983, although the per capita income of Brazil slightly exceeded average incomes in Malaysia in 1987, the bottom 20 percent of households (when ranked by income) received 4.6 percent of total income in Malaysia but only 2.4 percent of total income in Brazil. Consequently, the per capita incomes of the bottom quintile of households in Brazil were only 52 percent of the per capita incomes of the poorest fifth of households in Malaysia.

Among countries for which poverty data are available, the HPAE contingent once again outperforms all but one of the other countries.[14]

14. Mauritius has performed very well on both the growth and poverty dimensions, matching the performance of the lower echelon of the HPAEs. The country is more like a city-state comparable to Hong Kong and Singapore. But the existence of a sizable agricultural base differentiates it from the latter. Although sugar is a major product, the island nation has not gone the route of many other agriculturally rich countries but appears to have successfully moved resources into an export-oriented manufacturing sector. In 1976 sugar production was 23.3 percent of GDP and production at its export-processing zone was a mere .1 percent. By 1988 sugar's share was down to 12.8 percent and the EPZ share was up to 14.4 percent.

TABLE 1-4. *Absolute Income Share of Lowest Quintile, Selected Years and Countries, 1976–87*

Country and year	GNP per capita (millions of U.S. dollars)	Population (millions)	Total GNP	Income share of bottom 20 percent of households	Absolute income share of bottom 20 percent of households	Per capita income of bottom 20 percent of households[a]
Indonesia, 1976	240	135.2	32,448	6.6	2,141	79
Kenya, 1976	240	13.8	3,312	2.6	86	31
Malaysia, 1987	1,810	16.5	29,865	4.6	1,374	416
Brazil, 1983	1,880	129.7	243,836	2.4	5,852	226
Malaysia, 1987	1,810	16.5	29,865	4.6	1,374	416
Costa Rica, 1986	1,480	2.6	3,848	3.3	127	254
Korea, 1976	670	36	24,120	5.7	1,375	191
Botswana, 1986	840	1.1	924	2.5	23	115
Indonesia, 1987	450	171.4	77,130	8.8	6,787	251
Philippines, 1985	580	54.7	31,726	5.5	1,745	160

Source: World Bank, *World Development Report* (Washington, various years).

a. Absolute income share of bottom 20 percent divided by 20 percent of the total population.

Table 1-5 indicates the relative country performance in terms of an integrated poverty index (IPI). The IPI takes account of four measures: the percentage of the rural population below the poverty line, life expectancy at birth, the annual growth rate of per capita GNP, and the income-gap ratio. The income-gap ratio refers to the difference between the highest GNP per capita from among all the countries and the individual country GNP per capita divided by the former.[15] The IPI takes values between zero and one; the lower it is, the better off the country. Based on the index, the four East Asian successful economies clearly dominate most if not all the other countries.

The Sectoral and Household Distribution of Income

As per capita income of a country rises, the share of manufacturing in its GDP rises and the share of agriculture falls. This has generally

15. See Jazairy, Alamgir, and Panuccio (1992).

TABLE 1-5. *Integrated Poverty Index, 1988*

Region	Poverty index
HPAEs	
Korea	0.05
Indonesia	0.40
Thailand	0.28
Malaysia	0.26
Average	0.25
Other Asia	
Bangladesh	0.84
India	0.48
Nepal	0.59
Pakistan	0.27
Sri Lanka	0.42
Philippines	0.58
Average	0.53
Latin America	
Argentina	0.13
Bolivia	0.80
Brazil	0.45
Colombia	0.37
Chile	0.43
Mexico	0.37
Peru	0.60
Venezuela	0.22
Average	0.42
Sub-Saharan Africa	
Botswana	0.43
Côte d'Ivoire	0.24
Gabon	0.17
Ghana	0.52
Kenya	0.52
Malawi	0.83
Mauritania	0.77
Mauritius	0.09
Sudan	0.81
Zambia	0.79
Average	0.52

Source: Jazairy and others (1992).

Note: IPI measures the well-being of a country rather than that of an individual or household (based on Sen 1973's composite poverty index). The closer the IPI value to one, the worse the poverty.

FIGURE 1-2. *Ratio of the Real Value of Manufacturing Output to the Real Value of Agricultural Output*

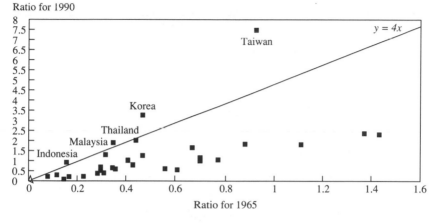

Source: World Bank, *World Development Report* (Washington, 1992), table 3.

been true for most low- and middle-income countries. Among countries that have had a sizable agricultural sector, the HPAE component has experienced the most rapid structural change. Over a twenty-five-year period (1965-90), the share of manufacturing has far outpaced the share of agriculture in Korea, Taiwan, Indonesia, Thailand, and Malaysia. As shown in figure 1-2 the ratio of manufacturing output to agricultural output rose at least fourfold in each of the HPAEs, sevenfold and eightfold in Korea and Taiwan, respectively. The ratio increased much less dramatically in other low- and middle-income countries.

When the impetus for growth switches to the manufacturing sector, productivity tends to increase. Again, the Kuznets hypothesis predicts that in the earlier stages of this transition, income inequality will tend to increase. The experience of the HPAEs for which agriculture has been an important sector suggests otherwise. Figure 1-3 plots the change in the Gini index against an index of the magnitude of the transition from agriculture-based to manufacturing-based growth between 1965 and 1990 for eleven countries.[16] Korea, Taiwan, Indonesia, and Malaysia

16. To construct the index, we used the following formula: let ISC denote the index, MFG manufacturing, and AG agriculture. Then

$$ISC = \frac{(\% \text{ of GDP in MFG, 1990})}{(\% \text{ of GDP in AG, 1990})} \div \frac{(\% \text{ of GDP in MFG, 1965})}{(\% \text{ of GDP in AG, 1965})},$$

FIGURE 1-3. *Gini Index and Structural Change*

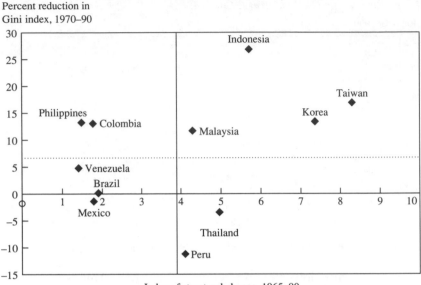

Percent reduction in
Gini index, 1970–90

Index of structural change, 1965–90

Source: World Bank, East Asia Miracle database, 1994; World Bank, *World Development Report*.

have had improved income distributions associated with the shift. That Indonesia and Malaysia are relative late starters suggests even more strongly that inequality need not necessarily increase during the early stages of the transition. They entered the initial stage of the transition fairly recently   in the late 1970s or early 1980s.

Wages, Employment, and Income Distribution

With rapid growth, both real wages and employment have increased dramatically in the high performers. Nowhere else in the developing world, or for that matter in the industrialized countries, has such performance been observed.

---

which is equivalent to

$$\text{ISC} = \frac{\text{(value of MFG output in 1990)}}{\text{(value of AG output in 1990)}} \times \frac{\text{(value of AG output in 1965)}}{\text{(value of MFG output in 1965)}}.$$

The larger the ISC, the greater the degree of structural change. The data on the percent of GDP are taken from World Bank, *World Development Report* (1992, pp. 222–23, table 3).

As indicated in table 1-6 Korea and Taiwan have experienced the most rapid growth in real wages averaging 8.15 percent and 7.7 percent a year, respectively, over two decades. In the other high performers, the rate of increase was slower but still significantly greater than in most other developing countries. Between 1980 and 1990 real wages increased 88 percent in Thailand, 77 percent in Indonesia, 63 percent in Singapore, 54 percent in Hong Kong, and 37 percent in Malaysia.[17] In contrast, real wages in several developing countries for which data are available actually declined. Moreover limited evidence suggests that urban unemployment rates have been steadily declining in most of the high performers, while they have been increasing in other developing countries (table 1-7). The magnitude of the unemployment rates provides an even starker contrast. For most of the 1980s, the rates have been in the low single digits in the high performers but in the double digits in the others. In sum, much of the labor force in East Asia's high performers has experienced rising real wages and with it a rising standard of living, while the labor force in others has suffered.

Infrastructure: Sectoral Distribution

Compared with most other low- and middle-income countries, the HPAEs have allocated more public investment and government effort to developing economic and social infrastructure in the rural areas. This has been important in promoting shared growth.

The contribution of rural infrastructure to growth is well known. Roads, bridges, ports, and airports link product and input markets in the domestic economy, and these domestic markets with the international economy. Water and electricity are crucial for industrial development. Telecommunications reduce transactions costs and thus facilitate the movement of goods and services. Improved health and sanitation facilities help develop human capital.

Less widely appreciated is that rural infrastructure also contributes to improved income distribution. The availability of electricity and telecommunications throughout a greater number of regions creates economic opportunities outside the metropolitan areas. Roads, ports, and telecommunications improve access to markets—both labor and

17. From 1980 to 1990, the average real earnings in manufacturing increased at an annual rate of 5.9 percent in Indonesia. This figure translates into an aggregate increase of 77.3 percent over the decade. The figures for the other countries are determined similarly.

TABLE 1-6. *Percentage Increase in Real Earnings per Employee in Manufacturing, 1970–90*
(1980 = 100)

Region	1970–80	1980–90	1970–90
HPAEs			
Korea	10.00	6.30	8.15
Taiwan[a]	7.80	7.60	7.70
Singapore	3.00	5.00	4.00
Indonesia	5.00	5.90	5.45
Thailand	1.00	6.50	3.75
Malaysia	2.00	3.20	2.60
Hong Kong	6.40	4.40	5.40
Japan	3.10	2.00	2.55
Average	4.79	5.11	4.95
Other Asia			
Bangladesh	−3.00	0.90	−1.05
India	0.40	3.00	1.70
Pakistan	3.40	6.10	4.75
Philippines	−3.70	6.40	1.35
Average	−0.73	4.10	1.69
Latin America			
Argentina	−2.10	−0.80	−1.45
Bolivia	0.00	−4.80	−2.40
Brazil	4.00	7.10	5.55
Colombia	−0.20	1.70	0.75
Chile	8.10	−1.00	3.55
Mexico	1.20	−3.90	−1.35
Venezuela	3.80	−2.90	0.45
Average	2.11	−0.66	0.73
Sub-Saharan Africa			
Botswana	2.60	−5.70	−1.55
Kenya	−3.40	0.10	−1.65
Mauritius	1.80	−0.60	0.60
Zambia	−3.20	6.50	1.65
Average	−0.55	0.08	−0.24

Source: World Bank, *World Development Report; Taiwan National Statistics Data Set.*
a. Index for Taiwan (1981 = 100).

TABLE 1-7. *Urban Unemployment Rates, Selected Years, 1980–90*

Region and country	1980	1985	1988	1990
East Asia				
Korea	7.5	4.9	3.0	2.9
Singapore	3.0	6.5	3.3	2.0
Taiwan	1.2	2.9	1.7	1.7
Hong Kong	3.8	3.2	1.4	1.3
Thailand	5.7	5.2	5.0	
Malaysia	5.0	6.2		
Indonesia		7.3		
Latin America				
Colombia	9.7	14.1	11.2	10.3
Chile		17.3	13.3	11.9
Ecuador	5.7	10.4		
Brazil	6.2	5.3	3.8	4.3
Costa Rica	6.0	6.7	6.3	5.4
Mexico	4.5	4.4	3.5	2.9
South Asia				
Philippines	8.2	11.8	12.6	12.6
Sri Lanka	14.2	19.4		
India	7.8	6.8	7.1	
Africa				
Kenya		14.1		
Nigeria		9.8	10.0	
Egypt			10.4	
Turkey		15.0	13.2	13.4

Sources: Fields (1992); World Bank (1993a); Turnham (1993).

product—for people and firms in these areas. Improved water, sanitation, and health facilities increase the employability of workers, raising their incomes. For these reasons, the development of rural infrastructure by the HPAEs has indirectly led to an improvement in income distribution.[18]

Most data on the allocation of public investment between rural and

18. The willingness of the HPAEs to invest in rural infrastructure can be directly related to the political basis of regime support. Unlike other regimes, for example, in Africa, the HPAE leadership does not depend on control over the capital city, and the regimes are not easily taken hostage by urban crowds or the discontent of labor unions.

TABLE 1-8. *Rural-Urban Disparity in Access to Service, 1987–90*

Region	Water[a]	Sanitation[a]
HPAEs		
Korea	54	101
Indonesia	168	113
Thailand	126	102
Other Asia	64.6	38.6
Latin America	58	46.5
Sub-Saharan Africa	43	30

Source: UNDP (1992).
a. One hundred means parity between rural and urban access. Figures >100 indicate that the rural average is higher than the urban average access to the service.

urban regions are too crude to provide accurate comparisons among countries. Nevertheless the available data suggest that the allocation has been less biased in the HPAEs. Among the HPAEs, Indonesia, Thailand, and Malaysia have large rural sectors, while Taiwan and Korea have modest rural sectors. For comparisons with other low- and middle-income countries, data on sanitation and water facilities are available for Indonesia, Thailand, and Korea. Table 1-8 gives a rough picture of the relative emphasis of public investment in sanitation and water facilities in these countries and other developing countries. As indicated there is a better balance between rural and urban sectors in the three HPAEs.[19]

The data on rural electrification also suggest that the HPAEs with nontrivial rural sectors have done better on average at providing electricity to the rural areas. "Less than 10 percent of electricity investment in the third world goes to the rural areas and in many countries that investment is less than 5 percent. . . . In Taiwan province of China, universal electrification has been achieved."[20] Since the early 1980s, electricity has also been universally available in Korea. As shown in table 1-9 Malaysia and Thailand have made great strides in rural electrification. Indonesia has not done as well. But the relative disparity between the urban and rural sectors is smaller compared with the

19. In Malaysia, as of 1987, 95 percent of the urban population and 68.6 percent of the rural population had access to safe water. See World Bank (1990a).
20. United Nations (1990, p. 132).

TABLE 1-9. *Percentage of Rural and Urban Population Served by Electricity, Selected Years*

Region and country	1983 population	Per capita GNP (U.S.$)	Urban	Rural	Year
HPAEs					
Indonesia	155.7	560	39	10	1984
Malaysia	14.9	1,860	85	55	1983
Thailand	49.2	820	78	40	1984
Other Asia					
Bangladesh	95.5	130	20	2	1981
India	733.2	260	<25	15	1981
Pakistan	89.7	390	<25	15	1981
Philippines	52.1	760	40	22	1980
Sri Lanka	15.5	330	35	8	1982
China	1019.1	300	>80	60	1982
Latin America					
Argentina	29.6	2,070	>95	5	1981
Bolivia	6	510	72	9	1981
Brazil	129.7	1,880	>95	19	1981
Chile	11.7	1,870	>95	42	1981
Colombia	27.5	1,430	84	13	1978
Costa Rica	2.4	1,020	>95	>95	1982
Ecuador	8.2	1,420	79	13	1980
Mexico	75	2,240		<20	1982
East and West Africa					
Burkina Faso	6.5	180	<15	1	1980
Ethiopia	40.9	120	10	<1	1982
Guinea	5.8	300	21	4	1982
Côte d'Ivoire	9.5	710	93	20	1981
Liberia	2.1	480	86	4	1982
Kenya	18.9	340	<10	<2	1982
Senegal	6.2	440	83	12	1982

Source: Munasinghe (1987, pp. 6–7).

disparity in countries with approximately the same per capita incomes (in 1983)—Liberia and Bolivia—or the same population (in 1983), Brazil.

On an aggregate level, it does seem that the HPAEs have invested more resources in physical infrastructure (though this should be interpreted with caution since the data are limited). Using population per

TABLE 1-10. *Population per Phone, Percentage Change from 1975 to 1985*

Region and country	1975	1985	Percent change
HPAEs			
Korea	25	5	80
Taiwan	4	2	50
Singapore	7	3	57.14
Indonesia	435	205	52.87
Thailand	133	68	48.87
Malaysia	42	12	71.43
Hong Kong	4	2	50
Other Asia			
India	352	203	42.33
Nepal	1167	903	22.62
Pakistan	296	186	37.16
Sri Lanka	187	135	27.81
Philippines	96	67	30.21
Latin America			
Argentina	13	10	23.08
Brazil	35	12	65.71
Colombia	19	14	26.31
Chile	24	16	33.33
Mexico	21	11	47.62
Peru	41	32	21.95
Venezuela	19	12	36.84
Sub-Saharan Africa			
Botswana	108	56	48.15
Ghana	164	179	−9.14
Kenya	113	72	36.28
Malawi	262	175	33.21
Mauritius	35	16	54.28
Sudan	281	281	0
Zambia	91	90	1.1

Sources: World Bank, Economic and Social database; International Telecommunication Union (1993).

phone as an index and 1975 as a base year of comparison, five of the HPAEs have significantly increased telephone service compared with other countries with roughly the same population per phone in 1975. For instance, as shown in table 1-10 over the ten-year period Malaysia reduced the population-phone density by over 70 percent while the comparable countries   Brazil, Peru, and Mauritius   achieved smaller gains. The quality of infrastructure may also be better in the HPAEs. Table 1-11 lists the percentage of roads that are paved in a relatively large selection of low- and middle-income countries. This percentage is distinctively higher in the HPAEs, indicating that roads there are on average of better quality.

Growth and Private Investment

A discussion of the growth-equity nexus in East Asia would not be complete without an overview of trends in private investment. Economic growth is stimulated by investment, a huge chunk of which comes in the form of plant, equipment, and technology. Without these productive assets, nothing else follows. With little investment there will be very little growth, and with little growth there will not be much to share.

In the high performers, investment as a proportion of GDP has been high compared with other developing countries. The difference stems mainly from private investment: the private sector has actively provided investments in the high performers. Though public investment as a proportion of GDP in the high performers has been roughly similar to the proportion in other developing countries, the proportion of private investment has been substantially higher, with the differential averaging about 8 percent of GDP a year.[21] Table 1-12 compares private investment in the high performers with that in some other developing countries. The difference is striking.

Private investment has been critical to the shared growth process in East Asia. Rapid growth is unlikely to be achieved without the full support of the private sector.

The data on growth, income distribution, and poverty indicate that the HPAEs have successfully promoted shared growth. The data on infrastructure and real wages support the same conclusion. Infrastructure development has been more evenly distributed between the rural and urban sectors in the high-performing Asian economies. As for wages, between 1970 and 1990 real wages have on average increased faster in the HPAEs than in other developing countries: 5.8 percent growth in the HPAEs compared with 1.7 percent in other parts of Asia, .73 percent in Latin America, and -.24 percent in Sub-Saharan Africa.

21. World Bank (1993a, p. 44, figure 1-7).

TABLE 1-11. *Percentage of Roads Paved, Selected Years*

Region and country	1971	1982	1986
HPAEs			
Hong Kong	100.0	100.0	100.0
Indonesia	25.0	58.7	62.3
Japan	18.0	50.7	60.2
Korea	14.2	35.7	54.2
Malaysia	85.0	82.0	80.0
Singapore	n.a.	88.0	95.8
Taiwan	n.a.	n.a.	91.0
Thailand	67.0	34.9	39.6
Average	51.5	64.3	72.9
Other Asia			
India	34.9	47.3	48.0
Pakistan	57.0	64.0	43.0
Philippines	n.a.	12.5	13.1
Sri Lanka	69.6	34.5	n.a.
Average	53.8	39.6	34.7
Latin America			
Argentina	13.0	10.0	23.1
Brazil	4.5	7.0	7.2
Chile	11.6	10.2	12.4
Colombia	11.3	9.0	8.0
Mexico	60.0	46.0	33.3
Peru	9.9	n.a.	n.a.
Venezuela	43.1	37.6	33.1
Average	21.9	20.0	19.5
Sub-Saharan Africa			
Côte d'Ivoire	0.0	7.9	n.a.
Gabon	2.9	6.8	n.a.
Kenya	7.0	11.9	n.a.
Malawi	8.0	18.0	n.a.
Mauritania	0.1	21.5	n.a.
Mauritius	0.9	92.0	92.0
Zambia	9.4	15.0	16.6
Average	4.0	24.7	54.3

Source: International Road Federation, *World Road Statistics* (Washington, various years).

n.a. Not available.

TABLE 1-12. *Share of Private Investment in Gross Domestic Product,*
1970–90
Percent

Private Investment/GDP	1970–75	1975–80	1980–85	1985–90
HPAEs				
Japan	25.58	21.89	20.69	22.70
Hong Kong	20.37	22.49	23.26	21.86
Indonesia	10.50	11.05	12.47	11.93
Republic of Korea	18.45	23.10	23.84	26.30
Malaysia	16.00	16.25	17.98	16.44
Singapore	28.26	26.04	31.38	26.26
Taiwan	14.13	14.02	12.97	11.81
Thailand	17.34	17.82	19.35	24.68
Average	18.83	19.08	20.24	20.25
Other countries				
Argentina	13.10	15.48	16.22	12.73
Bolivia	10.77	9.25	4.89	4.15
Chile	5.57	9.20	9.78	10.08
Côte d'Ivoire	13.64	13.97	8.92	4.75
Ghana	6.71	4.03	3.87	4.23
India	9.12	10.10	10.12	11.92
Mexico	12.60	12.88	12.63	13.42
Nigeria	9.53	8.28	4.68	3.95
Philippines	11.36	18.64	18.69	15.53
Sri Lanka	10.84	14.02	22.54	17.24
Turkey	12.18	11.78	8.45	11.20
Venezuela	15.74	18.51	9.32	9.89
Average	10.93	12.18	10.84	9.92

Source: World Bank, East Asia Miracle database, 1994.

Thus growth was more evenly distributed in the HPAEs than in other
regions undergoing industrialization. Even in Korea, where a small
number of firms dominate the economy, the Gini coefficients reveal
relatively egalitarian distribution of income. In Indonesia, despite explicit and extensive bureaucratic clientilism, growth has accelerated
and rural poverty has declined over twenty years. In short, not only
is East Asia a great success story for economic growth, but it is a rare
example of the benefits of early industrialization being more equitably
shared.

Two

Leadership and the Principle of Shared Growth

ALL THE leaders of what later became the high-performing Asian economies faced serious questions about their political legitimacy when they came to power, and most faced a formidable communist threat.[1] All responded by creating a broad social base that identified its economic interests with the success of the regime. This consensus for growth cut across social groups and strata, creating winning coalitions that supported these leaders and legitimized their rule.[2] This chapter examines how political and military threats prompted East Asian leaders to adopt shared economic growth as their legitimizing principle, and the ways that this choice contributed to political stability and economic growth.

Except in Japan, the leaders who set in motion the economic take-off in the HPAEs faced a political and military threat, either external or internal. South Korea was threatened by invasion from the North; Taiwan, from the mainland; and Thailand, from North Vietnam and Cambodia.[3] Thailand, Indonesia, Malaysia, and Singapore faced formidable internal communist insurgencies; Malaysia and Singapore had to contend with additional difficulties imposed by ethnic diversity.[4] Furthermore, because leaders in Korea, Taiwan, and Indonesia seized

1. Legitimacy refers to the right to rule. There are undoubtedly other definitions. See, for instance, Parker (1983), who summarizes different conceptions of the legitimacy of state that have been proposed by various political philosophers, for example, Hobbes.

2. On the failure of authoritarian regimes to generate legitimizing structures see O'Donnell (1973), who argues that regime failure occurs because mediations between capital-owning classes and labor are inadequate to respond to deteriorating economic conditions.

3. Cumings (1987); Wade (1990); Gold (1986); Wyatt (1982).

4. Schlossstein (1991); Turnbull (1977).

power by force, these military regimes needed to establish legitimacy in the eyes of the international community in order to obtain much-needed financial support from the industrialized countries. Even in Japan, where there was no immediate armed threat, leaders needed to reestablish legitimacy after the debacle of World War II.[5] For all these reasons, leaders in the HPAEs could not take their legitimacy for granted: they had to demonstrate that they should lead and not others.

They established legitimacy through *shared growth*.[6] This strategy had two primary components. First, it fostered growth by encouraging the business community, particularly big business, to make long-term investments and upgrade organization and management. Without the cooperation of economic elites, there would be little growth and thus very little to share. Second, the nonelite segments of the population were induced to make short-term sacrifices in exchange for larger benefits in the long term. Highly visible wealth-sharing mechanisms—such as land reform, free primary education, and free basic health care—were introduced to induce nonelites to support the growth process. Unlike simple income transfers, such as food or fuel subsidies, these mechanisms gave the population real assets that encouraged them to believe that they would indeed derive long-term benefits from growth.[7] Hence, these mechanisms signaled that all parties would share in the growing pie.

Few leaders would deny that shared growth is a desirable objective, but most have failed to develop the necessary means to achieve it.[8]

5. Johnson (1982).

6. Crone (1993) has presented a related thesis. He argues that states in which regimes have relatively broad political support have a greater capacity to promote economic change and that severe crises create the impetus for such regimes to introduce policy reforms. He states further that the extent to which reforms induce improvements in welfare depends in part on whether they are driven by a subset of elites that are strategic, that is, have a long-term perspective on regime maintenance. Our thesis differs slightly. We argue that the communist threat induced leaders to construct a broader base of political support which then allowed them to pursue economic reforms. In chapter 6, we discuss the important role of the economic bureaucracy, the analytical equivalent of Crone's "strategic elite."

7. This is not to say that the HPAEs have not provided food subsidies. Some have. But the point is, they did not rely on food subsidies to help the less fortunate but on mechanisms that gave people the means to acquire and increase their wealth. As discussed later, the latter have significant implications for long-term political stability.

8. In some countries, for example, Sub-Saharan Africa, sharing took precedence over growth and, as the pie shrunk and populations increased, the economy suffered. In others,

Why have East Asian leaders succeeded where so many others failed? The answer lies in mechanisms they created for achieving shared growth. These mechanisms in turn have their roots in the historical circumstances that each leader faced.

In seven of the eight HPAEs (Japan again being the exception), governments were prodded to adopt the principle of shared growth—and to deliver on their promises—by a fear of a communist takeover. In Taiwan (China), often cited as a model of growth with equity, the Kuomintang faced the threat of invasion by mainland forces and the potential opposition of native Taiwanese. In South Korea during the aftermath of the Korean War, the economy was stagnating while the communist North surged ahead, increasing the risk of communist-inspired political instability. Economic growth thus became the single objective of the military regime. Malaysia and Singapore illustrate how countries plagued by ethnic tensions can prevent political instability from undermining economic growth. In both cases, communist subversion magnified an ethnic problem, with left-wing groups exploiting these divisions. In Thailand, even before the onset of the Vietnam War, the potential for communist-induced chaos was already evident. The military, fearing such a development, took the reigns of government as early as 1948. In Indonesia, the rise of known members of the Communist Party into the upper reaches of government prompted the military to step in to prevent a communist takeover. And finally, Hong Kong received a flood of refugees from mainland China almost immediately after World War II, confronting the colonial government with the immense task of providing food, shelter, and jobs to an ever-increasing and potentially explosive refugee population.[9]

Political Contestability: The Communist Threat in East Asia

What motivated the leaders of East Asia's high-performing economies to take extra care to address the needs of the poorer segments of

---

for example, the Philippines, growth was pursued without changing the fundamental socioeconomic structure that would ultimately undermine that growth.

9. We do not ignore the history of repression in many of the HPAEs. This has been discussed in hundreds of articles and books. But it is not repression that distinguishes the HPAEs from other authoritarian regimes. The pursuit of the strategy of shared growth is one element that sets the HPAEs apart. For this reason, it is more fruitful to try to understand what led them to this strategy.

society? Surely, other leaders must have seen the benefits of shared growth. Yet, as the evidence in chapter 1 suggests, only the HPAE leaders delivered on their promises. The historical context provides an explanation. The triumph of communist forces in China in the late 1940s exerted considerable influence. The proximity of China to East Asia, cultural affinity, and the presence of large ethnic Chinese minorities in most East Asian countries meant that it would be easier for China to spawn insurgencies and spread communism in the HPAEs than in the rest of the developing world. The Korean War and the Vietnam War testify to the credibility of this threat. Nowhere else in the developing world has there been a confrontation between communist and Western forces on such a large scale involving so many countries.

For leaders in developing countries outside the region, separated from China by large differences in culture and vast distances or, in the case of South Asia, by nearly impassable deserts and mountains, the communist threat was far less palpable. Thus shared growth, though desirable, was not generally perceived by leaders outside the region as crucial to their political survival. In the eyes of these leaders, the politically difficult decisions sometimes necessary to deliver on the promise of shared growth—such as land reform or insisting that companies that benefit from state favors export aggressively—could be put off for a long time, perhaps indefinitely.[10]

Taiwan

Throughout Asia the threat of communist insurgency made more urgent the need to establish an equitable foundation for the distribution

10. The Philippines, although geographically in East Asia, has not adopted shared growth as a principle of legitimation. No government, for example, has succeeded in implementing a wide-ranging land reform (see, for instance, Hawes [1987] and Wurfel [1988]). The reasons are laid out in various historical accounts of the Philippines. See Karnow (1989); Wurfel (1988). The gist of these is that the United States traded military and financial support of the local elite, whose wealth had always been based on land (a legacy of Spanish colonialism), for continued long-term use of the two largest U.S. military bases outside the United States—Clark Air Force Base and Subic Bay Naval Base. This in turn attracted large inflows of U.S. investments, which were likely to be lost in the event of a communist takeover. Consequently, Philippine regimes could count more reliably on the United States for support in combating communist insurgency. Ferdinand Marcos was well known for exploiting this trump card to the fullest. Karnow (1989).

of the fruits of modernization. Nowhere, however, was the power and challenge of communist doctrine more familiar than to the Kuomintang (KMT) officials who moved to Taiwan in 1949.[11] Unlike other Asian governments that arose in the post-World War II era, the KMT came to power with a long list of lessons learned, which included the following diagnosis of the party's past failures: "(1) agricultural tenants rebelled against exploitation by landlords, while the Nationalists continued to be identified with the landlords; (2) the labor unions ran out of control; (3) bankers and financiers also broke loose, fueling catastrophic inflation; and (4) the government became beholden to 'vested interests.' "[12] These failures led the Kuomintang to adopt the shared growth principle in Taiwan, based on land reform and the development of small- and medium-sized enterprises (SMEs).

Because none of its members owned land on Taiwan, the KMT faced limited internal opposition to implementing land reform. Landlords were given bonds or shares in state enterprises in exchange for their land. Although the bonds were less than the market value of the land, they were nonetheless sufficient for some landlord families to become part of the new industrial elite. Peasants were given opportunities to buy the land at low prices and on generous terms. This opportunity for poor farmers to improve their lot is one important reason why wealth has been more equitably distributed in Taiwan than in most developing nations.[13]

These immediate equity benefits aside, land reform also removed two major obstacles that may have prevented the acceptance of growth-producing policies elsewhere: political destabilization by a radicalized peasantry and opposition to change from an entrenched rural elite. On one hand, the opportunity to acquire wealth drew peasants away from radical political activities. On the other, the large, rural middle class that arose as a result of land reform could not organize to pressure the government as efficiently as could a small class of landlords.[14]

---

11. We will not discuss the historical circumstances of Hong Kong and Japan. Haggard (1990) provides a brief but good account for the city-states (see his chapter 5). Pempel and Muramatsu (1993a) provide a brief analysis of the dominant political party in Japan, the Liberal Democratic Party (LDP), and its focus on shared growth as the basis for its political survival.

12. Wade (1990, p. 260).

13. Kuo (1976); Fei, Ranis, and Kuo (1979).

14. See Olson (1965) for the underlying logic.

Consequently, the agricultural sector as a whole was both less inclined and less able to block the government's development policies than would otherwise have been the case. Thus, in contrast with ruling groups in many developing countries, the Kuomintang had more room to formulate and implement policies that may have been unpopular with certain groups but were nonetheless conducive to growth.

To complement land reform, the Kuomintang encouraged and supported the proliferation of small- and medium-sized enterprises. Industrial parks were established to reduce entrepreneurs' high start-up costs and to spread industrial employment throughout the island. The government also provided financial, technical, and marketing support. By creating business opportunities for the native Taiwanese, the government diverted entrepreneurial energies from wasteful activities such as favor seeking toward industrial production. As with the development of a rural middle class, the proliferation of smaller, more numerous firms implied higher costs of organizing for industry and smaller potential gains from lobbying. Hence, as with land reform, the formation of vested interests was mitigated and capture of the state was avoided. The SME drive thus depoliticized the industrial sector, giving the KMT the flexibility to pursue growth-promoting policies.

Together with other reform measures that fueled economic growth, land reform and promotion of SMEs led to widespread prosperity.[15] As chapter 1 documents, income distribution in Taiwan has been among the most equitable in the world, and wealth, as measured by real per capita income, has increased at an average annual rate of about 7 percent. That helped, not surprisingly, to sustain the KMT's grip on political power in Taiwan.

Korea

Land reform did not come as easily to South Korea as it did to Taiwan. Southern landlords recaptured the state in 1945 and 1946. Two land reform programs were implemented, the first through the initiation of the U.S. military in 1947 and the second by the government in 1950. Civil war altered whatever vestiges of power the postwar coalition possessed. The war left behind a society in the South that in many ways resembled Taiwan: a standing army of 600,000, an economy bereft of heavy industry, and a large rural/agricultural base.

15. The details are discussed in chapter 3.

Winning the Korean War was not enough to get Syngman Rhee's government on the path of rapid growth. President Rhee's government (1948–60) was overthrown when a prolonged recession resulted in popular uprisings led by students. Prime Minister Chang's government came to power in the aftermath of the student rebellion. In less than a year a military coup led by General Park Chung Hee overthrew the Second Republic (May 1961). To solidify power and gain legitimacy, General Park led a movement for economic development that featured a populist campaign against the corruption of the previous regime. Beneficiaries of the import-substituting policies of the previous regime were marched down the streets bearing signs, "I was a parasite on the people." Park expropriated the fortunes he regarded as illicitly accumulated. His intention was to employ the proceeds for economic development. However, with most prominent businessmen in jail, the economy deteriorated, leading General Park to make a deal with the imprisoned business leaders: in exchange for freedom from persecution and future expropriation, the business leaders could establish industrial firms if they donated shares to the government.[16] As Young Back Choi put it, "From this initial attempt to reform society, the military junta emerged as the *encompassing organization*, after utterly destroying the old political network, often through brutal repression, publicly shaming the business leaders and charging them with a new patriotic duty to industrialize and export, having nationalized banking to tightly control credit, and having placed all stakes in the political game on economic development. The members of the junta were not ascetics, or inordinately public-minded, but they realized that their political survival, as well as material gain as the major stakeholders, depended on the overall performance of the South Korean economy."[17] As Woo states, "For economic growth to *substitute for* legitimacy, it has to be transmogrified into a symbol that appeals to some collective primordial sentiment— such as, for instance, nationalism. That symbol in Korea was a number: a talismanic double-digit GNP growth figure that was the Korean score in the race to catch up with Japan and also to surpass the DPRK's (North Korea's ruling party) economic performance."[18] The latter was of particular concern to Park, since growth rates in the communist

16. Haggard, Byung, and Chung (1990).
17. Choi (1984, p. 245). Emphasis added.
18. Woo (1991, p. 98). Emphasis added.

North surpassed those in the South, inspiring pro-North sentiment in the South.

Export-led industrialization began with Park's ascension to power. Under strong American prodding, Park devalued the currency to cheapen exports and reduced tariff barriers that protected domestic industries. Export-oriented firms were favored by the state bureaucracy, which employed licensing schemes to mediate the distribution of foreign credit. Tax holiday exemptions and directed credit were offered to firms willing to export: industries or projects were denied support once they were found to be unsuccessful in world markets. Park set up the Economic Planning Board (EPB) to centralize control over critical economic matters. A trade promotion agency (KOTRA) was also established. Foreigners were brought in as senior partners in consultation. From that point on the government concentrated on building up the private sector, allowing it to determine the best methods of meeting export targets and organizing production. As Woo put it, "The state has its hand on the tiller but business provides the motive force. The state is strong in that it can—and does—give and take life away from individual firms; but it is also constrained by virtue of being a capitalist state whose survival is contingent on the health and contentment of the business class."[19] The government tried to restrict competition by determining which firms entered which lines of production, especially the target industries. Nevertheless, as Lim points out, "The composition of actual exports differed drastically from the governments' projections, or targets. It was the private exporters who played a major role in identifying and taking risks, exporting unskilled-labor-intensive products in which Korea had a comparative advantage."[20]

Park's actions toward wealth holders of the previous regime is the most oft-cited example of an Asian regime behaving like an arbitrary dictatorship. But compared with the outright confiscations of socialist regimes in Africa and Latin America, Park did not permanently expropriate wealth. His government used state power to redirect the energies of the private sector and to make it capable of competing in international markets as equal to the firms of more developed nations. By contrast, in Africa, for example, governments have expropriated private sector

19. Woo (1991, p. 111).
20. Lim (1981, pp. 16–17).

wealth, firms have been less competitive after state takeovers, and capitalists have often been imprisoned and exiled. Their capital and expertise were exported rather than their production. Korea was governed by rules, though not necessarily democratically devised, and playing by the rules was rewarded and digressions were penalized.[21] The private sector wealth that was created in one period was not confiscated during the next but was used to create even more wealth.

The experience of many Latin American countries suggests that the military government could not sustain economic growth without offering a growth dividend to the general population. As discussed more extensively in chapter 3, one critical factor was the government's decision to invest heavily in primary and secondary education. This proved important in two ways. First, abundant skilled and semiskilled labor allowed Korea to pursue a labor-intensive, export-oriented manufacturing strategy. Second, economic growth permitted skilled labor to enjoy significant increases in real wages. Urban discontent was thus contained, enabling the military regime to implement growth-promoting policies.

Malaysia

Malaysia's approach to wealth sharing was designed to address ethnic divisions and conflict, a problem that has rarely been successfully addressed in developing countries. To make the promise of shared growth explicit Malaysia introduced a highly institutionalized form of wealth allocation. Frustration among the Bumiputras (native Malays), the most numerous but poorest of the three major ethnic groups, erupted in racial riots in 1969. Bumiputras had faced limited opportunities for upward mobility under the postcolonial regime between 1957, when Malaysia was granted independence from the British, and 1969, when inequality increased dramatically. To address this imbalance and to prevent the situation from degenerating into civil war, three dominant parties representing the major ethnic groups—the United Malay National Organization (UMNO) for the Bumiputras, the Malaysian Chinese Association (MCA) for the Chinese, and the Malaysian Indian Congress (MIC) for the Indians—formed a coalition that produced the New Economic Policy (NEP)—sometimes known as the

---

21. Selective, unusually detailed tax audits, for example, were sometimes used by the government to punish errant firms.

Bumiputra policy. The purpose of the NEP is best described in the Mid-Term Review of the Third Malaysia Plan (1971–75):

The NEP has as its overriding objective the promotion of national unity through the two-pronged strategy of

(i) eradicating poverty by raising the income levels and increasing employment opportunities for all Malaysians, irrespective of race. This is to be achieved by programs aimed at raising the productivity and income of those in low-productivity occupations, the expansion of opportunities for intersectoral movements from low-productivity to higher-productivity activities and the provision of a wide range of social services especially designed to raise the living standards of the low income groups;

(ii) accelerating the process of restructuring Malaysian society to correct economic imbalance so as to reduce and eventually eliminate the identification of race with economic function. . . . The objective is to ensure that Malays and other indigenous people will become full partners in all aspects of the economic life of the nation.

The efforts to attain these objectives will, in turn, be undertaken in the context of rapid structural change and expansion of the economy so as to ensure that no particular group experiences any loss or feels any sense of deprivation.[22]

Though significantly short of its targets, the NEP did produce results. Poverty declined dramatically over twenty years. Income distribution improved as well. "From .412 in 1957 the Gini coefficient rose to .537 in 1970, and declined to .479 by 1984 and to .447 by 1989." The ratio of the share of the top income quintile to the share of the lowest quintile dropped by 30 percent, from 16 percent in 1973 to 11.1 percent in 1987. Per capita incomes of the Bumiputras grew the fastest, at an annual average of 5.8 percent compared with the Chinese at 3.5 percent, and the Indians at 1.4 percent. Over twenty years (1971–90), Malaysia's GDP grew annually at an average rate of 6.8 percent.[23]

Growth might have been faster without the equity thrust of the NEP, but then insurgency in the rural areas and nationwide strikes in the cities (both rampant during the 1950s and spurred by left-leaning

22. Salleh and Meyanathan (1992, pp. 18–19).
23. Salleh and Meyanathan others (1992, for quotation see p. 5).

groups) could have resulted in political instability, and Malaysia would not have attracted sufficient foreign capital to develop its abundant natural resources and build a manufacturing base. By attacking the wealth-sharing problem at its source, the NEP prevented inequities from producing a social explosion. Although often criticized for creating inefficiencies, the policy reduced poverty and inequality and indirectly helped sustain two decades of uninterrupted growth. In 1995 the political coalition of 1970 remains intact, and UMNO, the largest of the three coalition members, remains the nation's dominant political party.

Singapore

Being the center of commerce and trade for the British-ruled Malaya Federation, Singapore became a hotbed of radical activity after World War II.[24] Its natural harbor had made it the entry point of most goods coming into Malaya and the exit point for the country's primary product exports. As a consequence, it had attracted a large labor force of mostly unskilled workers. During the war, leftist groups were instrumental in organizing opposition to the Japanese forces and hence gained the respect of many Singaporeans who even before the war agitated for independence from British colonial rule. Upon termination of the hostilities, leftists were positioned to organize dissent against British rule. A large labor force with high levels of unemployment was an easy target for their activities.

Dissatisfaction brewed among the students as well. In contrast with the rest of Malaya, about 78 percent of Singapore's population was Chinese, with the balance composed mostly of native Malay and Indian. British colonial policy was biased against Chinese education. "To the traditional Chinese, the most alarming aspect of colonial policy was its threat to Chinese education. The Singapore Chinese were concerned about a new education policy launched in the Federation in 1952, which concentrated on English and Malay schooling to the exclusion of Chinese. They also feared that the authorities were bent on suppressing Chinese education in Singapore, since in devoting the bulk of the finances to the English-medium schools it appeared the colonial government was content to see Chinese education atrophy and die."[25] This

24. Malaya then consisted of a loose assemblage of regions comprising the now Peninsular Malaysia, Singapore, Borneo, Sarawak, and Brunei.

25. Turnbull (1977, p. 246).

issue inspired protest against colonial rule and prompted leftists to infiltrate Chinese schools.

A combination of student and worker discontent led the then- nascent People's Action Party to seek support by appealing to the left. Although the leadership of the PAP was mostly English-educated, they perceived the necessity of gaining the support of the students and workers. Since the left had already successfully organized these groups, PAP leadership advocated alliance with the left. So ironically the PAP, which is today considered a conservative party, started out as an alliance between English-educated moderates and radical leaders whose common objective was to seek independence from Britain. Once independence was obtained, the moderate-left alliance broke down, and the left formed its own party, the Barisan Sosialis. Owing to a combination of fortuitous events and an effective strategy, the PAP managed to secure power solidly in the 1963 elections by capturing thirty-seven of the fifty-one parliamentary seats.[26] Since then the party has ruled the city-state without interruption.

The immense power of labor and the students made the PAP leadership realize the importance of well-paying jobs, reasonable housing opportunities for workers, and universal education. The end result has been a development strategy that has incorporated capitalist and socialist policies. Growth has been based on attracting foreign investment and technology. Its benefits have been directed largely at improving workers' welfare, most notably through housing, education, and productivity-based real wage increases. Leadership has promoted one of the most successful public housing and public education programs (discussed in chapter 3) and has successfully sustained harmonious business–labor relations over two decades (discussed in chapter 4).

Indonesia

Among the HPAEs, Indonesia came closest to officially recognizing the Communist Party's right to participate in government decisionmaking. As in Singapore, the communists gained wide recognition for their efforts in helping to secure independence from a colonial power, in this case the Dutch. With independence, they gained the right to participate in the nascent parliamentary democracy, forming their own party, the PKI.

---

26. See Turnbull (1977), chapter 8, for an extensive discussion.

After battling the Dutch colonialists for their independence, which they finally won in 1950, the Indonesians embarked upon nation building based on democratic politics. Wide ethnic, regional, and religious diversity gave rise to thirteen political parties, none of which commanded a majority. The largest controlled less than a fourth of the 232 seats in the legislature. Confronted with constantly shifting coalitions, President Sukarno, the hero and leader of the Indonesian struggle for independence, was forced to form six different cabinets between 1950 and 1956, resulting in chaos and government paralysis.[27] In 1957, with the support of the military, Sukarno declared martial law, dissolved parliament, and disbanded all political parties except one—the PKI. Because the communist-inspired PKI strongly supported his policy of anti-imperialism, the bedrock of his ideology, and because he needed a counterweight to the military, Sukarno permitted the PKI to continue, delicately balancing the power of one against the other. "Sukarno was well aware of the potential danger to his own position of excessive reliance on the army, so, in addition to exploiting rivalries within the armed forces, he encouraged the activities of civilian groups as a counterweight to the military. Of these groups by far the most important was the PKI."[28] As Schlossstein put it, "By 1962, the PKI had become the most powerful political party in Indonesia and the largest Communist Party outside the Soviet Union and China."[29]

Sukarno's leadership during the campaign against the Dutch made him a national hero revered by the general population. The army avoided direct confrontation with him despite its discomfort with his association with the communists. Even when Sukarno withdrew his country from the United Nations and realigned with China, the army stayed quiet, not intervening until the bloody events of September 30, 1965, when the army under General Soeharto stepped in and forcefully took power from Sukarno.

The immediate catalyst for the takeover was the abduction and murder of six army generals. To this day it remains unclear who was behind the attack. Interviews, trial records, and newspaper accounts point to a group of disgruntled junior officers in the army and senior officers of the air force. Be that as it may, the army seized the opportunity to eradicate the PKI and depose Sukarno in what it called a counter coup

27. Schlossstein (1991).
28. Crouch (1978, p. 43).
29. Schlossstein (1991, p. 47).

to preserve the republic. In the military's view Sukarno had leaned too heavily on the PKI, the military's principal political adversary. A bloodbath ensued in which hundreds of thousands of alleged communist supporters were killed. From this bloody confrontation arose Soeharto's New Order Regime.

The New Order regime inherited a sick economy, plagued by hyperinflation, deteriorating infrastructure, worsening poverty (especially in the rural areas), and declining GNP. To differentiate itself from Sukarno's "Guided Democracy" regime, Soeharto and his generals confronted these problems directly and used their success as the rationale upon which to base their continued rule.[30] They hoped to gain legitimacy through sustained economic development despite their repression of electoral politics.[31]

The success of the New Order is now well documented. Inflation fell from a high of 1,000 percent in 1965 to under 10 percent by the early 1970s, where, except during the two oil crises, it has remained.[32] Infrastructure was expanded and improved over the past twenty-five years.[33] And, as documented in chapter 1, per capita income increased tremendously while poverty and income inequality declined significantly. Except for the other Asian high performers, no other developing country has achieved such remarkable gains. This record highlights the importance of shared growth to the success of the New Order and Soeharto's continued hold on power, which to this date has not been challenged.

Thailand

Compared with its East Asian neighbors, Thailand seems the most unstable politically. Since Thailand's transformation from an absolute monarchy to a constitutional monarchy in 1932, the country has experienced ten coups and sixteen failed coup attempts.[34] In stark contrast,

---

30. This is not to say that military officers did not have any material self-interest in the perpetuation of their rule. As discussed in chapter 5, they accumulated wealth. But this accumulation was linked to the sustainability of growth and the spread of benefits to the more general population.

31. Crouch (1978); Liddle (1991).

32. See figure 6-3 in chapter 6.

33. World Bank (1990b).

34. Morell and Samudavanija (1981); Schlossstein (1991). In essence, the constitutional monarchy embodied a sharing of power between the military and the king, though from 1932 to 1957, the king held very little sway over political events. It was not till 1957

Indonesia and South Korea have each had one (two in South Korea if the assassination of President Park is included) and the other high performers *none*. Remarkably, the country has not disintegrated and, despite constant threats from communist-backed groups in the 1960s and 1970s, did not succumb to the peasant-based insurgency that displaced Western-aligned governments in neighboring Vietnam, Laos, and Cambodia.

The communist threat has hovered over various Thai governments since the thirties. The 1932 coup, which brought the military to the forefront of politics, was instigated in part because of the fear of rising communism. Among the first acts of the new government was to promulgate a harsh anticommunist law. It "passed a law legitimizing the change of administration by coup d'etat and at the same time adopted a decidedly anti-communist stance."[35] The communist threat persisted, occasionally erupting in armed conflict, and worsened during the Vietnam War. With the fall of the military government in 1973 and the restoration of democratic politics, the left emerged as a powerful political force with the support of students in Bangkok and farmers primarily from the Northeast.[36] The three chaotic years that followed saw labor strikes, student protests, and rural insurgency. When the military seized control again in 1976, it enjoyed broad support from the monarchy, the business community, and the middle class. Since then the threat of communist takeover has subsided, though until recently intermittent skirmishes with Vietnamese troops took place on the Cambodian border. Students, workers, and farmers have shifted their political focus from overthrow of the establishment to demands for increased participation in policymaking through democratic processes.

Nevertheless the coups have continued. General Prem successfully staged one in 1980 and put down two attempts, one in 1981 and another in 1985. In 1988 he stepped down when the first popular elections in more than a decade were held. In 1990 the military once again stepped in but quickly abdicated to civilian authority in the face of mounting local and international pressure.

---

when General Sarit lifted the monarchy to a more prominent role in politics (largely to legitimize his own rule) that the king has been able to influence the government.

35. Wyatt (1982, p. 247).

36. Wyatt documents the proliferation of communist literature among students and farmers, for example, Mao's famed red book, during this period. The availability of radical writing was largely circumscribed before this period.

The survival of the Thai state despite the continuing change in regimes seems nothing short of a miracle. Several analyses evolve around the role of the monarchy since 1957.[37] In essence, they argue that Field Marshal Sarit's use of then-young King Bhumibol in 1957 to build political support for his military regime immersed the monarchy once again in the thick of politics. Since then, say these studies, the monarchy has become the arbitrator of last resort whose role is to resolve conflicts among the different factions that make up the elite. His role as such has led to stability despite numerous coups.

This explanation is weak in one way. Why would the elites, the military in particular, grant the king so much leverage when the king has little or no coercive capacity? The citizenry's respect and reverence for the king has never stopped military regimes in other developing countries from deposing a king and permanently eradicating the monarchy.

The answer perhaps lies in the economy. The different elite factions have carved out their own respective portions of the economy. Different military groups have established ties with business elites and have developed a significant material interest in the success of the economy.[38] The monarchy has as well. "Today, the Crown Property Bureau, which manages the royal wealth, owns 31.75 percent of the Siam Commercial Bank and 37.4 percent of Siam Cement, in addition to 13,000 acres of prime real estate in central Bangkok. Altogether the royal family has shareholdings in some forty Thai companies, including 10 percent of Honda (Thailand), 10 percent of YKK Zipper (Thailand), and 7.5 percent of Minebea Electronics, all major Japanese affiliates."[39] Furthermore, twenty-five years of economic development have created a wealthy middle class. Real per capita incomes have more than doubled since 1960. Poverty in the country has declined significantly from 57 percent in the early 1960s to 25 percent in the late 1980s. Although some regions have remained poorer, especially in the Northeast, in each place the incidence has declined considerably.[40] And finally, income inequality as measured by the Gini index has declined slightly from around .43

37. Several explanations for this exceptional phenomenon have been proposed, including those of Morell and Samudavanija (1981) and Wyatt (1982).

38. Riggs (1966) provides some documentation, and Schlossstein (1991) offers some anecdotal evidence.

39. Schlossstein (1991, p. 178).

40. World Bank (1993b); Oshima (1993, p. 214).

in the late 1960s to around .40 in 1990, with a slight rise to .45 in the mid-1980s because of the second oil crisis and the drop in farm prices.[41]

Given that a relatively broad cross section of society has benefited from economic growth, including the growing numbers of middle-class workers, one would expect conflicts among elite factions to be resolved quickly to prevent damage to the economy. With the monarchy as final arbiter, most coups have been bloodless, with the king tipping the balance in favor of or against the coup plotters. Leaders of the defeated camps are normally exiled.[42] Even those coups that were relatively violent never approached the magnitude of violence of coups in other countries. The coup of 1976, which resulted in fewer than one thousand deaths, pales in intensity when compared with the estimated hundreds of thousands that disappeared during and immediately following the 1965 coup in Indonesia.[43] Hence, although regime legitimacy has been premised on the support of the monarchy, that support ultimately flows from the prosperity enjoyed by important groups, including the growing middle class.

Wealth Sharing, Regime Stability, and Growth

Wealth sharing has been critical to the HPAEs. It has resulted in relatively high political stability and, consequently, higher levels of

41. Oshima (1993, p. 202). Oshima's data also show that inequality has generally been lower in Thailand than in Singapore or Malaysia even though inequality has fallen more sharply over time in the latter countries. It should also be noted that in a fair number of countries in Latin America and Africa, inequality has not only been much higher but has also increased over time (see chapter 1). The latest World Bank report on Thailand (1993b) indicates that income distribution has not improved since the early 1980s, contrary to Oshima's findings, with regional disparities increasing.

42. The monarch, King Bhumibol (1946–present), is widely known to be a fair and forgiving man. Interviews with various officials and researchers suggest that his reputation has been key to giving him the influence to resolve conflicts. There is strong evidence that this may be true. The king has three daughters and one son. His son, the crown prince, Maha Vajiralongkorn, is widely known to be his "black sheep" and to be unpopular with the people. In contrast, one of his daughters, Princess Sirindhorn, is seen as much like her father. In 1977 the king had the succession law (with respect to the monarchy) amended to allow women to ascend the throne and has been grooming the princess to succeed him.

43. Morell and Samudavanija (1981); Crouch (1978). Other estimates of deaths have ranged from 78,500 to 1 million.

investment. It has also indirectly muted the impetus for lobbying, which also has led to more investment.

Much debate about the impact of income inequality on political stability has occurred.[44] The experience of the HPAEs may help clarify this debate. The wealth-sharing mechanisms found in these countries essentially involve asset transfers as opposed to pure income transfers, for example, land reform versus food subsidies. Asset transfers represent a future stream of income. That stream is dependent on the performance of the economy over time. Because assets assure individuals that they will share in some of the benefits of growth, giving them assets (in the form of skills and physical property) will encourage them to support growth-promoting policies and inhibit them from disrupting the economy. In other words, wealth-sharing mechanisms in the HPAEs have acted as credible signaling devices to the general population that they will benefit from growth.

Some recent econometric work strengthens the argument that lower inequality, which wealth sharing promotes, leads to greater political stability. It also clarifies the link between income distribution and growth. Alesina and Perotti conducted a cross-section econometric analysis of the relationship among income distribution, political instability, and investment for a sample of sixty-four countries.[45] Their analysis suggests that improvements in income distribution reduce political instability, which in turn has a modest impact on the percentage share of investment in GDP. As an index of income distribution, they use the share of income received by the third and fourth income quintiles. These quintiles roughly represent the size of the middle class. For a measure of political instability, they adopt a sociopolitical index developed by Dipak Gupta.[46] The index is a weighted average of various social and political variables: the nature of the political regime (democratic or otherwise); the number of strikes, coups, protests, deaths from political violence, politically motivated attacks, assassinations, and executions that occurred in a country during the period of investigation. They conclude that "an increase by one standard deviation of the share of the middle class causes a decrease in the index of political instability of about 1.2, which corresponds to about one-fifteenth of the average

44. See, for instance, the review article by Lichbach (1989).
45. Alesina and Perotti (1992).
46. Gupta (1990).

TABLE 2-1. *Income Share of the Middle Class in HPAEs, 1973*

Country	1973
HPAEs	
Hong Kong	46.00
Indonesia	41.20
Korea	48.40
Malaysia	37.50
Thailand	44.80
HPAE average	43.58

Source: World Bank, *World Development Report* (Washington, Various Years).

value [of the index]. This in turn causes an increase in the share of investment in GDP of about 1 percentage point."[47]

Assume that the Alesina-Perotti analysis holds for a more general population of countries.[48] Then the suggestion is that by the creation of a relatively stable political environment, wealth sharing in the HPAEs has resulted in a modest increase in the share of investment in GDP. Table 2-1 shows the average income share of the middle class in five of the HPAEs for 1973. The Alesina and Perotti data on the share of the middle class are for years surrounding either 1960 or 1970. The mean for all countries that they compute is 33.27, and the standard deviation is 5.57. Based on the data in table 2-1 the HPAEs are approximately 1.85 standard deviations above the mean. If one takes this deviation as reflecting the impact of wealth sharing, then the Alesina-Perotti model implies that wealth sharing may have contributed approximately 1.85 percentage points to the share of investment in GDP in the HPAEs. Figure 2-1 compares the average share of investment in GDP between the HPAEs and other developing countries for the period 1970–88. The average for the HPAEs is approximately 8 percentage points higher. This increase suggests that wealth sharing may well have accounted for 23 percent of the HPAE differential in investment shares with the other countries.

In fact, the contribution of wealth sharing may be larger. Many

47. Alesina and Perotti (1992).

48. We recognize that this is a very strong assumption. It is, however, reasonable to assume that their policy implications—reducing income inequality leads to an increase in investment—hold. Hence, at the very least, the qualitative aspects of our argument hold.

FIGURE 2-1. *Share of Investment in Gross Domestic Product, HPAEs, and Other Developing Countries*

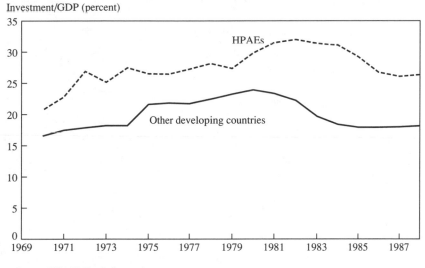

Investment/GDP (percent)

Source: World Bank (1993a).

scholars have argued that lobbying necessarily retards growth. In the first place, it diverts resources to unproductive uses.[49] In the second, it creates uncertainty in the policy environment since it puts pressure on the government to change policies. The first affects growth directly by wasting resources. The second does so indirectly by discouraging private investment.

Wealth sharing in the HPAEs was pursued primarily to build a broader base of political support. A broad support base gives a political regime greater freedom to pursue economically rational policies since they are better able to reject demands from particular interest groups. Regimes whose support is based on narrow interests have to cater to the demands of those interests whether they like it or not (and whether the demands are economically rational or not). Otherwise, they are likely to lose power. The returns to lobbying differ between these two types of regimes. In particular, under broad-based regimes, returns are likely to be lower since the probability of success is lower. Given lower returns, interest groups will thus allocate fewer resources (at the margin) to lobbying, leaving more for investment. Furthermore,

49. Bhagwati and Srinavasan (1982); Olson (1982).

TABLE 2-2. *Survey Rankings: Effectiveness of Lobbying in Fourteen Newly Industrializing Countries*

Region and country	Rank
HPAEs	
Singapore	1
Hong Kong	2
Malaysia	3
Korea	5
Taiwan	6
Thailand	10
Indonesia	13
Average	5.7
Other countries	
Mexico	4
South Africa	7
Hungary	8
Venezuela	9
Brazil	14
Pakistan	11
India	12
Average	9.3

Source: World Bank (1992).

because there is less lobbying activity, the uncertainty surrounding the policy environment is likewise reduced. This, too, leads to increased investment.

We of course are not claiming that there is little or no lobbying in the HPAEs. On the contrary, there has been, but as table 2-2 suggests, it has been less effective and thus (given rational behavior) may be less extensive. The table shows the rankings of fourteen newly industrialized countries (inclusive of seven HPAEs) based on the effectiveness of lobbying by special interest groups.[50] A low number indicates that lobbying is relatively less effective. A remarkable positive correlation between the HPAEs and the rankings exists. Although not definitive,

50. We emphasize that we are not claiming that no lobbying occurs in the HPAEs. On the contrary, we presume there is, but we argue that the efforts are less effective. If individuals are rational, then if their efforts bring less return, they will reduce them *at the margin*.

this suggests that, for most of the HPAEs, wealth sharing may well have contributed more substantially to investment and growth than has been indicated above.

The notion that legitimacy would be based on the promise of prosperity raised the issue of how prosperity would be shared. The principle of shared growth or what has been called "developmental policy without losers" was adopted by all the high-performing Asian economies to differing degrees. As the discussion in this chapter suggests, wealth sharing was accomplished differently according to national circumstances.

Three

Wealth-Sharing Mechanisms

IN CONTRAST with leaders in many other developing countries, leaders in the high-performing Asian economies (HPAEs) recognized the importance of establishing broad support for the regime. Obtaining the support of ordinary people was essential to the leaders' development strategy. Wealth-sharing mechanisms were designed precisely to achieve this objective. These mechanisms ranged from coercive, such as land reform, to more discrete measures, such as public investment in rural infrastructure. All were intended to raise the standard of living of the general population.

The mechanisms differ fundamentally from the subsidies for food and fuel typically found in other developing countries. Instead of these direct income transfers, which may alleviate hardship in the short run but do little to improve the recipients' long-term prospects, wealth-sharing mechanisms offer nonelites opportunities for upward economic mobility.[1] For instance, land reform in conjunction with the necessary support, for example, credit facilities and farm-to-market roads, enables peasants to participate actively in agricultural markets. Moreover, since they own the land, they can invest in improving productivity with some assurance that they will benefit from increased yields year after year. In contrast, kerosene or fertilizer subsidies, while helpful to peasants, depend on government whim and thus implicitly on the capacity of peasants to organize, demonstrate, and possibly riot.

In general, then, wealth-sharing mechanisms give the broader population real assets that, if used productively, will provide a continuous stream of returns over the long term. Income transfers are one-shot deals that could conceivably be repeated each year but could also be reduced or terminated at any time. Wealth-sharing mechanisms increase the beneficiaries' self-reliance and give them a stake in the contin-

1. Ranis (1989) makes a similar argument for Taiwan.

ued stability and success of the regime. Income transfers induce dependence while simultaneously offering incentives for recipients to press demands on the government or even to destabilize it if the subsidies are withdrawn.

Land Reform and Rural Development

Land reform has been successfully implemented in very few societies. Among the successes, Taiwan is perhaps the best known. Given the Kuomintang's tenuous position in Taiwan, the party needed the support of the native Taiwanese. Land reform was used to build broad support among the island's predominantly rural population. The KMT's land reform program, introduced in 1949, began with the establishment of a rent ceiling. A tenant's rent was limited by law to 37.5 percent of the annual crop yield. By lowering the effective return on land, this restriction lowered land values, thus lowering the opportunity cost to landowners of disposing of their land. In the same year, public land was sold to tenant farmers. "The size of the parcels was limited according to predetermined fertility grades, and the average size was 1 chia.[2] Selling prices were 2.5 times the value of the annual yield of the main crops; payments in kind were set to coincide with the harvest season over a ten year period."[3] This was then followed by the Land-to-the-Tiller program, which required landowners to sell excess land to the government, which in turn would sell it to tenant farmers on the same terms as the sale of public land. Landowners were allowed to retain three chia (approximately nine acres) of medium-grade land and were paid in bonds (70 percent) and stocks (30 percent) in four public enterprises (which were previously owned by the Japanese) for their excess land.

Besides redistributing land, the government took measures to integrate the production of the peasants-turned-farmers with the market. The regime understood that the quality of information in agricultural markets can increase the importance of the middleman and can deter small farmers from getting maximum benefits. Public policies, including the supervision of uniform weights and measures, engineering standards, and social surveys, were introduced to reduce the costs to

2. One chia is equal to 2.97 acres.
3. Fei, Ranis, and Kuo (1979, p. 40).

TABLE 3-1. *Distribution of Land and Owner-Cultivated Households in Taiwan, by Size of Holding, 1939 vs. 1960*

Size of holding[a] (chia)	Percent distribution of owner-cultivated households	
	1939	1960
Less than 0.5	43.2	20.7
Between 0.5 and 1	20.9	45.9
Between 1 and 3	24.6	30.1
Greater than 3	11.3	3.3
Total	100.0	100.0

Source: Fei, Ranis, and Kuo (1979).

a. One chia is equal to approximately .97 hectares or 2.47 acres. The 1960 data exclude public and private commercial farms, which are all larger than 10 chia and account for about 6 percent of total land and less than .1 percent of the number of holdings.

the small farmer of participating in markets. Price information was disseminated to the peasantry, and marketing channels were provided to reduce the rents extracted by middlemen. Village councils were created to discuss local land and market management issues such as irrigation. As a result, today Taiwanese farmers receive a far greater share of the final price for their produce than do farmers in Africa.[4]

The direct impact the land reform program had on asset ownership is demonstrated in table 3-1. In 1939, 11.3 percent of the farms had an area over three chia (14.85 acres), and 43.2 percent had an area of less than one-half chia (1.485 acres). By 1960, only 3.3 percent of the farms were larger than three chia and 20.7 percent smaller than one-half chia. Table 3-2 shows that the number of landowners increased and the number of tenants declined substantially between 1939 and 1960.

Land reform combined with the various support programs mentioned dramatically influenced income distribution. As table 3-3 demonstrates, owner-farmers and part-owners (those who work their own land as well as rent from other owners) tend to earn more than the tenants. The implication is that an increase in ownership leads to an increase in incomes of farmers. One analysis has "estimated the shares of farm income by recipient before the land reform, using the 1936–

4. In general, African farmers receive 30 to 60 percent of the terminal market price of their goods, whereas Asian farmers receive from 75 to 90 percent. See Raissudin and Rustagi (1987, p. 109).

TABLE 3-2. *Percent Distribution of Farm Families and Agricultural Land in Taiwan, by Type of Cultivator, 1939–40 vs. 1959–60*

Period	Distribution by farm families			Land distribution	
	Owner	Part owner	Tenant	Owner	Tenant
1939–40	32.0	31.2	36.8	43.70	56.30
1959–60	64.0	21.0	15.0	85.60	14.40

Source: Fei, Ranis, and Kuo (1979).

TABLE 3-3. *Farm Incomes by Category of Farmers in 1963, Taiwan*
In Taiwan dollars

Category	Per family farm	Per hectare	Per person
Owner-farmer	34,853	26,998	4,019
Part-owner	39,095	25,252	4,274
Tenant	29,377	17,754	3,038

Source: Fei, Ranis, and Kuo (1979).

1940 average, and after the land reform, using the 1956–1960 average. According to these estimates the share of cultivators in farm income increased from 67 percent to 82 percent; the share of government and public institutions, which received repayments from new landowners, increased from 8 percent to 12 percent; but the share of landlords and money-lenders declined from 25 percent to 6 percent."[5] In short, income inequality declined.

Land reform was also an important wealth-sharing mechanism in South Korea, where an initial attempt was undertaken at the prodding of the United States in 1947, and a subsequent, more extensive round of reform was instituted at the government's initiative after the Korean War.[6]

In a rather elaborate simulation-planning exercise, Irma Adelman and Sherman Robinson have investigated the interactive effects of various rural development programs on income distribution and poverty

5. Fei, Ranis, and Kuo (1979, p. 44).
6. One of the first policies implemented by the South Korean leadership after the civil war was land reform. The government took over landlord properties, paid the latter nominal compensation, and distributed the land to more than 900,000 tenants. The effort practically eliminated tenancy.

TABLE 3-4. *Overall Effectiveness of Simulated Experimental Programs in South Korea, 1978*
Percent

	Rural		Urban	
Simulated program	Income of bottom decile	Households in poverty	Income of bottom decile	Households in poverty
		Changes in indicators		
Land reform	28.7	−4.6	n.a.	n.a.
Public works and small-scale industry	30.4	−4.7	2.8	−0.6
Cooperatives	5.7	−2.1	n.a.	n.a.
Productivity and marketing	3.4	−0.9	n.a.	n.a.
Consumption subsidy	5.9	−1.4	1.0	−0.4
Education and demographic change	7.9	−1.1	−3.5	0.7
All programs	77.6	−10.7	n.a.	n.a.
All programs but land reform	63.5	−9.6	n.a.	n.a.

Source: Adelman and Robinson (1978).
n.a. Not available.

in South Korea. Land reform is one component.[7] Their objective was to determine what types of programs would yield the largest impact over the medium term. They constructed a basic model of the Korean economy, taking great pains to calibrate it so that its predictions came close to actual outcomes over a predetermined period; for example, the predicted distribution of national income across standard categories corresponds roughly to the actual GNP accounts during the period. In essence, the basic model was made to mimic the development of the Korean economy over a nine-year period, 1964 to 1972. Having satisfactorily established a representative model, they conducted several simulation experiments or programs including one on a simulated land reform. Because the model incorporates all the interactive effects of the various simulated programs, the simulated outcomes represented the predicted overall effect of each program.

Several observations are pertinent (table 3-4). First, among the indi-

7. Adelman and Robinson (1978).

TABLE 3-5. *Sources of Income of Farm Families by Decile, 1966, 1975*
Percent

Decile[a]	Agricultural income	Nonagricultural income	Agricultural income	Nonagricultural income
	1966 farm families		1975 farm families	
1	54.7	45.3	33.9	66.1
2	55.3	44.7	37.3	62.7
3	57.3	42.7	39.0	61.0
4	61.0	39.0	40.6	59.4
5	64.3	35.7	43.1	56.9
6	65.5	34.5	44.4	55.6
7	68.5	31.5	46.0	54.0
8	70.1	29.9	48.4	51.6
9	70.2	29.8	50.8	49.2
10	67.6	32.4	52.4	47.6
All deciles	65.9	34.1	46.3	53.7

Sources: Calculated from DGBAS, *Report on the Survey of Family Income and Expenditure,*
1966 and 1975.
a. Arranged from lowest to highest income.

vidual programs, land reform has the most favorable impact on income
distribution. Second, land reform and the public works and small-scale
industry programs are much more effective in reducing poverty than
are the other programs. Third, promoting rural development, that is,
implementing all the simulated programs, leads to greater reductions
in the incidence of poverty and income disparities than either of the
two programs taken individually or jointly. And fourth, without land
reform, rural development programs would be less successful at addressing both poverty and income inequality.[8]

Adelman and Robinson also conduct experiments tailoring some of
the above programs to urban areas. As table 3-4 suggests, the retrofitted
urban programs were less likely to affect poverty or inequality. Rural
development would go much further in improving income distribution
and reducing poverty. Taiwan's experience bears out this observation.
Table 3-5 compares the proportion of incomes of farm families stem-

8. The effect of excluding land reform may likely be greater. By the 1960s land
distribution in the rural areas of Korea was much more equitable than in most other
developing countries, perhaps better than all of them except Taiwan and Japan. The
basic model already embodied this observation.

ming from agriculture and nonagricultural sources in 1966 to the proportion in 1976. During this decade almost a 50 percent jump occurs in the proportion attributable to nonagricultural sources. "For rural families agricultural income consistently was less equally distributed than non-agricultural income. . . . Thus, the steady increase of opportunities in rural by-employment available to members of rural families, especially the poorer ones . . . contributed favorably to FID equity."[9] The implication is clear. Rural development matters for income distribution.

Investing in Education and Promoting Labor-Intensive Manufacturing

Economists have often argued that education's contribution to human capital accumulation is critical to the development of a country. All of the HPAEs have invested heavily in education and, unlike many other developing countries, have concentrated on primary and secondary schooling. The share of the educational budgets allocated by the HPAEs to basic (primary and secondary) education is significantly higher than the share allocated by other developing countries. Tertiary education has been left largely to the private sector.[10]

The benefits of focusing on primary and secondary education are substantial. The higher the enrollment rates in primary and secondary education, the higher the growth in a country's per capita gross domestic product. Nancy Birdsall and Richard Sabot estimate that "a 10 percentage point increase in primary school enrollments in 1970 (among a sample of 98 developing countries) would have increased average annual growth in real per capita GDP between 1980 and 1985 by .21 percentage point; a 10 percentage point increase in secondary enrollments would have increased the growth rate by .33 percentage point."[11] An increase in human capital is one outcome caused by increased education. But another reason has to do with the potential spillover

9. Fei, Ranis, and Kuo (1979, p. 315). An important component of rural development in Taiwan was the diversification of agricultural production to include fruits, vegetables, and livestock, all of which led to the proliferation of small- and medium-scale industry in the rural areas, for example, processing plants. See Oshima (1993).

10. World Bank (1993b). For an extensive analysis of human capital formation, education, equity, and growth, see Birdsall and Sabot (1993). The discussion in this section is based on their work.

11. Birdsall and Sabot (1993, p. 96).

effects of education. The social return to primary education is much higher than to tertiary education, and the return to secondary education about equal to tertiary education.[12] Hence, countries that invest more in primary education are more likely to experience larger spillover effects. Faster growth occurs in these countries because of the larger spillovers. Furthermore, primary school graduates increase secondary school enrollments while secondary school graduates increase the proportion of college-age students enrolled in universities. Therefore the absolute magnitude of spillovers from secondary and tertiary education for any given time will be higher than in countries that invest less in primary education, resulting in a higher annual growth rate on average.

A focus on basic education also leads to a reduction in income inequality. Basic education increases the number of skilled workers. When skilled workers are in short supply, they are likely to earn much more than unskilled or semiskilled workers. That is, the difference between the wage of a skilled worker and other workers will be higher. In the terminology of Birdsall and Sabot, skilled workers will earn a scarcity premium. This premium (and thus inequality) contracts with the expansion of basic education.[13]

A significant negative correlation exists between enrollment rates in basic education and income inequality.[14] Moreover, a comparison of Brazil and Korea shows that in Korea (when standardized for other characteristics such as employment experience) "in 1976 workers with high school education earned 47 percent more than primary school graduates; by 1986 that premium had declined to 30 percent. Similarly, the premium earned by workers with higher education declined from 97 to 66 percent. . . . The net effect of educational expansion was to

12. World Bank (1993a); World Bank, *World Development Report*. Whenever social returns are higher than private returns, there are positive externalities. For example, a worker's productivity is likely to increase with increased literacy among his or her coworkers. Literacy makes a worker more capable of doing a job efficiently. However, if coworkers are also literate, then a worker can become even more efficient since his or her coworkers are less likely to make mistakes, can understand instructions more quickly, and so on.

13. Birdsall and Sabot also make a case for reducing the gender gap. They show that, in East Asia, the difference in male-female enrollment rates has declined substantially (especially at the primary level) relative to other developing countries. Given that returns on education to men and women are more or less the same (see their figure 9), a narrowing of inequality is implied.

14. See Clarke (1992). Based on a sample of eighty countries.

TABLE 3-6. *Educational Composition of Male Wage Labor Force*

Educational level	Brazil		Educational level	Korea	
	1976	1985		1976	1986
Uneducated	25.6	20.5	Elementary and below	19.6	7.5
Primary (lower)	45.5	40.8	Middle	30.5	25.4
Primary (upper)	17.8	21.6	High school	32.2	43.5
Secondary	6.7	11.1	Junior college	2.6	4.8
University	4.4	6.0	University	15.1	18.8

Source: Birdsall and Sabot (1993).

reduce substantially, by 22 percent, inequality of pay over the decade. . . . *By contrast, over the same period, in Brazil* the wage premium earned by university leavers was 159 percent in 1976 and 151 percent in 1985. . . . The net effect of educational expansion in Brazil over the decade was to increase inequality of pay roughly by 4 percent."[15] The difference in outcomes is clarified in table 3-6. During the decade in question, the composition of the labor force that had less than an elementary education remained high in Brazil but fell drastically in Korea. The composition with a secondary education increased only slightly in Brazil but jumped substantially in Korea. The implication is that Korea's emphasis on primary and secondary education provided skills for a larger proportion of its labor force. An increase of skilled workers lowered the scarcity premium.

Among the HPAEs, Korea has put the most emphasis on public provision of universal primary and secondary education and the promotion of labor-intensive manufacturing as a means to reduce wealth disparities. The expansion of primary and secondary education began almost immediately after the Korean War and perhaps was partly a consequence of the war. With little else to invest in, the education of children, especially given the cultural importance of education, became an attractive option to parents.

The ascension to power of Park Chung Hee and the concomitant switch to export-oriented industrialization in 1964 led to a rapid growth phase in the economy. As in Taiwan, Korea depended heavily on

15. Birdsall and Sabot (1993, pp. 106–07). Emphasis added.

the production of labor-intensive commodities. Industry continuously absorbed growing numbers of workers, reducing the ranks of the unemployed and attracting labor from the rural sector. As firms moved up to more sophisticated stages of production, the literate and educated work force was able to meet the firms' changing and growing demands. From 1970 to 1990, wage employment as a percentage of total employment in Korea increased from 39 percent to 60 percent, and urban unemployment rates declined from 7.4 percent to 2.4 percent.[16] At the same time, as shown in chapter 1, real earnings in manufacturing per employee in Korea increased by an average of slightly more than 8 percent a year during the same period. Hence, as the demand for labor increased, so did the real incomes of workers.

The Korean leadership may not have consciously attempted to link distribution with growth. Nevertheless a relatively egalitarian distribution emerged because favorable initial conditions were already in place, that is, high levels of basic education and land reform; labor-intensive production permitted the full exploitation of the initial conditions.

We need look no further than Thailand to see the price paid for underinvesting in education. The experience of Thailand highlights the importance of more active government intervention in distributing the benefits of growth. Thailand underinvested in postprimary education, which had a deleterious effect on income distribution in the 1980s as the economy shifted to more skill-intensive manufacturing.

In Thailand, the proportion of the population completing some postprimary education has been lower than in the other successful Asian economies. Secondary enrollment rates have been much lower than the rates in the other HPAEs—in fact, lower even than the average for low-income countries (table 3-7). Birdsall and Sabot present a simple regression of secondary enrollment rates with per capita income. Thailand was barely at the mean enrollment rate in 1965 given its per capita income then; in 1987 it fell far below the corresponding mean.

The economy has also been undergoing a major restructuring, moving from a largely primary-product-based one to a more skill-based manufacturing economy (table 3-8). This transition has produced an increasing demand for more skilled workers. Both industry and services have gradually emphasis impetus from workers with primary education to those with secondary, vocational, and tertiary education

16. Birdsall and Sabot (1993, tables 14, 15).

TABLE 3-7. *Primary and Secondary Enrollment Rates in the High-Performing East Asian Economies*

Region and country	Primary		Secondary	
	1965	1987	1965	1987
High-performing East Asian economies				
Indonesia	72	118	12	46
Thailand	78	95	14	28
Malaysia	90	102	28	59
Korea	101	101	35	88
Singapore	105	n.a.	45	n.a.
Hong Kong	103	106	29	74

Source: World Bank, *World Development Report* (Washington, 1990).

TABLE 3-8. *Distribution of Exports: Thailand*
Percent of total exports

Export products	1970	1979	1986
Heavy manufactures	12.3	10.9	4.5
High-skill light manufactures	0.8	6.4	17.1
Low-skill light manufactures	1.9	13.1	19.6
Primary products	83.3	66.8	54.4

Source: Dollar (1991).

(table 3-9). This suggests that the supply of better-skilled workers has failed to keep up with the demand, and wages for such workers have increased faster. Two effects follow: firms tend to substitute capital for labor, and skilled workers earn much higher scarcity rents. Both results lead to a deterioration in income distribution.[17]

Promoting Small- and Medium-Sized Enterprises

To encourage the broad-based development of the private sector, most of the HPAEs introduced support systems for small- and medium-

17. As a corollary, because the lack of skills restricts a still-large proportion of the work force to agricultural work, a change in the terms of trade between agriculture and industry (in favor of the latter) can make matters worse. The decline in world prices for primary products in the 1980s did indeed turn the terms against agriculture. World Bank (1993b).

TABLE 3-9. *Educational Composition of the Thai Labor Force, by Sector*
Percent

	Agriculture		Industry		Services	
Education	1977	1986	1977	1986	1977	1986
Less than four years						
of primary school	17.7	11.1	12.1	8.1	13.9	8.3
Elementary	81	85.3	77.1	69.8	57.4	51
Secondary	1.2	3	7	13.9	13.9	15.8
Vocational	0	0.3	2.3	4.5	4.9	7.6
Teacher	0.1	0.1	0.2	0.5	6.2	8.1
University	0	0.1	1.3	3.2	3.6	9.2

Source: Dollar and Brimble (1990).

sized enterprises (SMEs). SMEs generally have difficulties obtaining long-term credit to finance capital improvements. They also find it hard to obtain better technology and acquire the necessary skills to use the technology and break into markets, particularly export markets. Hence, a nontrivial SME sector cannot be established without external assistance. The support programs in three of the first-tier (more advanced) HPAEs—Japan, Korea, and Taiwan—have produced modestly positive results.[18] It is still too early to tell whether the programs of the southern-tier HPAEs—Thailand, Malaysia, and Indonesia—will be as effective. But the three have established such programs. Unlike many other developing nations, these countries have made a conscious effort to promote a broader-based private sector. Taiwan has been notably successful. The creation of industrial parks in the rural areas and introduction of government support activities has produced one of the most dynamic and vibrant SME sectors in the world.

In stimulating the economy, the Kuomintang strongly encouraged the development of small- and medium-sized enterprises. Again, this action was a response to its defeat in the mainland. While asserting strict control over politics, the Kuomintang encouraged economic mobility through a proliferation of SMEs. As shown in table 3-11, SMEs compose at least 90 percent of enterprises in any given sector; the average across all sectors is 97 percent. Not surprisingly, the SMEs also dominate exports, producing about 60 percent of the total value (table 3-10).[19]

18. Levy (1994); Wade (1990).
19. Taiwan (1990).

TABLE 3-10. *Exports of Small and Medium Enterprises in Taiwan*
Hundreds of millions of U.S. dollars

Categories	Value of exports	Export value of small and medium businesses	Percent of small and medium businesses
Manufacturing	436.89	264.26	60.49
Trade business	235.25	120.96	51.42
Total	672.14	385.22	57.31

Source: Ministry of Finance, *Statistics for Small and Medium Enterpieces* (Taiwan, 1990).

TABLE 3-11. *Statistics of Small and Medium Enterprises in Taiwan*

Categories	Total enterprises	Number of small and medium businesses	Percent of small and medium businesses
Agriculture, fishing, livestock, forestry	3,256	3,171	97.39
Mining and quarrying	1,390	1,360	97.84
Manufacturing	157,965	155,263	98.29
Electric, gas, and water	186	168	90.32
Construction	28,419	26,456	93.09
Commerce	489,864	475,106	96.99
Transport, storage, and communication	36,897	35,818	97.08
Finance, insurance, real estate, business service	30,534	28,263	92.56
Community, social, and personal service	69,550	69,229	99.54
Total	818,061	794,834	97.16

Source: Ministry of Finance, *Statistics for Small and Medium Enterprises.*

Given the opportunities provided by the Kuomintang, the native Taiwanese have realized the ancient Chinese proverb, "Better the head of a chicken than the tail of a horse."

Of particular importance are the programs of the Medium and Small Business Administration (MSBA). Despite its small size—approximately fifty employees—the agency has effectively assisted SMEs by contracting out functions to the private sector. For instance, its credit guarantee program uses commercial banks as evaluators and monitors of SME projects. To obtain financing, an SME approaches a commercial bank. The bank evaluates the potential of the project and, if it decides affirmatively, forwards the application to the MSBA for a credit guarantee. Repeated transactions between banks and the MSBA reduce potential moral hazard problems. The MSBA also provides extensive technical and managerial assistance. But it does so not through direct provision but by bringing together private sector consultants, either foreign or domestic, and SMEs in need of such assistance. And the MSBA pays up to 50 percent of the total cost of these services.

Japan's SME sector differs fundamentally from Taiwan's. It is largely based on a three-tier, pyramidlike, subcontracting system. At the top of the pyramid are the large companies and trading houses who do most of the marketing and exporting. One level down are the first-tier SMEs who generally subcontract with those companies, providing them with semifinished or finished products. The second- and third-tier SMEs usually handle part of the process in the manufacturing chain, for example, weaving in the apparel industry, subcontracted from upper-tier firms. The government has established support programs in marketing, technology acquisition, and financing. The marketing and technology support programs have not been very helpful because the subcontracting system has provided most of the benefits that these programs were designed to deliver. But the financial assistance programs have proved important, especially in times of transition and rapid change.[20] The development of the subcontracting system may in no small part have occurred because of the establishment of industrial parks in the various prefectures (towns). Hence, as in Taiwan, the government's provision of such parks has helped the SME sector.

Korea's economic development has largely been characterized as conglomerate driven. Growth is frequently associated with the expansion of the *chaebols* (business conglomerates). Rarely mentioned is that beginning in the early 1980s, shortly after the Heavy and Chemical Industry (HCI) drive was halted, the SME sector began to grow rapidly.[21] The share of SMEs in manufacturing employment has risen from 37.6 percent in 1976 to 51.2 percent in 1988; similarly, the SME share

20. Itoh and Urata (1993).

21. In fact, the SME sector started to decline only when the HCI push was initiated in the mid-1970s. The HCI drive diverted scarce financial resources toward heavy industry. SMEs, whose growth requires financial support (as the experience of Japan, Taiwan, and Korea indicates), were thus starved for funds during this period (approximately 1972 to 1978).

in manufacturing value added has risen from 23.7 percent in 1976 to 34.9 percent in 1988.[22] Like Japan and Taiwan, Korea established an extensive support system for SMEs. Although marketing and technology support systems have played minor roles in expanding the sector, as in Japan, financial support systems have been important (for example, export financing and credit guarantee programs). Overall, "SME support systems sometimes appear to be more effective than those in other developing countries."[23]

A link among industrial structure, income distribution, and poverty has yet to be established. Nevertheless the Adelman-Robinson simulation discussed earlier suggests that promoting small-scale industry in the rural areas combined with improvements in rural infrastructure (which is certainly needed to encourage the growth of industry) can reduce poverty.[24] The experience of Taiwan suggests that the proliferation of rural industries and services in Taiwan led to increased nonagricultural employment in the rural areas, increased rural incomes, and ultimately to an improvement in income distribution. Although Fei, Ranis, and Kuo do not provide any evidence of the structure of industry in the rural areas, it seems unlikely that rural industries would be oligopolistic, especially because more than 90 percent of enterprises in each of the country's manufacturing sectors are SMEs, and more than 60 percent of manufactured exports are accounted for by SMEs.[25] Hence, it is quite likely that the promotion of SMEs in Taiwan has contributed partly to the reduction in inequality and poverty.

Developing Rural Infrastructure

Disparities between rural and urban areas help increase income inequality. Neglect of the rural sector, common in many developing

22. Kim and Nugent (1993).

23. Kim and Nugent (1993, p. 39).

24. There is also some evidence from Korea that rural-based enterprises are significantly more labor intensive than urban-based ones. See Kim (1988, table 4). Since the chaebols (large conglomerates) are located in the cities, then it is reasonably safe to assume that rural enterprises are small to medium sized. This suggests that SMEs increase wage employment more than large enterprises. Thus SMEs can be more effective in absorbing unemployment and underemployment, which at the very least will tend to reduce poverty.

25. Fei, Ranis, and Kuo (1979).

countries, leads to growing unemployment and underemployment in the rural areas. Thus people migrate to the cities where the supply of jobs is rarely adequate. Consequently, urban unemployment and underemployment increase while wages stagnate.[26] And income disparities persist if not widen.

To minimize outmigration, it is necessary to create income-producing opportunities in the rural areas. An essential component of any strategy is to build up rural infrastructure. Land reform will be much less effective if farmers do not have roads and bridges to take their produce to markets. Without irrigation, farmers may not be able to plant crops outside of the rainy or main planting season. Unless farmers can plant during the off season, rural unemployment and underemployment will persist.[27] The influx of nonagricultural firms can help alleviate these problems. But manufacturing and service enterprises need water and electricity. In short, building up rural infrastructure is essential to creating jobs and opportunities in the rural areas.

Indonesia's funding of rural infrastructure development is notable. During Sukarno's Guided Democracy period, much of the country's inadequate infrastructure was left to deteriorate. Following the advice of its technocratic core, the New Order government embarked on a development program that consisted of successive five-year development plans. REPELITA I, II, and III, the first three five-year development plans, were almost exclusively dedicated to the rebuilding of infrastructure and development of the rural sector. Although the plans did not specifically incorporate objectives of achieving equity, they were designed to promote growth and reduce poverty. Because most of the population was poor, the plans indirectly led to an improvement in the distribution of income.

The first five-year plan focused on rural and agricultural development: self-sufficiency in rice production and the provision of irrigation facilities. Most of the effort was concentrated in Java and Bali. The second and third five-year plans, buttressed considerably by the increase in resources made possible by the oil boom, continued the emphasis on rice production while adding physical and social infrastructure—roads, bridges, school buildings, health facilities—and promoting human resource development. Universal primary education

26. Todaro (1969); Harris and Todaro (1970).
27. Oshima (1993).

became a principal objective. So, unlike many other oil-exporting countries, Indonesia allocated a substantial share of the oil windfall gains to poverty-reducing programs.[28] These funds were used to create income-generating opportunities for the rural poor by improving their productive capabilities and access to markets and by enhancing their human capital. By the late 1970s, the government's development program began to bear fruit. From a high of 60 percent in 1970, the proportion of the population falling below the poverty line had dropped to 40.1 percent in 1976, 33.3 percent in 1978, and 28.6 percent in 1980.[29] Not surprisingly, income inequality steadily improved with the Gini index declining from .40 in the late 1960s to .30 in the late 1980s (table 1-1).

An important component of the government's development program was the INPRES expenditure program, which institutionalized a formula for allocating revenues among various levels of government—central, provincial, district, and village level. It established "a system of flexible direct subsidies (to provinces, districts, and villages) with the aim of reducing interregional disparity and building infrastructure in the provinces."[30] The small-scale rural infrastructure projects that it financed created substantial employment opportunities among unskilled workers.[31]

The drop in oil prices in the early 1980s brought Indonesia to the brink of economic crisis. Despite the fall in oil revenues, however, the government persisted in its poverty reduction program, while at the same time it avoided incurring large budget deficits.[32] To do so, it adopted a strategy that included macroeconomic adjustment measures and structural reforms designed to maintain export competitiveness while protecting poverty-related expenditures. Between 1983 and 1987, development expenditures were reduced by 43 percent.[33] Routine expenditures, which financed a large share of the operational and mainte-

28. Evidence of this is presented in chapter 5.

29. World Bank (1990b, p. 6). For the impact of the rice program on income distribution see Manning (1987).

30. World Bank (1990b, p. 4).

31. See Gelb (1985).

32. In Indonesia, foreign grants and loans are included in the calculation of the government's revenue.

33. Development expenditures are generally expenditures on capital or public investment (in both human and physical capital). Some are poverty related, for example, building new schools. But not all poverty-related expenditures are development expenditures, for example, routine expenditures on social infrastructure.

nance costs of social infrastructure, for example, teachers' salaries, were increased by 7 percent.[34] Moreover, remaining development expenditures were retargeted toward other poverty-related sectors. The share of mining and industry fell substantially, and the shares of human resource development and regional development increased. INPRES was instrumental in protecting the share going to regional development.[35]

The New Order government did not have to deal with large inequities in land ownership. As early as the turn of the century, land was already evenly distributed among the land-owning population. Most landowners in Java then had less than three acres.[36] Fifty years and two world wars had not changed this distribution.[37] The radical land reforms undertaken in Taiwan and Korea underscore the importance of this initial condition for a government's success (in countries where land is scarce relative to the population). Concentrated land ownership would have impaired strategies to reduce poverty and for that matter income inequality.

Allocating Corporate Equity

Malaysia introduced the most aggressive and explicit mechanism for sharing growth. The New Economic Policy (NEP), promulgated in 1970 as a response to the racial riots of 1969, was to govern economic policymaking for twenty years, 1971–91. The NEP was a growth-sharing scheme: increments to the economic pie were to be shared among all Malaysians. The government justified growth as a means to eradicate poverty and produce a more equitable distribution of wealth.[38]

Among the more specific goals of the NEP was the attainment of equity targets for the Bumiputras (ethnic Malays). By 1990 Bumiputras

34. World Bank (1990b).
35. World Bank (1990b).
36. See Husken and White (1989, table 12.4).
37. Husken and White (1989, table 12.4). We note that the land problem in Indonesia has more to do with the problem of titling. Traditional property rights systems have made it somewhat difficult to establish clear titles. Nishio (1993).
38. Arguments have been made that Malaysia may have indeed grown faster were it not for the NEP. There is, however, a competing argument that growth might not have occurred in any substantial way if the NEP were not introduced to promote and sustain political stability. Some econometric work tends to support the latter (see our discussion of Alesina and Perotti's recent work in chapter 2).

were targeted to hold 30 percent of the equity in the corporate sector. To meet this mandate, statutory bodies were established that essentially managed equity funds for the Bumiputras. The most important of these was the National Unit Trust Berhad (ASNB). The government gave it initial capital for investment. Like any trust fund, the ASNB manages a portfolio of investments, except that only Bumiputras can buy units in the fund. The ASNB was thus designed to provide opportunities for the Bumiputras to hold an equity stake in the economy.

The ASNB and similar statutory bodies were supported by licensing requirements for manufacturing concerns. The Investment Coordination Act of 1975, the main legal instrument governing the promotion of investment and exports under the NEP, mandated that "enterprises with 25 or more employees or paid up capital greater than M$250,000 were to obtain a license to manufacture. Its key provision made the granting of licenses conditional upon compliance with the NEP guidelines."[39] This requirement was relaxed in the early 1980s in response to the recession: the minimum paid-up capital requirement was raised to $M2.5 million. The NEP mandated that 30 percent of newly created stock was to be sold to the Bumiputras (at their issue price).

Although the NEP fell short of its objectives, it did produce tangible gains. As shown in table 3-12 the Bumiputras share of equity in the corporate sector increased tenfold over the twenty-year period.

Sharing with Labor: Effective Tripartism

Labor in Taiwan, Korea, Singapore, and Japan was restructured by replacing existing unions with new state-controlled ones. The restructuring produced two immediate consequences. First, in the absence of an independent organization capable of coordinating union activities nationwide, labor could not engage in effective and potentially violent lobbying activities. Second, because representatives of unions were government appointed, the government had greater control over business-labor relations. Thus labor could not and did not engage in paralyzing strikes or similarly disruptive activities. Moreover, not charged with curing social ills, firms imposed fewer demands on the government for subsidies. Government in turn could concentrate on growth-producing policies rather than short-term redistribution of profits.

39. Salleh and Meyanathan (1992, p. 41).

TABLE 3-12. *Malaysian Ownership of Share Capital of Limited Companies (at par value 1969–90)*
Percent

Year	Bumiputra	Other Malaysian residents	Foreign residents
1969	1.5	59.6	62.1
1970	2.4	34.3	63.4
1971	4.3	33.9	61.7
1975	9.2	37.5	53.3
1980	12.5	44.6	42.9
1982	15.6	49.7	34.7
1983	18.7	47.7	33.6
1985	19.1	54.9	26.0
1988	19.4	56.0	24.6
1990	19.2	46.8	25.4

Sources: Second Malaysian Plan, 1971, p. 1984; Third Malaysian Plan, 1976, p. 184; Fourth Malaysian Plan, 1981, p. 62; Mid-Term Review of the Fourth Malaysian Plan, 1984, p. 101; Fifth Malaysian Plan, p. 107; Mid-Term Review of the Fifth Malaysian Plan, 1989; Mid-Term Review of the Sixth Malaysian Plan, 1993.

Ironically, although labor was politically disabled, its economic needs were largely met. Chapter 1 documents the increase in real earnings in manufacturing in the HPAEs and other developing countries. On average, real earnings in the HPAEs rose three times faster than in South Asian countries and about seven times faster than in Latin American countries.

Singapore's approach to labor deserves special attention. Its combination of union restructuring, which is antisocialist, with explicit sharing, which is usually considered prosocialist, reflects the pragmatic nature of policymaking in the country. As in the other HPAEs, ideology of any form has taken a back seat.

In the early postindependence years, the ruling People's Action Party (PAP) set out to weaken the trade unions. Recognizing that Singapore lacked exportable natural resources, the PAP wanted to woo multinational firms to relocate labor-intensive operations in Singapore. But to attract the multinationals, it had to guarantee industrial peace. The trade unions had to be controlled and pacified. As the first step, the PAP introduced draconian labor control measures. In 1967 it passed the Trade Unions Amendment Act, which specified the terms of union membership and affiliation. The act was used to purge the unions of radical elements. In 1968 the Employment Act established the rights and duties of employees and standardized bonus payments, the work week, retrenchment and retirement practices, and fringe benefits. The objective was to contain labor costs by linking wages to efficiency and productivity. In the same year, the PAP also passed the Industrial Relations Amendment Act, which gave greater powers to employers and removed from the collective bargaining process such functions as staff recruitment, promotion, internal transfer, work assignment, retrenchment, dismissal, and reinstatement. By restraining the power of the trade unions these laws improved the investment climate.

However, the PAP also realized that industrial peace could not be guaranteed for long if labor did not benefit from industrialization. In 1969 the PAP called on the National Trade Union Congress (NTUC), the organization officially recognized as the representative of labor interests, to organize a seminar on the "Modernization of the Labor Movement" to chart new directions for the union movement. The seminar produced two key recommendations: to promote tripartite relations involving government, employers, and labor aimed at achieving cooperation among the three parties and avoiding potentially antagonistic and destructive wage negotiations; and to establish worker cooperatives to give labor a stake in the economy.

To promote tripartism, the government created the National Wages Council. Briefly, the NWC is an advisory body composed of representatives of government, employers, and labor. Each year it reviews wage rates and trends in relation to economic performance and prospects and then makes recommendations on wage adjustments and other related matters. Its recommendations have always been adopted by government, labor, and the private sector. Since its formation, the NWC has helped to keep wage increases in step with overall economic growth. Its role was clearly demonstrated during the 1985–86 recession, when it persuaded labor to accept wage cuts of about 12 percent in return for a promise that wage increases would resume as soon as the economy recovered. Wages were increased in 1987 on the council's recommendation.

The HPAEs have frequently been criticized for excluding labor from the political process.[40] The labor strategy of Singapore suggests a differ-

40. See Deyo (1987).

ent interpretation. Although the government initially outlawed independent trade unions, it also incorporated a much broader labor base into the consultation process. In most of Africa and Latin America, the regimes have depended on a much narrower labor support base, that of organized labor. Singapore and the other HPAEs have not found the need to nurture such a narrow relationship because they have established a broader base of support.

In contrast with Latin America and Africa, East Asian regimes established their legitimacy by promising shared growth, so that the demands of narrowly conceived groups for regulations that would have long-term deleterious consequences for growth were resisted. In particular, broad-based social support allowed their governments to avoid making concessions to radical demands of organized labor. By appealing to a broad constituency, the goal of growth enhancement dominated the selection of economic policies. As long as the benefits of that growth were perceived to be widely distributed, the government could resist buying the support of narrow segments of labor with privileges that could restrain overall productivity. Thus the common notion that labor in East Asia was weak or bamboozled does not tell the whole story.

Worker Cooperatives

To complement the National Wages Council, the Singaporean government empowered the NTUC to establish worker cooperatives, among which the Comfort taxi service, the Income insurance enterprise, and the Welcome supermarket chain are the best known. The cooperatives were created to enable workers to acquire assets and thus to give them a greater stake in the economy.

The NTUC Comfort Cooperative was established in 1970 as a transport cooperative primarily to provide more efficient and reliable taxi and minibus transport services to the commuting public and to give taxi drivers and minibus operators an opportunity to become owner-drivers. Before its launching, taxi service in Singapore was provided by 3,800 registered Yellow-top taxis and numerous unlicensed (pirate) taxis. The Yellow-top taxis belonged mostly to fleet owners and financiers, who would hire out the taxis to the 13,500-plus holders of vocational taxi licenses. Because of the limit on the allowable number of registered taxis, fleet owners and financiers could and did charge rates with substantial premiums. Consequently, many of the taxi drivers resorted to driving pirate taxis. But these vehicles posed a serious safety hazard, since they were generally inadequately maintained and uninsured (a consequence of ill-defined property rights).

The Singaporean government provided an initial loan of S$13.5 million to Comfort for the purchase of vehicles in bulk and thus at discount prices. A vehicle ownership scheme was established. Under the scheme, a driver obtaining a Comfort taxi through a drawing was required to pay an initial deposit and weekly installments that covered the cost of the vehicle, insurance, road and diesel tax, and administrative costs. The payments were much less expensive than rent for a Yellow-top taxi. Consequently, pirate taxi drivers gradually disappeared as most opted to join NTUC Comfort. The quality of taxi service improved significantly. In later years, a co-ownership scheme was introduced to reduce the financial burden on an owner-driver and to maximize use of the vehicle through shifts.

The statutory life span of a taxi in Singapore is seven years. To help its members replace their vehicles, the NTUC established a savings scheme in 1974. When a member has completed the installment payments, the payments continue but are instead deposited into his savings account. By the end of the seven years, the savings account is large enough to cover the initial outlay for the vehicle. Should a member decide to leave the cooperative, his or her savings are then returned with interest.

As of the end of 1991, NTUC Comfort accumulated a surplus of S$63.8 million. A major share is used to finance the purchase of taxis and other capital equipment needed to upgrade the service. The remainder goes to dividends (about 10 percent) and to funding of various educational, social, cultural, and safety net programs for the benefit of members and their families. NTUC Comfort has recently incorporated. Its objective is to increase its capital base and expand operations through issuance of shares in the Singaporean stock exchange. It has initiated a joint-venture operation in South China and plans to use most of the capital increase to expand this operation.

Singapore's use of worker cooperatives may be replicable in other developing countries. In Indonesia, for instance, worker cooperatives have also been created. The Indonesian Workers' Cooperative Alliance (INKOPKAR) essentially performs functions similar to those of the NTUC in Singapore although on a much smaller scale. It helps improve the welfare of workers not through collective bargaining but through financial assistance and services. It has a transportation cooperative modeled after the NTUC Comfort taxi cooperative. This entity operates minibuses for workers and leases taxis to worker-drivers. A driver can negotiate to own the taxi after five years. INKOPKAR also operates a housing cooperative, which provides low-interest loans and low-cost housing to member workers. It owns a cooperative bank, which finances housing, educational, and business loans, and it buys stocks in private corporations, thereby providing workers with equity shares in the corporate sector.

The urban population is growing rapidly in Indonesia as in other developing countries. Industrialization has increased the demand for urban housing. However, imperfections in the real estate and financial markets keep housing out of the reach of the typical blue-collar Indonesian worker (most likely a rural migrant). Slum creation in the industrial areas has emerged and with it many undesirable social, political, and economic problems.

To respond to this potential crisis, INKOPKAR in Indonesia has launched a low-cost housing program targeted to member workers in industrial areas. The program offers a basic house of very simple construction at terms the workers can afford. The house, with an area of twenty-one square meters, sits on a lot of sixty-six square meters. It has clean water and electricity (450 watts) and can be improved and expanded later when the owner can afford it. This arrangement parallels the tradition in rural communities of building houses step by step as resources become available. Each house costs approximately U.S.$2,000 and is payable under very liberal terms: a 10 percent down payment, which most workers can obtain from their employers and monthly installments ranging from $16 to $35, which is within the income range of many workers.[41] INKOPKAR makes a profit of 1 percent to 5 percent, which it reinvests. To date, INKOPKAR has built and sold about 8,000 units in industrial areas throughout the country. During the next five years, it plans to build 30,000 units in the Cibinong industrial area about twenty-five kilometers from Jakarta.

The government has provided assistance in various ways. It opened up a loan facility at the State Savings Bank to finance INKOPKAR's

41. Per capita income in Indonesia is about $680. At $16 a month, a worker with this average income would be allocating about 28 percent of income to housing. Interestingly, 28 percent (or thereabouts) is the cutoff point for eligibility for mortgage finance in the United States.

lending program. It has helped in land preparation and has provided basic infrastructure. And it has greatly simplified the administrative procedures governing the assemblage and acquisition of land.

Public Housing Programs

Although Hong Kong has generally followed a laissez-faire approach to the economy, the government has intervened heavily in the housing market. During the 1950s, the city-state was inundated with refugees and migrants from the Chinese mainland. Population increased from 600,000 in 1945 to more than 2.4 million in 1950. The influx continues today although at a lesser rate; the flow was largest during the 1950s and 1960s.

The large influx led to the creation of slum areas coupled with high unemployment and poverty. These conditions contributed to social disturbances that culminated in riots in 1967. To alleviate the tension and reestablish stability, the government embarked on a fast-track public housing program targeted to low-income households. The Ten-Year Housing Program initiated in 1972 proposed to develop enough housing units for 1.8 million people by 1983. Although short of its target (largely because of overoptimism and miscalculations), the program has successfully provided reasonably good public housing to a large share of the population. As of 1986, more than 45 percent of the population lived in public housing.[42]

Like Hong Kong, Singapore experienced a dramatic influx of migrants in the late 1950s and early 1960s, which led to similar problems: slums, poverty, unemployment, crime, and social disturbances. Singapore's expulsion from the Malayan Federation made matters even worse. The government responded by creating the Housing Development Board (HDB) in 1960 and granting it the mandate and authority to develop a public housing program for low-income families. The government's strong commitment to the program is indicated by the share of total social development expenditures allotted to the program—43 percent.[43]

As the housing needs of low-income families have been met, the HDB has developed middle-income public housing and has established

42. Castells, Goh, and Kwok (1990).
43. Yeung (1973, chap. 2).

self-sufficient new towns outside the city proper, much like those in Hong Kong. By the late 1980s, more than 80 percent of the population lived in HDB housing, and 90 percent of those households have purchased their units.[44]

Summary

Wealth-sharing mechanisms signal the polity, especially those near the bottom of the economic pyramid, that they will share in the benefits of growth. Thus these measures help persuade nonelites to make sacrifices needed to initiate and sustain economic growth. Land ownership gives peasants reasonable faith that growth will bring increased personal wealth: at the very least, the value of their land increases. The lower unemployment rates that accompany the proliferation of SMEs inspire confidence that jobs will be available. Education gives the less fortunate segments of society hope that their children will have better access to higher-paying jobs. The development of rural infrastructure makes it easier for budding rural capitalists to gain access to markets in urban areas. Worker cooperatives offer opportunities to blue-collar workers for small business ownership. Public housing programs make home ownership less of a dream and more of a reality. All these mechanisms make the broader population more cooperative, willing to make sacrifices in the expectation of future returns.

44. Castells, Goh, and Kwok (1990, chap. 7).

Four

Wooing the Business Sector

To achieve their economic goals, leaders in the high-performing Asian economies needed to win the support and cooperation of economic elites. Without the investment and expertise of these groups—by definition the wealthiest and better-educated members of society—HPAE leaders would not have been able to achieve sustained, rapid, and relatively equitable growth. Winning and keeping the support of these groups without compromising necessary economic policies was tricky. To do so, leaders had to avoid a common mistake of dictators: fearful of losing power, a typical dictator prizes loyalty and gives high priority to preserving it.[1] Rather than encourage competition, for example, dictators grant monopolies to businesses that can be relied on to repay the favor by supporting the dictator—and often by sharing part of the proceeds. Thus dictators typically build loyalty, and enrich themselves, by tying the fortunes of those who control economic resources to those of the regime.

A typical dictator rewards his followers with assets taken from those who refuse to profess loyalty or who have been associated with a political rival. Inevitably economic decisions become embroiled in political machinations; economic rivalry is resolved in the political sphere, as insiders use their influence to hinder their competitors. The privileged insiders will be depicted as patriots as long as they do the dictator's bidding. But they know if they become too wealthy they, too, may become targets. Because the ruler enforces his will with threats, his followers fear that their good fortune can be rescinded at any time. Those who benefit from largess today know that the ruler's promise not to harm them in the future carries little credibility: because the dictator is above the law, his promises are unenforceable.[2]

1. Tullock (1987); Wintrobe (1994).
2. Root (1989, 1994); Weingast and North (1989).

This uncertainty about the ruler's future behavior induces firms to be secretive. Firms know that their assets can be confiscated, so they attempt to keep them hidden. Rather than register their assets, firms hide accounts and expatriate capital to safe havens abroad. Similarly, investors hesitate to put their capital at long-term risk. They therefore prefer trade activities or activities with a short time horizon to the long-term investments in fixed assets that are necessary to build up industrial capacity.

Frequently, a dictator's subjects attempt to protect themselves from censure by making the dictator feel admired. They therefore provide the dictator only with the information he wants to hear.[3] The more power the dictator accumulates, the less willing his subjects are to risk disclosing unpleasant information. For similar reasons, government officials will avoid delivering bad news or reporting activities that run contrary to the expectations of the ruler. Lacking a method to learn about the impact of a given policy from those most directly affected, most dictators are unable to formulate effective economic programs.

Despite the violent origins of the political authority held by many of the HPAE leaders, this all-too-familiar scenario clearly does not apply to East Asia's high performers. Indeed, some observers have suggested that the East Asian economies succeeded precisely because the region's leaders were relatively unconstrained by institutions in the choice and implementation of government policy. In this view, authoritarian rule was not a hindrance but an aid to sound economic policy.

This chapter and the next offer a different hypothesis about the institutional foundations of East Asia's success. We argue that the East Asian leaders secured the support of economic elites without compromising sound policy through mechanisms designed to facilitate consultation, cooperation, and coordination.

To understand what East Asian leaders did, it is useful to look more deeply into the problems that beset authoritarian leaders. A dictator, by his nature, does not generally entertain checks (and balances) against his authority. But this absence undermines credibility for the long term: how do firms know he won't change policies tomorrow? If dictators want information to determine the appropriate choice of policies, they must ensure that the disclosure of information will not result in the direct (through expropriation) or indirect (through adverse changes in

---

3. Wintrobe (1994).

policies) confiscation of assets. To solve this commitment problem and to institutionalize the flow of information between the private and public sector, East Asian leaders traded authority for information, in effect tying their own hands by establishing institutions that restricted their scope for arbitrary action. Their design of institutions to limit sovereign discretion is rich in implications for the governments of other developing nations, including those governed by democratic constitutions.

The need to gain the cooperation of the economic elites illustrates the importance of institutions that facilitate the exchange of information between the public and private sectors. Each of the high performers had to overcome leadership's credibility deficit in order to win the confidence of those groups that had the capability, knowledge, and capital to build a dynamic industrial sector. One critical but often overlooked institutional device to achieve this is consultative committees, which five of the successful Asian economies—Singapore, Thailand, Korea, Japan, and Malaysia—have used.[4] In these countries, these committees, sometimes called deliberation councils, have been active and often critical in the formulation of policies, rules, and regulations that eventually govern a sector, industry, or in some cases the macroeconomy.[5]

The Deliberation Council

A deliberation council consists of representatives from the private sector and public sector.[6] The constitution of its membership depends

4. Although consultation processes have also permeated policymaking in Hong Kong, they have not been extensively documented. The process of consultation in Hong Kong begins at the executive council, which in 1986 consisted of five ex officio high government officials—the governor, the chief secretary, the financial secretary, the attorney general, and the commander of the British forces—and ten nominated members who do not hold public office. Although formally empowered to override advice given by members of the executive council, the governor is unlikely to do so as he depends heavily on the cooperation of nongovernmental council members for their contacts among the broader community. The executive council as well as the legislative council, the urban or regional councils, the district boards, and the many advisory boards and committees appointed by the government all depend on private sector participation.

5. We should note that the councils described here should not be equated with the *deliberative* councils in Japan. Many of the Japanese councils perform perfunctory roles and do not possess the fundamental characteristics that make a deliberation council effective. Only some (and these tend to be the more important ones) such as the industrial structure council are consonant with our concept.

6. Councils are not the only mechanism through which business and government interact. Many informal devices permeate this interaction. But councils are the most

on the policies over which it deliberates. For example, a council formed to discuss regulations governing the electronics industry would include representatives from the biggest electronic firms. If the industry has an active association, several members of the association would normally act as representatives. It would also include several midlevel and senior bureaucrats from the ministry of trade and industry. A council established to discuss international trade policy, however, would be larger and would enlist representation from all major industries and from many more government ministries. It may also include representatives of labor and consumer groups and is likely to be chaired by the deputy prime minister, if not the prime minister himself.

Generally the deliberation council has a quasi-legislative authority, and policies cannot be introduced or changed without its recommendation or approval. In this sense, it is like a legislative committee in a typical western democracy. But unlike a legislative committee, its private sector representatives are not selected by the electorate. Instead they are chosen by their respective sectors, for example, industry or labor. Its government officials become representatives by virtue of appointment. The principal task of a council is to assist the government in formulating policies that would enhance the performance of a particular segment of the private sector (if not the private sector as a whole). Within this context, a council is designed to reduce the high transaction costs of coordination; to overcome asymmetric information and rent seeking; to stabilize the policy environment; and to legitimize economic policies. More specifically, its cooperative format reduces the cost of obtaining and transmitting information about the design, implementation, and modification of existing policies. Second, it provides private sector participants with a transparent forum in which to bargain over the rules that determine how rents are to be allocated. Thus it diminishes the importance of patron-client relations and reduces the need for lobbying. Third, it gives the government a mechanism to instill confidence among investors that policies will not be altered without appropriate consultation and support from the private sector. Thus government can credibly commit to policies that enhance private sector development. And fourth, private sector participants gain a forum to express their views about policies that affect their industry and to

---

visible and can be documented more easily. Furthermore, agreements between the two parties are formalized in councils.

have those views incorporated into the formulation or alteration of the policies. Thus councils create a channel for government to establish the legitimacy of the policies it promulgates and implements. Councils vary by country and sector in the relative importance they assign each function.

National Wages Council: Singapore

Singaporean independence was marred by worker and student unrest. Tensions between labor and government had a long history. As discussed earlier, leadership understood that resolving labor tensions was critical if Singapore were to enjoy the prospect of development. Aggressive efforts to attract multinational corporations were the main feature of Singapore's development strategy. But multinationals have generally been hesitant to move their labor-intensive operations to countries with an unstable labor regime or an uncertain policy environment. The People's Action Party (PAP) thus focused on facilitating cooperative business-labor relations to help stabilize the policy environment. An important component of the strategy was the creation of the National Wages Council (NWC).

As noted earlier, the NWC is a tripartite advisory body composed of government, employer, and labor representatives. Multinationals are also represented. Each year the council reviews the past performance of the economy and evaluates prospects for the coming year. Based on the findings, members deliberate on employment-related issues generally and specifically on the appropriate guidelines for the year's wage increases. A key feature is tying the increases to gains in productivity, estimates of which are based on the past and projected performance of the economy. Meetings are held in the first half of each calendar year. Public views are sought for each year's deliberations although the deliberations themselves are kept private. Meetings follow two working rules, the Chatham House rule on nonattribution and the decision rule of unanimity. Under the Chatham House rule, statements and comments made by members are not to be publicly attributed to any individual. The rule thus promotes a freer discussion of the issues. Unanimity requires that each of the three groups—government, labor, and business—must support the proposed guidelines. Deliberations continue until all three agree to the provisions. Once an agreement is reached, the agreed-on guidelines are announced to the general public. The council's recommendations are nonbinding but, largely because of the unanimity rule, both business and labor have accepted them as an impartial benchmark of a reasonable wage settlement achieved through compromise. The government has always accepted the guidelines and usually is the first to adopt them.

The NWC incorporates all four functions of a deliberative council. It has been the primary channel through which government and the private sector share market information, especially information on improvements in productivity and trends in global markets. Orderly wage increases have resulted from its deliberations: (quasi) rents are allocated transparently and objectively between business (profits) and labor (wages).[7] Both labor and business have been granted veto power over wage policy (via unanimity) and thus have had real input into the decisionmaking process. In effect, the council resembles a legislative committee with limited jurisdiction. And finally, precisely because of its veto power, the council has helped maintain order and stability in wage negotiations, providing assurances to business and labor that wage policies will not be reversed arbitrarily or forcefully, for example, through strikes.

The unanimity rule has resulted in the implicit devolution of authority over employment policies by the government to the NWC: unanimity has assured each party that employment policies cannot be altered without their consent. By granting the council this authority over employment policies, the government has imposed on itself a very high cost to changing employment policy "from above." Forcing such a change could undermine the growth process since, fearing the onset of arbitrary policymaking, businesses may decide to move out and labor may decide to resort to more disruptive expressions of its demands. Should any of the parties take unilateral actions that challenge the council's legitimacy or jurisdiction, they would reduce the future value of the council as an instrument for coordination, consent, and commitment.[8] In short, the council has given the government the capacity to credibly commit to a stable, rational policymaking process.

7. Quasi rents are to be interpreted as gains over and above marginal cost.
8. There is a related argument that has permeated the study of American politics. One of the principal theoretical results of positive theories of U.S. congressional politics is that legislative institutions, for example, the committee system and its associated rules,

Japan

As a democracy with a free press and an established tradition of freely electing the legislature, Japan is unique among the high performers. However, like Singapore, it has made extensive use of deliberation councils. Its experience thus highlights the potential adaptability of a council system to different political circumstances.

After World War II the newly formed legislature earned its legitimacy as representatives of the people; the bureaucracy, however, was held over by the occupying forces and lacked a comparable claim to democratic legitimacy. Moreover, owing to the demise of the military as a political force and being the only surviving institution from the prewar era, the bureaucracy had become powerful.[9] Thus, although a parliamentary democracy, Japan's government had a credibility problem. It was dominated by a single party, which had at its service an administrative apparatus (imposed by the occupying forces), which did not have a democratic mandate and yet could intervene directly in the economic decisions of the private sector. To remedy this condition, councils were introduced and were especially important during the first two decades of Japanese democracy as a method for the bureaucracy to break with the past. In dealing with the Diet (the Japanese parliament), councils allowed the bureaucracy to make a claim to being representative of a constituent group.[10]

Among the HPAEs, Japan's councils are the most well developed

---

enable legislators to exploit gains from trade—vote for my project and I will vote for yours—which otherwise would not materialize because of majority rule vote cycling. Legislators, it is argued, support the maintenance of such institutions precisely because it allows them to exchange votes in ways that make everyone better off (for a concise explanation, see Shepsle and Weingast [1994]), that is, they allow bargains to be struck and to stick. In the context of the NWC, each party gains from having the NWC function as it has. The government manages to attract and keep investment, especially foreign investment, in the country; labor is assured that wages will track productivity gains and will be applicable to all workers; firms, especially multinationals, can be certain of a stable work environment. Hence, each party has incentives to keep the NWC as is.

9. Johnson (1982).

10. This would inevitably mean that bureaucrats would have to show the consensus of the relevant council before bringing a policy up for parliamentary approval. See chapter 6 for an extensive discussion.

and widely recognized. However, they are also the least transparent.[11] The Japanese deliberation councils included private sector representatives from the large industrial sector and in some cases from labor and consumer groups. Two categories of deliberation council allowed the Japanese government and private industry to cooperate on economic policy since the late 1940s. The first type is organized along functional or thematic lines, for example, industrial rationalization, pollution, and finance; the second is organized according to industry or sector, for example, iron and steel, automobile, and chemical. The councils are established by a government ministry and are formally associated with specific bureaus within that ministry. Table 4-1 lists the councils attached to the Ministry of Trade and Industry (MITI). The Industrial Structure Council, the Industrial Property Council, the Export and Import Transaction Council, and the Industrial Technology Council are examples of the first type. The Mining Industry Council and the Textile Industry Council are examples of the second. A functional deliberation council is normally divided into special committees. As shown in table 4-2 the Industrial Structure Council, one of the most influential during the 1960s, had eighteen such committees, each consisting of representatives from government and the private sector. Table 4-3 identifies the composition of the Industrial Structure Council.

Figure 4-1 illustrates the typical process involved in the formulation of policy in MITI. In the initial stage, MITI calls a hearing and invites various parties to participate. It compiles the data and integrates the results of the hearings into a draft. The draft report goes to the appropriate research group in MITI, which then prepares a report for discussion in the appropriate council. In the council, the views of industry officials, academics, consumers, and other interested parties are solicited and incorporated into a plan. The research group then makes changes to the report based on the feedback from council members. The last stage of the process resembles an advertising campaign through which MITI explains to the general public the objectives and reasons for the new policy.

As in Singapore, a Japanese council is essentially a forum through which government officials and representatives from the private sec-

11. Much of the information is contained in files of MITI to which access is limited. The discussion presented here comes from background papers by researchers in academia and government and from interviews with Japanese academics and government officials.

TABLE 4-1. *Major Regular Deliberative Councils Attached to MITI, 1990*

Council name	Affiliated bureau or agency	Date founded
Commodity Exchange Council	Industrial Policy Bureau	1950
Export and Import Transaction Council	International Trade Administration Bureau	1953
Coal Mining Council	Agency of Natural Resources and Energy	1955
Mining Industry Council	Agency of Natural Resources and Energy	1962
Small and Medium Enterprise Policy Making Council	Small and Medium Enterprise Agency	1963
Industrial Structure Council	Industrial Policy Bureau	1964
Textile Industry Council	Consumer Goods Industries Bureau	1964
Electricity Utility Industry Council	Agency of Natural Resources and Energy	1964
Industrial Location and Water Council	Industrial Location and Environmental Protection Bureau	1966
Industrial Property Council	Patent Office	1966
Data Processing Promotion Council	Machinery and Information Industries Bureau	1971
Industrial Technology Council	Agency of Industrial Science and Technology	1973
Large-Scale Retail Stores Council	Industrial Location and Environmental Protection Bureau	1974
Chemical Product Council	Basic Industries Bureau	1974
Traditional Craft Industry Council	Consumer Goods Industries Bureau	1974
Petroleum Council	Agency of Natural Resources and Energy	1978
Aircraft Industry Council	Machinery and Information Industries Bureau	1986

Source: Japan Development Bank and Japan Economic Research Institute (1993).

tor—industry, academia, the press, and in some instances, labor—exchange views on policy matters, discuss trends in markets and products, and more generally, share information.[12] The councils have provided the government the means to create a consensus on a particular policy matter: when the council does not agree on a policy, it is unlikely

12. Extensive informal information networks supplement the meetings of the deliberative council.

TABLE 4-2. *Committees of the Industrial Structure Council*

Committee name	Main items of deliberation	Year established
Central Committee	Basic direction of overall industrial policy	1964
Distribution Committee	Survey the actual state of distribution system and basic issues with respect to its modernization	1964
Industrial Pollution Committee	Measures to cope with industrial pollution	1964
Industrial Fund Committee	Formulating appropriate annual capital investment plans from the viewpoint of upgrading the industrial structure and strengthening international competitiveness; formulating plans for procuring necessary funds	1964
Management Committee	Financial, labor, and production management	1964
Cinema Committee	Liberalization measures and promoting exports	1964
Nuclear Power Industry Committee	Development of nuclear power and related businesses	1964
Energy Committee	Comprehensive energy policy	1964
International Economy Committee	Understanding and taking measures for the direction of the international economy, focusing mostly on the North-South problem, East-West problem, and problems of advanced industrialized nations	1964
Consumer Economy Committee	Analysis of the consumption structure and providing for a sound consumer life-style	1964
Heavy Industry Committee	General measures for promoting the machinery industry; analysis of the market for heavy industrial products and measures to promote exports	1964
Chemical Industry Committee	Measures to guarantee long-term supplies of naphtha for the petrochemical industry; analysis of the export market for chemical products and measures to promote exports	1964
General Merchandise and Construction Materials Committee	Grasping the current state of the general merchandise distribution system and formulating measures for the future; measures to promote the export of general merchandise; survey of the current condition of the gravel supply; basic direction of the pre-fab industry	1964

TABLE 4-2. *(continued)*

Committee name	Main items of deliberation	Year established
Textile Committee	Grasping the actual condition of the distribution system for textiles and policies for its normalization	1965
Industrial Finance Committe	Industrial finance policies for normalizing finance, consolidating equity, and upgrading the industrial structure	1965
Industrial Labor Committee	Measures for the effective application of industrial labor potential	1965
Industrial Location Committee	Appropriate placement of industry; preparing the conditions for locating industry	1966
Industrial Technology Committee	Measures to strengthen the development of technology	1965

Source: Japan Development Bank and Japan Economic Research Institute (1993).

the policy will be approved by the legislature even if it is supported by the bureaucracy.

Hence, it was important for MITI to achieve consensus within the deliberation council, for it is here where success or failure of a policy initiative was essentially determined. For example, "the plans for the concentration of the automobile industry, which in fact never materialized, were both strongly opposed at the council level. In the end a consensus within the industries concerned was not obtained."[13] Three times MITI proposed rationalization of the auto industry. The first national car plan basically gave the rights of production to a single winner. In 1955, MITI formulated the National Car Project and attempted to execute it, its purpose being concentrated production of low cost, small cars for the general public by a single manufacturer.... The Concept concerned a car accommodating (1) four passengers (2) costing about 250,000 yen (3) with a displacement of 350 to 500 cc (4) weighing 400 kg, and (5) with a maximum speed of 100 km/h. Concentrated production of this car by a single manufacturer was proposed.[14] The second was a partitioning of the industry into three groups, each group producing a specific vehicle cate-

13. Japan Development Bank and Japan Economic Research Institute (1993, chap. 2, p. 42).
14. Itoh and Urata (1993, p. 14).

TABLE 4-3. *Composition of Industrial Structure Council*

Industries and business representatives (20)	*Academics (7)*
Japan Committee for Economic Development, secretary general	National University, professor
Japan Chamber of Commerce and Industry, managing director	National University, professor
	Private university, professor
Osaka Chamber of Commerce and Industry, president	Private university, professor
	Private university, professor
Kansai Economic Federation, chairman	Private university, professor
National Federation of Small Business Associations, chairman	Economic commentator
Synthetic fiber company, president	*Journalists (2)*
Chemical company, honorary president	Newspaper advisor
Chemical company, president	Broadcast station analyst
Petroleum Association of Japan, president	
Oil company, advisor	*Consumer and labor representatives (3)*
Steel company, chairman	
Electronics industry association, chairman	Consumer association, director
Electronics industry promotion association, chairman	Labor association, director
	Labor association, director
Electrical manufacturing company, president	*Financial representatives, others*
Electrical manufacturing company, president	
Automobile industry association, chairman	City bank, chairman
Retail company, chairman	Long-Term Credit Bank, chairman
Retail company, president	Japan Development Bank, governor
Railway company, president	Shoko Chukin Bank, president
Federation of Electric Power Companies, chairman	Prefectural Governor
	National Mayor's Association, chairman
Electric Power Company, president	
Former bureaucrats (4)	Total 42
Think tank, managing director	
Think tank, managing director	
Think tank, managing director	
Japan Foreign Trade Council, chairman	

Source: Management of Coordination Agency; Japan Development Bank and Japan Economic Research Institute (1993).

gory. "In May 1961, MITI proposed to split the automakers into three groups of mass production, special passenger cars (high class cars and sports cars), and mini passenger cars, each group consisting of two to three manufacturers."[15] Both times, council members rejected MITI's

15. Itoh and Urata (1993, p. 15).

FIGURE 4-1. *Industrial Vision Formulation and the Deliberation Council*

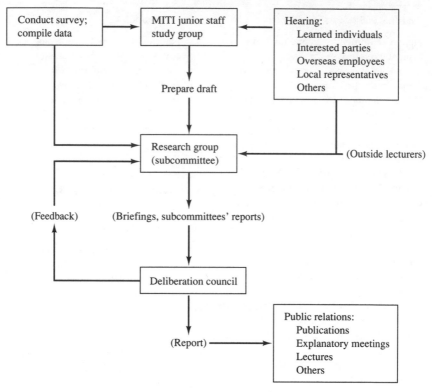

Source: Ono (1992).

proposals. And both times, MITI resisted forcing the issue in the Diet. In its third try, MITI managed to obtain a consensus among the manufacturers. Import protection was agreed to in exchange for exporting: every manufacturer could participate.[16] Shortly thereafter the Diet (the legislature) passed a new automobile industry rationalization law embodying the agreement.

The auto industry example illustrates two functions of a council. First, transparent rules for the allocation of rents among firms were established. Manufacturers agreed to a plan that gave each one opportunities to earn rents through protection of the domestic market in exchange for successful expansion into export markets. Second, while

16. Itoh (1993).

providing inputs into legislation, manufacturers had veto power. As a consequence, automobile manufacturers could be confident that policies would not be changed without their consent and therefore were relatively durable.

Why does government not overturn those council decisions it opposes and abide only by those it prefers? The answer is rather subtle. Given that councils have permeated many industries and sectors in the country, by unilaterally imposing its will on a single industry or sector, the government risks undermining the value of councils and thus subverting the whole system of cooperative decisionmaking. This in turn would increase the transaction costs of policymaking and thus could retard economic growth.[17] Should that happen, the legitimacy of the government could be more easily challenged. Tying the fortunes of many groups to the continued use of a particular system raises the cost of altering that system. Hence, the more closely groups are tied together, the more credible a system becomes. By institutionalizing councils, the government has limited its discretionary power over economic policy but in turn has created an environment that has given big business confidence in the stability of policies agreed upon.

Korea

Rebuilding private sector confidence was a priority for an obscure group of military officers who violently took power in Korea in 1961. Those officers were willing to place all political bets on economic growth. After first shattering existing old-boy networks, they struck a deal with the heads of the big conglomerates (chaebols) they had imprisoned: the private sector would deliver development and, as part of the bargain, confiscated wealth would be released. After this initial heavyhandedness, consultation between government and the chaebols greatly helped to win back private sector support. Political leaders helped to coordinate private sector effort but left the actual work to the business community.

In Korea from the mid-1960s to the early 1980s, government and private sector relations were characterized by frequent, regular meetings between leaders of both groups. These meetings were less formal than the council meetings in Japan or Singapore, but they had similar objectives: information exchange; rent allocation; elite participation in

17. This argument is derivative of Grief, Milgrom, and Weingast (1994).

policymaking; and stability of the policy environment. President Park Chung Hee's presence at monthly export promotion meetings gave authority to the meetings.[18]

The meetings were the barometer for the country's export push and thus critical to its overall economic performance. The ministries' commitment to building up the private sector went as far as bullying it into accepting export markets.[19] However, bureaucrats did not decide what to produce. Rather they coordinated and ensured the sharing of relevant information among all parties that had bargaining power, specifically, big business. These meetings and the informal consultations that followed facilitated early recognition of problems encountered in expanding Korean export markets. The primary focus of these meetings was the joint determination of export targets for various industries by private enterprises and government officials. The Ministry of Commerce and Industry collected information from individual exporters on a monthly, weekly, and sometimes even daily basis. It also monitored and analyzed changes in market conditions. Export targets and policies were altered when necessary so that the government and private sector could respond rapidly to fluctuations in world markets. Short-term changes in government policies could then reflect world market conditions. The system reduced the risks to private enterprise of engaging in export activity.

Lower-level meetings between middle managers in private industry, mid-level officials in government, and experts and scholars supplemented the monthly export promotion meetings. Meetings took place in the form of industrial discussion groups. There were basically two types: the functional (for example, taxation) and the sectoral. The former was centered around the presentation of various viewpoints from known experts on topics normally identified and chosen by the bureaucracy, for example, the Ministry of Finance. The experts provided their analyses and opinions; the government bureaucrats normally just listened. Though the final decision was made by the bureaucracy, the

18. "The establishment of this well-publicized meeting had a significant effect in exploring profitable markets and in implicitly promising government-wide support for private sector activities designed to achieve those export targets." Chang (1992).

19. Samsung lost a fertilizer factory when it refused to support Park's initiative. This confiscation, however, was conducted according to rules: the stick was applied when the company refused to cooperate. This information is based on an interview with Professor Bong-Joon Yoon in October 1992.

policies adopted generally attempted to incorporate the various viewpoints. The second type of industrial discussion group involved representatives from an industry, usually from the corresponding industrial association, who discussed their perspectives on an issue with representatives from the Ministry of Trade and Industry. At this level, the process was primarily one of gathering information rather than collaborative decisionmaking. Nevertheless, vocal industry representatives often helped shape the final product.

Deliberation councils, especially the monthly export promotion meetings, were important in coordinating the export drive. During the meetings, obstacles to achieving competitiveness were discussed and solutions were often recommended and implemented.[20] The meetings presided over by Park were devoted to monitoring export targets and solving export-related problems. The criteria for access to subsidized credit and to production licenses became more transparent as a result of the councils. Firms seeking credit and licenses had to meet Park's basic criterion: "How much have you exported for me lately?"[21] Export performance was used to allocate preferential credit and to determine who would get valuable licenses from the government to produce promoted products.[22] The council's principal function was to extract the necessary information to formulate better export promotion policies and to allocate rents, that is, credit subsidies and production licenses, in a systematic, transparent, and objective fashion.[23]

20. Amsden (1989).

21. Amsden (1989) refers to this system as reciprocal exchange.

22. The meetings were designed to be genuine dialogues between firms and the government. Participants were chosen by business associations. Moreover Park made a policy of never meeting with representatives of firms privately. He met with business people in groups and as representatives of their industry, not their particular firms (interview with Chang-Yum Kim, January 1995). In this way, rent allocation was based on transparent and objective criteria.

23. Exporting, which began in the more neutral environment of the 1960s, continued to be a major criterion for allocating credit during the 1970s Export promotion consisted not only of preferential credit but of other policies as well. See Rhee and others (1984) for a comprehensive review of Korea's export-promoting policies. Enforcement of the performance criteria was possible because the government possessed strong leverage over firms: it controlled the sources of loans, for example, banks, and the authority over industrial licensing. Haggard (1990); Amsden (1989). As Wade (1990) notes, the debt-equity ratio of firms in Korea has been historically higher than in Japan or Taiwan, suggesting that much of the firms' initial growth was debt driven. Since loans often had to be rolled over, the threat of terminating loans could jeopardize the existence of highly

Once established, the country's export orientation was difficult to alter. Firms had come to expect significant rewards for success in exporting and thus had oriented their production, management, and marketing capabilities to world markets. Changing the rules of the game would have had serious consequences on firms' operations and thus on economic growth, undermining the legitimacy of the military government. The councils in Korea helped make export policies durable and credible to the private sector, coordinating the move from an inward-looking, protectionist trade regime to an outward-oriented one, institutionalizing a process that made exporting virtually irreversible.[24]

Thailand

Before 1981, Thailand's relationships between the public and private sectors were characterized by "a prevailing sense of distrust, and elements of arrogance on both sides. The public sector regarded the private sector as selfish entrepreneurs and thinking only of their personal profits with little sense of social responsibility. The private sector, on the other hand, suspected government officials of being extremely inefficient, corrupt, and bureaucratic. . . . The two points of view were rarely reconciled as there was no formal mechanism to bring about more fruitful dialogues."[25] The sources of the mistrust had deep historical roots. Since the turn of the century many commercial enterprises have been controlled by the Chinese minority causing the majority native Thai to perceive them as capitalist exploiters. From the overthrow of the monarchy in 1932 to the late 1970s, under successive governments, mostly military, the public sector was the exclusive domain of native Thai counteracting the economic power of the Chinese. As a result, business-government relations had come to be governed by military-bureaucratic *clientilism* (that is, a relationship in which

---

leveraged firms. In some cases, the government refused to bail out failing companies unless the firm agreed to changes in the management.

24. Irreversibility is related to the concept of path dependency. Path dependency refers to historical constraints imposed on the trajectory of an economy. For example, David (1985) argues that the initial development of the QWERTY keyboard for the typewriter has constrained the adoption of more efficient keyboards primarily because the former has come to be accepted and used by a very large number of people and establishments. Changing to a new system would involve enormous coordination. Irreversibility stems largely from the costs of coordinating a switch.

25. Muscat (1994, p. 183).

public officials are "patrons," providing some protection or security from harassment to private business groups who are "clients."[26] To protect their business interests, the Chinese resorted to "outright bribery or [sought] patron-client relationships with the military-bureaucratic leaders, mainly by inviting the latter to join executive boards or to hold stock in companies at no cost."[27] The presence of military-political leaders on the boards of twelve of Thailand's sixteen commercial banks in 1972 illustrates the extent to which this protection system was institutionalized.[28]

But although the protection system allowed economic activity to flourish, it failed to alleviate the basic mistrust between the public sector and the private sector. Entrepreneurs presumed (correctly) that they needed strong patrons in government to prevent harassment. Bureaucrats and military officers had come to expect board memberships in exchange for their consent to and protection of commercial activity.

In the early 1980s, partly to help overcome the tradition of mistrust, the orchestrators of Thailand's liberalization drive championed the need for better and more formal communication between the public and private sectors. Designating the private sector as the engine of growth, the Prem government's Fifth National Economic and Social Plan proposed a mechanism for public and private sector collaboration. "The National Joint Public and Private Consultative Committee (JPPCC) was formed, with the Prime Minister as Chairman and the Secretary General of the National Economics and Social Development Board (NESDB) as Committee Secretary. Other members were the deputy prime ministers, ministers and deputy ministers of economic ministries, the Governor of the Bank of Thailand and the Secretary General of the Board of Investment. The private sector was represented by three representatives from the Thai Chamber of Commerce (TCC), three from the Federation of Thai Industries (FTI), and three from the Thai Bankers Association (TBA)."[29]

26. Clientilism refers to the personalized pairing of partners in recurrent exchanges. Ties are developed to cope with the cost of contract uncertainty. Thus promises are likely to be honored despite the absence of a public enforcement authority, and social or political rank will heavily influence the terms of trade.

27. Laothamatas (1988, p. 451).

28. See chapter 5. Business-government relations in pre-1981 Thailand share many of the features of the relations in post-1965 Indonesia.

29. Samudavanija (1992, p. 26).

In Thailand much of the initiative to establish peak industrial associations came from the private sector, for example, TCC, FTI, and TBA. Although the government legally chartered these bodies, it did not intervene extensively in their development and management.[30] Hence, in contrast with their status in other corporatist states, industrial associations evolved more independently of government in Thailand than elsewhere.[31]

The industrial associations enabled businessmen and bankers to develop their own networks and to participate with the military-bureaucratic elites in the task of developing the economy. This partnership took a new face in the early 1980s as Thailand attempted to recover from the impact of the second oil crisis. In 1981 General Prem, who headed the government from 1980 until 1988, sought the assistance of the private sector to help stimulate the Thai economy. The quadrupling of oil prices increased the balance of payments deficit to alarming levels. Prem asked the representatives of the peak industrial associations for help in addressing the external deficit problem. The creation of the JPPCC, where development policies could be discussed jointly and openly by high-ranking government officials and private sector representatives was their response to Prem's request. With the active support of government technocrats, their recommendation became a reality.[32]

30. "Weak as they might have been as interest groups, business associations were at that time (circa 1970) much stronger than any functional group. . . . Almost all of them were created and/or sponsored, and closely controlled by the government for security and agricultural development purposes. . . . By comparison, business associations were largely independent of the government. . . . No public officials sat on the executive boards of business associations. Official control of their operation, internal regulation, and leadership selection, though harsh in theory, was mild in practice. No closures of associations or bans on their functions or leadership selections had been reported." Laothamatas (1992, pp. 31–32). The impetus for the JPPCC came from the combined efforts of prominent members of the business community with proactive support from technocrats, particularly from Dr. Snoh Unakol, Secretary General of the NESDB during most of the 1980s.

31. Military-bureaucratic governments often create corporate bodies to represent key sectors of the polity and then control these bodies by designating the representatives. This is generally referred to in the literature as *bureaucratic corporatism* (see, for instance, Staniland (1985, chap. 4).

32. The NESDB and in particular, its director, Dr. Snoh, convinced the government to establish the JPPCC. Laothamatas conjectures that Prem may have given serious thought to creating the JPPCC, which the peak associations had long been clamoring for, in order to establish an alternative base of political support. In 1980 he barely survived an attempted coup by so-called Young Turks in the military. Laothamatas (1988).

To contain if not resolve the balance of payments problem, the Prem government recognized that Thai firms had to export. But to export successfully, firms had to be internationally competitive. Hoping to reinvigorate the economy, the Prem government adopted the recommendations of the JPPCC. Through the JPPCC, information about the impact of regulations, tax measures, and trade policy on the performance of firms and more generally on the economy was transmitted back to officials more quickly, thereby focusing the government's response to problems. Moreover, various industrial conglomerates were able to express their concerns over trade policy and to have those concerns addressed in a transparent (to members) forum. Big business was incorporated into the policymaking process, especially trade policy.[33]

But perhaps the most important contribution of the JPPCC was the reduction of bureaucratic clientilism through the creation of an alternative, more transparent system of rent allocation. The need to minimize the adverse consequences of bureaucratic clientilism was one of the principal motives for the Thai technocrats to actively support the creation of the national JPPCC. The principal sponsor among the technocrats, Snoh Unakol, had a very clear position on this matter. "In Snoh's view, Thailand had been close to the decadent model of capitalism. Government-business relations in the past had served only those few who had massive financial resources or good personal connections with high officials. These relationships created resentment among the business community, as well as the general public. . . . Snoh's proposal for government-business dialogues was guided considerably by his conviction that a new system must be built in which under-the-table dealings were reduced by the availability of on-the-table consultation, by the government's responsiveness to the legitimate requests of business, and by the deregulation of the economy."[34] Similarly, Robert Muscat explains that the experience "and the whole arrangement based

33. In some developing countries where big business dominates, trade policy has generally had a protectionist character, for example, in the Philippines. In contrast, in the HPAEs, government has dominated the private sector by controlling the extent to which the private sector participates in decisionmaking. Historical factors are responsible for the difference. See, for instance, Hutchcroft (1991) and McCoy (1993) on the Philippines, Haggard (1990) on Korea, and Amsden (1979) on Taiwan.

34. See Laothamatas (1992, p. 82). In interviews, a business tycoon who is a member of the Malaysian Business Council and a senior fellow of a local think tank raised similar points.

on organizations, issues, and transparency, rather than inside dealings and the pursuit of individual commercial advantage, would promote the 'maturation' of the Thai business sector and contribute to the reduction of particularistic or corrupt relationships between business and officialdom."[35] An important component of the business sector's maturation was the acquisition of "a professional capability for open policy discussions." Some of the leading associations commissioned research teams to persuade the government with analytical data. Among others, this included contracting with Chulalongkorn University to research the effect of the tax structure on key industries.

The Thai consultative meetings differed from the meetings in Japan and Korea. Only matters of general interest were discussed, that is, problems that applied to a majority of, if not all, large firms. The Thai meetings were also open to the press, which put pressure on the prime minister to respond to business's proposed reforms. Among the innovations that occurred as a result of the JPPCC dialogue were the development of graduate education in modern business management, incentives for family firms to go public by issuing equity, and establishing standards for disclosure. Investment by multinationals was encouraged in joint ventures with Thai firms. The JPPCC was critical in orienting the economy toward manufactured exports. Significant progress resulted toward establishing international competitiveness and modern business practices. In particular, rules, regulations, and tax measures that governed the export of domestically produced or processed manufactured goods were streamlined and rationalized in order to reduce the production costs of manufacturers and to enable them to compete internationally.

Nevertheless, the consultative process in Thailand has been faulted for failure to develop channels for the representation of small farmers and nonunionized labor. The JPPCC does not represent labor, farm, or public enterprises. At the very least, the councils helped the new professional business sector to establish a foothold in the policy dialogue and to challenge the practice of clientilism. It also signaled the government's commitment to professionalism and to international business practices.

The blatant exploitation by the business sector of public officeholders to obtain privileged access to government favors by the (big) business

35. Muscat (1994, p. 183).

sector resurged, however, during the Chatichai (July 1988–February 1991) administration.[36] Although the Chatichai government represented the political ascendancy of business and was democratically elected, it has less successfully advocated consistent business policies than its predecessor. The pursuit of the spoils of office once again disrupted the dialogue for a coherent policy framework.[37]

The shift to an export-oriented economic strategy is perhaps the greatest achievement of the expanded government-business dialogue. But the sources of mistrust have not yet been eliminated. The JPPCC format did not evolve into a framework for close collaboration between business and government characteristic of Japan or Korea. Measurements of transparency and predictability in the regulatory environment still rank Thailand lower than the more advanced high performers— Japan and the four tigers (see chapter 6).

Malaysia

A lack of confidence stymied the collaboration of business with government until the early 1990s, when Malaysia too learned the benefits of formally coordinating the flow of information. There, business-government relations have evolved through three phases: the free market phase (postindependence to 1970); the Bumiputra or New Economic Policy (NEP) phase (1972 to 1985); and transition to the New Development Policy (NDP; 1986 to the present).[38] In phase one, the government basically allowed the private sector to function freely and was primarily concerned with infrastructure building. In phase two, in response to

36. Muscat (1994).

37. Muscat (1994, p. 184) speculates that the JPPCC declined when the Chatichai business cabinet (July 1988–February 1991) made it unnecessary. "The policy and regulatory framework that is the natural subject of interest to the private sector across the board receded into the background as the rivalries among a handful of individual businessmen and groups, then having captured the very mechanisms designed to regulate them and dispense public resources, took center stage. The further evolution of institutionalized relationships between government and business organizations was put on hold as the individual businessmen/politicians and government leadership became one and the same." His conjecture suggests why councils in other parts of the world might not work: if the business community has viable, alternative means for communicating and influencing government, then councils may have less value and thus may not be as highly valued by their members.

38. The New Development Policy was introduced officially in 1991 as the successor to the twenty-year program embodied in the NEP.

the racial riots of 1969, the government introduced the Bumiputra Policy. As discussed earlier, the policy was designed to narrow the wealth gap and enable native Malays to participate in trade and industry by requiring minimum Bumiputra participation in economic activities. During phase three (which roughly coincides with Prime Minister Mahathir's leadership), the antagonism that characterized government-business relations in the second phase was gradually redressed. For example, firms with less than M$2.5 million capitalization were no longer subjected to the requirement that 30 percent of their stock be sold to Bumiputras. The NEP was transformed into the NDP, in which big business has been given the primary role of leading the development of the country. This thrust characterizes Mahathir's Look East Policy. The first sign of a change was the creation of the so-called Budget Dialogue in which captains of industry were called in to discuss the national budget with finance officials. Then advisory groups for certain sectors were formed. Each group included representatives from industry and government. The members helped formulate policies and developed strategies for implementation. Finally, the Malaysian Business Council (MBC), which included sixty members from private industry, some members of labor, several government ministers and deputy ministers, and the prime minister as chairman, was established. The MBC facilitated direct communication between big business, labor, and the prime minister.

The use of councils dates back to 1981. A confidential government study of business-government relations in the mid-1980s uncovered informal councils tied to government ministries. An informal council basically made evaluations of a ministry's regulations. It was further discovered that a council's effectiveness depended on the participation of individuals from the private sector. Those that had members from the private sector produced output useful to the ministries as well as to the private sector groups the latter regulated: rules and regulations were revised to reduce the burden on the private sector. Those that did not failed to provide useful solutions to problems they were asked to address. These findings largely influenced the formation of the Malaysian Business Council and the Budget Dialogue Group in which private sector representatives participate as active and equal members.[39]

It is still too early to evaluate the effectiveness of the MBC and the

39. Critics point out that labor is not adequately represented in these consultations.

Budget Dialogue Group and to establish exactly what their functions are. Personal interviews with some participants suggest that, like the JPPCC in Thailand, the MBC has helped move rent seeking from covert, under-the-table dealings to more transparent, over-the-table transactions.[40]

The Implications of Councils for Economic Performance

As the preceding examples illustrate, deliberation councils yield economic benefit.[41] A council serves as a convenient channel for collecting relevant information from, and distributing it to, its participants. It thus improves economic efficiency: it supplements the allocative function of markets by facilitating coordinated responses to changes in economic conditions. A council also helps reduce the opportunities for and welfare losses from rent seeking.[42] Furthermore, a council performs a commitment function, binding sovereign authority to a set of rules governing economic policymaking. Hence, it helps minimize economic distortions attributable to the nonsimultaneity of the costs and benefits of a policy.[43]

Improving Coordination

Although the HPAEs have all established various mechanisms to reduce the costs to firms and the government of obtaining information

40. Malaysia's most recent advertising campaign to promote business and investment highlights the importance of the MBC to the country's thrust toward achieving Mahathir's Vision 2020. A video featuring the role of the MBC was played for participants at an ASEAN conference on governance in Vietnam in September 1994.

41. Ideally, we would have wanted to link councils with their welfare consequences. Unfortunately, this would require constructing an experiment that would provide measurable criteria. In general, the state of the art in evaluating the welfare impact of institutions is still primitive compared with evaluation in other more developed fields. Campos and Lien (1994) have shown theoretically that councils can reduce the amount of directly unproductive profit-seeking (DUP) activities. See Bhagwati and Srinivasan (1982) for a definition and discussion of DUP activities.

42. That is, it not only reduces the size of the "Harberger" triangles but also the magnitude of the "DUP rectangles." Harberger triangles refer to a measure of efficiency losses and DUP rectangles to a measure of losses from DUP activities.

43. See Rodrik (1989) and Campos and Esfahani (forthcoming) for a discussion of the problem of promises and the lack of credibility within the context of policy reform.

about markets, councils stand out as particularly useful mechanisms to transmit information. Changes in world markets, new trends in technologies, and perverse effects of regulations domestically and abroad are all communicated to the bureaucracy by private sector agents. In turn, the bureaucracy synthesizes the different pieces of information and communicates this synthesis through proposed plans. The potential effects of these plans are relayed by private agents back to the bureaucracy for possible alterations. This interactive process continues until a consensus is reached. In short, deliberation councils provide a built-in feedback mechanism that helps the public and private sectors adjust to an ever-changing environment. They "can acquire more information than any one individual (member) for it has each member performing different experiments. Thus, the limitations on an individual industry's or firm's capacity are overcome."[44] Although deliberation councils cannot substitute for the informational attributes of markets, they certainly supplement them.[45]

Problems involving synchronization frequently arise in development.[46] They arise for instance in new industries with potentially large-scale economies. As Paul Milgrom and John Roberts have pointed out, "Economies of scale that are achieved in the manufacture of components of several products increase the need for coordination because the optimal scale of each product is an increasing function of the anticipated scale of the other products that use the same components."[47] From this perspective consider the following advantages of councils as coordination mechanisms: if a new airport is to be built, roads and trains to the airport must be ready by a target date. To induce a company to invest in creating the roads might require assurances that another firm has agreed to construct the airport. Similarly, hotelkeepers will invest once they are assured of the behavior of other relevant investors. Information demanded to achieve coordination required for a new airport may not be efficiently conveyed by the price system. Councils offer supplemental sources of information, providing decisionmakers with information about how parts of a large project fit together. They provide a forum

44. Lim (1981, p. 15).

45. In fact, councils work because they use markets as their guide. The plans developed jointly by the public and private sectors are tested against the realities in the marketplace.

46. See Gershenkron (1962).

47. Milgrom and Roberts (1991, p. 117).

to communicate strategy to all members of an industry. When a lack of synchronized behavior may be costly to several parties, the council can be especially helpful. For example, the price system does not take into account the true marginal cost of the early introduction of a product. Knowing the number of possible delivery dates requires communication not necessarily conveyed by prices. A council meeting can more easily reveal the marginal costs of a speedup for each supplier, making it possible to predict the cost of the final product. Inducing private sector actors to make one set of investments sometimes requires assurances that a related set will also be made. In those cases councils are helpful because they facilitate coordination.

Deliberation councils also help resolve externality problems (which in essence are also coordination problems). For example, an exporter who breaks into a foreign market bears all the costs, while results can easily be copied by firms that did not pay the initial costs of gaining entry. In the council, the costs of learning about new markets are distributed among council membership.[48]

A council might also help distribute burdens from future crises, thereby reducing the overall risk of a project.[49] For example, in Japan members of a council will shoulder the costs of a collective decision that causes a weaker member to go bankrupt. When downsizing is called for, the biggest firm in the industry may be asked to absorb smaller companies that take the loss.[50]

Taming the Rent Seekers

Whereas an absence of transparency has allowed governments of many developing nations to reserve economic opportunities for their clients, councils have permitted most of the HPAE regimes to avoid this pattern. In the council, information about the policy environment is shared among all players. Each has access to the same information, and information flows both ways. By contrast, in many developing countries, policy-relevant information is asymmetrically distributed. Private sector firms do not know what their competitors know and hence are uncertain about what their competitors will do; even announced government plans cannot be trusted. In essence, when the

48. World Bank (1993a).

49. In a discussion of risk sharing, credit markets, and participatory government intervention in Korea, Cho and Hellman (1993) make a similar argument.

50. Yamamura (1986).

parties have unequal information they will mistrust one another and will hesitate to cooperate on joint projects.

Mistrust creates a strong impetus toward rent seeking. In the absence of a credible and transparent policy regime governing market competition, pressure groups have incentives to lobby government officials. Lobbying can be viewed as a defensive measure that often occurs when each group assumes that others will lobby to acquire as large a share of the market either directly, for example, logging concessions, or indirectly, for example, import quotas. Hence, to protect its turf, each is induced to engage in as much lobbying as can be afforded. Seeking special deals or privileges thus becomes the modus operandi of groups. A council can eliminate this uncertainty and reduce mistrust by making policies transparent to all affected parties; by making information available to all, a council makes it more difficult for individuals or groups to obtain special favors from the government and for government officials to provide special treatment to individuals or groups.[51] Welfare losses attributable to directly unproductive profit-seeking (DUP) activities can thereby be reduced.

In many developing nations, patronage is the main source of rents and thus is central to the political support base of the regime. Informal political structures nourish the proliferation of patron-client ties. Impersonal institutions such as deliberation councils, by diffusing access to regime officials, can weaken patron-client ties and help the regime reduce the costs of rent seeking.

During the early stages of development, political and economic elites constitute small and overlapping circles. The closer an individual's ties to a regime, the more difficult it is for the regime to enforce rules that would alter that individual's behavior. Therefore, it is necessary to protect government ministries from individuals who wish to use connections to win exceptions, privileges, or modifications to rules. The advantage of policies approved by councils is that members will have to accept changes and adjust to rules that apply to all, since if they seek exceptions their lobbying will quickly become known to other members of the council. Through councils the government acquires greater capability to resist pressures from powerful individuals.

In sum, when rules, procedures, and regulations are discussed openly

51. Campos and Lien (1994) show that, if firms can reveal information without fear of being taken advantage of, the level of rent seeking falls, that is, firms have less incentive to engage in lobbying.

among the relevant parties and input from all parties is encouraged, a more transparent and impartial policy environment emerges. This constricts the possible avenues for seeking or granting special favors and raises the cost of and reduces the potential gains from rent seeking. Councils help limit the perverse effects of rent seeking: members effectively agree to the rules of the game that ultimately determine how rents are to be distributed among them. The rules could directly specify the distribution as in the case of industry downsizing in Japan or indirectly as in the case of export performance criteria in Korea.[52] In either case, rent shares are negotiated in a relatively open forum, making it difficult for individuals or special interest groups to seek special treatment and thus to derail good policies.

An Implicit Constitution: Councils as Commitment Devices

The use of deliberation councils to coordinate economic policy creates a structure of rights and expectations that induces investor confidence. In effect, a de facto constitutional framework to direct economic decisionmaking is erected. Violating the implied norms imposes costs on the government and on the private sector operators. To violate the procedural norms or etiquette that governs economic decisionmaking would require altering the rules governing the creation of policy.

Changing the rules imposes costs of its own. The party that forces those changes may ultimately wish for the protection they have abandoned. To avoid risks that disagreements over procedural changes may lead to unexpected outcomes, officials may decide to stay with the rules already in place. Moreover, an attempt to force a change in the rules without private sector participation would undermine the future value of the councils as a coordination and rent-sharing mechanism. That in turn would make policymaking more difficult.

Ultimately, the councils are commitment devices that restrain governmental discretion.[53] By granting authority to deliberation councils

52. Yamamura (1986); Lim (1981); Amsden (1989); Haggard (1990); Chang (1993). In Korea firm subsidies are based on their export performance and thus on the ability of firms to compete; in the former, the government, through the council, determines which firm(s) absorb the less profitable ones in the industry.

53. It is often argued that Korean business-government relations consist of the government's bribing, cajoling, or coercing private sector firms. See Amsden (1989); Haggard and others (1990); Lee (1992). But it should be emphasized that the government has applied the carrot and the stick impartially and consistently. If a firm fails to deliver, it

the government gains authority. As Daniel Okimoto puts it, "Without industry's willing cooperation, the Japanese state would not be nearly as powerful or effective."[54] An agreement from a deliberation council represents unanimity within an industry and increases the likelihood of legislative approval. In effect, the government relinquishes authority to gain the possible consent of the private sector to promote a government program. By granting authority to the councils, the government gains credibility that it can implement its programs. This in turn makes the government a more credible player nationally and internationally. An investor will choose a country where the government has the capability to protect the property rights of investors. The councils provide some of this capability because they imply that policies have the implicit consent of the relevant private sector actors.

Councils provide rules for gaining a consensus on economic policy. These rules are an implicit constitution offering guarantees against the imposition of policies detrimental to council members. Revisions of the rules or of policies are subject to the councils' purview, thus providing economic actors with assurances against sudden policy shifts. By imposing restrictions on its ability to alter policy, the state makes the property rights of council members more durable.[55] Economic entrepre-

---

is penalized; if it delivers, it is rewarded. That is, the Korean state has refrained from the predatory behavior characteristic of many dictatorships.

Of course, the question then is how credible is the state's commitment to impartial and consistent implementation of the carrot and stick? Reputation is critical. If the state's goal is to promote growth, and it depends fundamentally on the help of the private sector (which was certainly true in Korea), then it must necessarily obtain the cooperation of the private sector by building a reputation for impartiality and consistency. By contrast, favoritism encourages DUP activities, which results in uncertainty about the "rules of the game." This restrains growth by making it difficult to obtain the needed cooperation. In short, the long-run cost to the state of ruining its reputation is a disincentive to playing favorites.

54. Okimoto (1989, p. 145). "Instead of labeling Japan a strong state, therefore perhaps it would be more accurate to call it a 'societal,' 'relational,' or 'network' state, one whose strength is derived from the convergence of public and private interests and the extensive network of ties binding the two sectors together."

55. Economic policy can be viewed as a contract between government and the private sector. Williamson (1985). However, contracts cannot address every possible contingency. To induce investments in fixed capital assets whose value is greatly reduced in alternative uses, that is, asset specific investments, the government must be able to commit to not expropriating those investments whether directly through confiscation or indirectly through arbitrary and frequent policy changes, that is, not reneging on ex ante

neurialism is encouraged by the knowledge that today's policies will not create the profits for tomorrow's confiscations.

An Implication: From Import Substitution to Export-Oriented Industrialization

Deliberation councils can be critical in facilitating the change toward export orientation from import substitution (ISI). By abandoning the relative comfort of the ISI regime, established firms open themselves up to the danger of losing market share by reducing their comparative advantage, for example, knowledge of the domestic market and control over distribution, and over other potential domestic competitors who may be much smaller. Deliberation councils can be harnessed to reduce this uncertainty and thus to provide better incentives for firms to support the export drive. Through these mediating institutions, information about developments in world markets is shared among all firms, giving each equal opportunities to respond. Subsidized credit can be directed to good performers to reduce the risk of breaking into world markets. In some cases, established firms and the government can agree to limit entry in the initial stages. In other words, these institutions help provide the necessary coordination needed to move from a low-level equilibrium to a higher-level equilibrium: because they guarantee the existing (and more often than not the major) players that none will be disfavored in the change of regimes (in the sense of fair application of the new rules and regulations), they induce the players to participate more willingly in the new programs; a larger pie and Pareto superior allocations result.

Public sources of credit are often necessary to promote an export drive. Private financiers have the means to test the waters in domestic markets but very rarely in foreign markets. Financiers are therefore reluctant to lend for exports and will consistently ration credit in favor of domestic production. Consequently, when domestic bankers combine with large, indigenous merchants, their preferred policy is a secure domestic market characterized by import substitution as opposed to exporting. But government-subsidized credit is not sufficient to guarantee good export performance. The carrot, that is, subsidized credit,

---

agreements. But at the same time, the government must also have enough flexibility to change policy when external circumstances warrant. A council can serve as a "flexible" commitment mechanism.

without the stick, that is, penalties, may result in investment without accompanying export growth. Firms may take advantage of the credit but allocate it to nonexport activities.[56] Councils can be especially helpful in providing information that will help the government to direct credit to high-performing exporters.

The Political Role of Councils

The East Asian experience reveals that access to information by all parties is essential for economic development. Information to make effective economic decisions is usually lacking in autocratic governments because the private sector has incentives to dissimulate and deny information to autocrats that can later use their knowledge to expropriate profits, to penalize dissent, and to provide privileges to insiders and allies. Information is usually used to maintain power, not to promote welfare-enhancing policies. As a result, autocrats typically lack information about private sector development, and the private sector usually has unreliable information about government programs and intentions. Thus autocracies have a problem of credibly committing to growth-enhancing policies. Dictators are unreliable partners in trade because of their above-the-law status.

In all the HPAEs, the legislature is significantly weaker than the executive branch. Even in Japan, where the Diet plays a more active role in policymaking, until recently the ruling Liberal Democrat Party (through the prime minister) has generally dictated the thrust of policies. This top-down approach to policymaking has earned the HPAEs the reputation as authoritarian states. Modifications to this conception are needed, especially if one considers that surveys of democracy typically correlate Asian governments with those of Africa as examples of autocratic rule.[57] Because the standard indexes of democracy are not

56. See, for example, the study of Boyce (1992) on the Philippines.

57. The Freedom House correlates the political systems of Korea, Malaysia, Singapore, Taiwan, and Thailand at the same antidemocratic extreme as a number of African regimes. The definition of political rights and civil liberties used in the rankings do not prioritize transparency of the regulatory environment, bureaucratic integrity, equal access to information by private sector operators, consultative instruments, security of property rights, freedom to contract, and the reliability of government commitments. The survey leaves out the factors contributing to private sector strength and government credibility. Thus results do not touch on the conditions that ultimately create a firm foundation for an independent civil society.

sensitive to the participation in policy by consultative bodies, they fail to reflect a fundamental difference between the polities of Asia and, for example, those of Africa. Consultative polities differ from autocratic regimes as much as they differ from representative regimes. Councils allow select groups in the private sector (based on function rather than on personal ties) to express their views on economic policies and have those views integrated into the final policy output. This feature gives councils credibility and legitimizes government economic policies; councils grant the private sector participants some influence over the rules that are to govern their sector and prevent those rules from being altered without consultation.[58]

Summary

Japan, Korea, Malaysia, Singapore, Thailand, and Hong Kong have developed mechanisms for interaction between state and society, allowing the private sector to contribute effectively to the policymaking process. Consultative bodies induced private sector cooperation with the regime and helped to draw the elites into the process of market-led growth. Similar assurances of consistent private sector input into policy formation are rarely provided by autocratic governments. Nevertheless observers have all too often confused effective governance with the type of political regime and thus have failed to see the universal implications of East Asian experience. That experience suggests that the foundations of effective economic governance—commitment, coordination, and consultation—are likely to be independent of regime type. But it also suggests that consultative committees may fail to produce similar results in other developing countries unless a reputable economic bureaucracy exists to impose discipline among private sector members of a council.

As chapter 6 explores, each of these high performers created and murtured a competent, relatively independent but accountable, economic bureaucracy. Unless the economic bureaucracy can deflect external pressures from regime insiders or powerful interest groups, agreements arrived at in a council could be easily undermined. To

---

58. It should be pointed out that in the early stages of English parliamentary government, representation was limited to a small privileged group, that is, those who could pay taxes to the king. See Root (1994). The councils are in a way functionally similar to England's ancient parliamentary system.

enable that bureaucracy to perform its role as arbiter, it must be able to resist such pressures. A weak arbiter cannot induce cooperation or compromise among rival groups; it cannot punish detractors nor reward performers. Similarly, a corrupt or incompetent arbiter cannot gain the confidence of participants. Therefore measures to prevent the arbiter's abuse of power must also be introduced.

Five

Coordinating the Public and Private Sectors: Taiwan and Indonesia

A KEY ELEMENT in the success of the high-performing Asian economies (HPAEs) was the creation and maintenance of institutions to coordinate public and private sector activities. The choice of institutions, however, differed among the eight governments. In Japan, Korea, Singapore, Malaysia, Thailand, and to a lesser extent, Hong Kong, governments established deliberation councils to promote the flow of information, clarify the division of rents among the elites, signal commitment to announced policies, and provide ways for the private sector to participate in economic policymaking. In Taiwan and Indonesia, however, governments undertook these activities without the benefit of formal deliberation councils. Taiwan depended on indirect mechanisms for coordinating public and private sector activities, and Indonesia relied on an informal and opaque mechanism. This chapter examines these mechanisms and the historical circumstances that shaped their evolution.

Both governments took power through military domination and faced a similar political challenge: determined to retain power by promoting growth, they also recognized that growth would require the support of groups that for varying reasons were not viable political allies. In Taiwan the politically marginal group was the native Taiwanese; in Indonesia it was the ethnic Chinese business elite. Neither government could expect to sustain rapid growth without the participation of the politically excluded group. In Taiwan the Kuomintang (KMT) sought a way out of this dilemma by encouraging entrepreneurship among native Taiwanese while maintaining tight control over the state. The KMT, rather than establishing deliberation councils that might have eroded its grip on power, built large public enterprises and worked with a few prominent business families to spearhead industrial development in strategic areas. Most economic activity was diffused into thousands of small- and medium-sized enterprises. In Indonesia, where the weak bureaucracy and the need to appease the military made deliberation councils impractical, a less predictable, more patronage-based form of coordination emerged.

Taiwan

The KMT's defeat by the communists on mainland China drove home the importance of shared growth. But at the same time the same experience made the transplanted mainlanders too distrustful of the native Taiwanese economic elite to share political power with them. Hence, the KMT preferred policies—such as land reform and limits on firm size—that spread the benefits of growth while simultaneously ensuring that local economic elites did not become powerful enough to challenge the party's monopoly on political power.[1] Although the KMT did make some exceptions for the few Taiwanese whose political loyalty it trusted, it was careful not to empower a business elite it could not dominate.

KMT measures to prevent the emergence of a powerful native business elite took many, often subtle, forms. For example, under Taiwan company law, holding companies are prohibited, and private, nonbank financial institutions such as insurance groups may not own industrial firms. "Banks are prohibited by law from taking shares in the companies to which they lend or from having representatives on the board of directors in sharp contrast with Japan. . . . Restrictions on entry to an industry have also sometimes been used to prevent individuals not closely connected with the regime from acquiring excessive power, as in the case of Y. C. Wang's attempts to integrate backwards into naphtha production. . . . (Up till recently, the party's control over the Securities and Exchange Commission gave it control over the stock exchange.) The commission has had great discretion about how carefully it checks a company's balance sheet before allowing the company to proceed with a share issue. Many businessmen *avoid* the stock exchange because

1. As indicated in chapter 3, landowners were required to sell any land over three chia to the government. The government resold the purchased land to the tenants. See Gold (1986).

TABLE 5-1. *Characteristics of Business Groups in Taiwan, Korea, and Japan*

Type of group and characteristics	Taiwan	Korea	Japan
Number of groups	96	50	16
Total sales (billions of dollars)	NT634	W54,663	Y217,033
Equivalent in U.S. dollars (billions)	16.48	68.32	871.26
Number of firms	745	552	1,001
Firms/business group	7.8	11	62.6
Workers/firm	444	1,440	2,838
Percentage of total work force	4.7	5.5	9.5

Source: Hamilton, Orru, and Biggart (1987, table 1).

to issue shares on it exposes them not only to possible loss of control of their own companies, but also to Nationalist party arm-twisting."[2]

Among the KMT's range of instruments to guide business development, control of the banking and financial system (mostly through state ownership) was perhaps the most important. The KMT gained leverage over credit, allowing it to direct entrepreneurial activity toward desired or targeted sectors and to control entry into sectors characterized by potentially large-scale economies.[3] This meant medium and large enterprises had to depend upon government discretion to finance their activities. By rationing credit, however, the KMT indirectly encouraged the development of the curb market where small entrepreneurs could borrow funds without being subject to legal restrictions.

Combined with land reform, control over the formal banking sector restricted the accumulation of capital by Taiwanese elites. Land reform ruled out speculation in land; banking controls limited the growth potential and business orientation of firms. Though the ownership structure of Taiwanese firms is extremely opaque, these and other more subtle restrictions on accumulating capital seem to have resulted in a loose-knit industrial structure not dominated by interconnected business groups as in Japan or Korea. Although 40 percent of Taiwan's largest 745 firms are members of groups, many large firms remain detached. Sales for the 745 firms in the top ninety-six groups are relatively small. The interconnections are weaker and, as table 5-1 shows,

2. Wade (1990, p. 270). Emphasis added.
3. Wade (1990).

the groups are smaller than business groups in Japan and Korea. More-over, in the aggregate, private investment as a share of GDP has been one of the lowest among the HPAEs—only Indonesia has a lower ratio (see table 1-12).[4]

The looser organization of Taiwan's industrial structure, although reducing the threat of capture, raised the problem of how to coordinate public sector and private sector activities. The party eliminated or restricted groups that could independently articulate interests and thereby become an opposition force. The result was an agglomeration of small and medium enterprises, making formal consultations through deliberation councils impractical (in 1990 approximately 97 percent of all private sector enterprises were classified as small- or medium-sized ones).

Resolving Rent Allocation

Putting political considerations aside, "smallness" was consonant with the KMT's goal of retaining control over the commanding heights of the economy so it could direct industrial development.[5] Risky up-stream sectors that required substantial investments became the do-main of public enterprises. Contrary to the popular image of Taiwan as a freewheeling capitalist economy, public enterprises account for a larger share of investment in Taiwan than in Korea and Japan or even India, where central planning has played a key role (table 5-2).

The SME thrust limited the private sector's capability of making huge investments even in projects for which it potentially could have raised sufficient capital, for example, petrochemicals. Public enterprises were used to create many industries for which large investments were needed.[6] From synthetic fibers and petrochemicals to steel and ship-building, public enterprises led the way. Public enterprises promoted developments in fuels, chemicals, mining, metals, fertilizer, and food

4. Gross domestic investment as a share of GDP, however, has been as high if not higher on average in Taiwan than in Korea, Hong Kong, and Malaysia over the period 1960 to 1985. See Wade (1990, table 2-11).

5. A debate about the role of industrial policy in Taiwan was provoked by Wade's (1990) documentation of the KMT's intention to influence the development of industry in ways not necessarily consonant with static comparative advantage. The debate, about the effectiveness of this type of intervention, is far from resolved despite the conclusions reached in the World Bank's *East Asian Miracle* report (1993a).

6. Wade (1990).

TABLE 5-2. *Output and Investment Shares of Public Enterprises in Taiwan, South Korea, and India, Various Years, 1954–77*

Country	Period	Percent share of GDP at factor cost	Percent share in gross fixed capital formation
Taiwan	1954–77	13.3	32.3
	1978–80	13.5	32.4
South Korea	1963–64	5.5	31.2
	1970–77	6.7	23.4
India	1962–77	7.4	32.3

Source: Wade (1990).

processing. Among the upstream industries where state leadership was critical were synthetic fibers, plastics, basic metals, and advanced electronics. Although some of these were eventually sold to private interests (undoubtedly those close to the party), they began as public enterprises.

Taiwan diverges from other developing countries where public enterprises have generally performed poorly, often requiring government subsidies to survive.[7] "Overall, public enterprises [in Taiwan] have more than covered costs of production. Over the 1970s their surpluses contributed an average of 10 percent of the government's net revenue, which makes Taiwan an exception to the familiar thesis that government-owned corporations tend to deplete rather than add to government revenues. Moreover their profit rate (operating surplus/(capital + net worth)) has generally been positive, negative only in two years."[8]

Regime survival often dictates the use of public enterprises as instruments to allocate rents to a political regime's supporters; thus profit and efficiency are secondary considerations.[9] The management of Taiwan's public sector differed for several reasons. First, not owing their power to the native Taiwanese, KMT leaders were not pressured to allocate employment in public enterprises as patronage. Second, the leadership established party enterprises to provide for the party faithful, who could expect financial rewards if the enterprises were profitable. The

7. See World Bank (1995).
8. Wade (1990, p. 180).
9. Campos and Esfahani (forthcoming).

KMT's Central Investments Holding Company "owns a range of manufacturing and service enterprises. During the 1970s, for example, the party's finance department directly owned six companies and through these seven more: in textiles, paper and printing, cement, pharmaceuticals, fiber and glass, electronics, electrical construction, insurance, and the investment and trust business. . . . Altogether the party owns about fifty firms."[10]

Third, the military, the only force that might have successfully challenged leadership, was provided with a conglomerate that serviced the needs of ex–military officers.[11] "The Vocational Assistance Commission for Retired Servicemen (VACRS) is in part a huge holding company, probably the biggest conglomerate on the island (one estimate put the employees in its firms at well over one hundred thousand in the mid-1970s). VACRS provides equity capital and management. It runs . . . dairy and trucking farms, orchards, restaurants, trucking companies, and construction firms that have built dams and highways in Taiwan, roads and runways in Vietnam and other Southeast countries, and miscellaneous construction projects in countries as far east as Saudi Arabia. It even operates a Royal Crown bottling company."[12] In sum, the two groups that provided the leadership with the political muscle to wield power—party members and the military—were directly awarded rents in the form of privately owned enterprises.[13] Party members and military personnel became the residual claimants to firms whose growth depended on a strong economy, and their interests were thus tied to those of leadership.

10. Wade (1990, p. 273). One of the economic advisers to an opposition party (of which there are now several), expressed concern over party-owned enterprises. The interviewee lamented that state funds were used to finance these enterprises.

11. Gold (1986, p. 63).

12. Wade (1990, p. 266).

13. There was actually a third group. The KMT leadership fled the mainland with remnants of its supporters. The accompanying supporters could be categorized into three groups. The first consisted of military personnel, the second of party members, and the third of bureaucrats. As chapter 6 mentions, bureaucrats were granted considerable influence over day-to-day affairs, especially over economic policymaking. Moreover mainlander bureaucrats were given priority over native Taiwanese in assignments to middle- and especially senior-level positions. "For most of the postwar period the native Taiwanese, in an 80 percent or more majority, have held few top positions in the state. . . . The cabinet during the 1950s and 1960s included hardly any; over the 1970s and 1980s the number increased gradually to reach ten out of thirty-one in 1987. Of posts of vice-ministerial rank and above, however, only 14 percent were held by native Taiwanese in 1987." Wade (1990, p. 236).

The preceding argument suggests why public enterprises have performed relatively well in Taiwan. But it also outlines the rules that governed rent allocation among the governing elites: investment funds were allocated to create elite-owned private firms, but financial rewards depended on the firm's performance. Interestingly, this condition mimics the rules that established a rents-for-performance criterion among the other HPAEs.

Making Credible Commitments

The same circumstances that induced the KMT to promote a relatively diffused private business sector created credibility problems for the KMT. Among the governments of the HPAEs, the KMT was the most powerful in comparison with civil society. Taiwan had always been subjugated to external rule: various mainland authorities ruled before the turn of the century, followed by the Japanese until 1945. By the time Taiwan became the KMT's base (in 1948), civil society had little organizational capacity. Moreover, the KMT leadership fled the mainland with a self-selected loyal cadre of military and bureaucrats. Other military-backed regimes among the HPAEs—Korea, Thailand, and Indonesia—could not rely on such loyalty, especially among military personnel.[14]

Hence, the domination of civil society by government, a characteristic of all the HPAEs, was strongest in postwar Taiwan. This meant that government had wider discretionary powers to expropriate private investments directly through confiscation or indirectly through random and irresponsible changes in economic policy. Given the immense concentration of power, today's promises could easily be broken tomorrow. This potential for arbitrary government behavior was a source of uncertainty that could have discouraged domestic or foreign businesses from investing in long-term projects, especially those with large sunk costs. However, several factors mitigated the "political" risk implicit in this imbalance and helped Taiwan resolve the commitment problem.[15]

First, as colonial rulers, the Japanese had invested in large-scale industry and infrastructure. Many of these investments were intact at

14. General Park Chung Hee of Korea was assassinated in 1978 by his own personal appointee to the KCIA. For many years, Thailand experienced frequent palace coups Wyatt (1982); Schlossstein (1991). And the New Order government of Indonesia came to power in rather fragile conditions and had to carefully craft a military coalition to secure power. Crouch (1978).

15. Weingast (1993) discusses the problem and analyzes the technical aspects of the implied "political risk" of investment.

the time of Japan's surrender at the end of World War II. The KMT incorporated many of these industries into public enterprises with the intention of transferring ownership to private individuals. Thus many sunk costs had already been borne by the Japanese, and additional investments were undertaken by the KMT. In this way, the state solved the credibility problem in part by internalizing the risk—if the state's policies waffled, so would its revenues.

Second, in implementing land reform, the party coopted several large landlords, offering them shares in public enterprises. "Landlords were compensated 70 percent with land bonds in kind (rice for paddy land, sweet potatoes for dry land) and 30 percent with shares of stock in four government enterprises earmarked to be transferred to private ownership—Taiwan Cement, Taiwan Paper and Pulp, Taiwan Agriculture and Forestry, and Taiwan Industry and Mining. . . . *Small* landlords regarded the government enterprise bonds skeptically and sold them off below par value to speculators. In contrast, the large landowners made out quite well. . . . They accumulated shares in the four enterprises. . . . In 1954, the state began to transfer these firms to private ownership amidst a flurry of stock price manipulation. The main beneficiaries were the biggest landlords. . . . The five families *who were the prominent pro-Japanese collaborators* concentrated on the Taiwan Cement Corporation. Lin Po-shou of the Pan-ch'iao clan became the first post-transfer chairman. . . . A seat on the board became a coveted status symbol for later generations of Taiwanese capitalists)."[16] Again, in this case, the investors did not incur the sunk costs, and moreover they mitigated the risk of expropriation by having established themselves as key supporters of the KMT.

Third, as discussed earlier, the party itself took on the task of investing in industry and created avenues for ex–military personnel to engage in productive activity as well. This gave added incentive for government to avoid undermining the profits of party- and military-owned firms. Maintaining sound macroeconomic policies was important.[17]

Robert Wade has argued that government control of the commanding heights of the economy enabled it to direct economic activity into selected areas in order to foster dynamic comparative advantage. "The

16. Gold (1986, pp. 66, 71).

17. Macroeconomic policies have remained remarkably stable. Wade (1990); World Bank (1993a).

public enterprise sector is also used, whether for military or civilian production, as a substitute for attempts to induce private firms to enter new fields with high entry barriers. . . . Moreover the fact that public enterprises are concentrated in upstream sectors gives the government indirect influence over the downstream sectors. . . . Through the Chinese Petroleum Corporation, for example, the government has indirect leverage on synthetic fiber and textile producers."[18] This suggests a fourth factor: the viability, if not profitability, of public enterprises depended on the profitability of the downstream (mostly small- and medium-sized) enterprises; irresponsible policymaking would diminish the latter's profitability. Frequent visits by lower-rank officials of the Industrial Development Bureau (IDB) to SMEs suggests that the impact of policies on private firms was of deep concern to government.

Fifth, a subtle theoretical argument suggests why SMEs might not face the same "political risk" as large enterprises. Because SMEs have been highly labor intensive (at least until recently), their sunk costs are generally smaller. Thus they have a greater capacity to vary products or even switch industries. This mitigates the risk of investing in an uncertain policy environment.[19] By biasing industrial structure toward SMEs, the KMT indirectly reduced the "political risk" to native Taiwanese entrepreneurs. This would suggest that private investment (as a share of GDP) should be higher than in many other developing countries outside of the high performers, which in fact is true.[20]

18. Wade (1990, p. 180).

19. Rodrik (1993) offers empirical evidence that on a product-per-product basis, the Korean version fetches a higher unit price than the Taiwanese version. This occurs, he says, because of the large size of Korean firms that have an incentive to establish a good reputation for their products. The smaller Taiwanese firms, however, are caught in a collective action problem in which every firm would be better off if each maintained quality but individually each has an incentive to exploit the absence of monitoring for its own advantage. Esfahani (1992) has presented a different argument: firms with small sunk costs will tend to produce a product of lower quality relative to that produced by firms with large sunk costs. Firms with large sunk costs must pay close attention to quality in order to sell their product (or version of the product at a price high enough to cover the larger sunk costs). With smaller sunk costs to cover, small firms have less incentive to maintain quality. In equilibrium, consumers recognize this fact and so are willing to pay a higher price for the high-quality product—if they do not, then eventually the high-quality product will disappear through adverse selection. The implication is that sunk costs are a less important consideration in the decisionmaking of the Taiwanese SMEs than the Korean ones.

20. See table 1-12 in this volume.

Finally, the KMT also actively encouraged the development of SMEs. It sent clear, concrete signals that government was seriously promoting SMEs.[21] The activities of the Medium and Small Business Administration have already been noted. But there were other signals.

The government financed the establishment of industrial estates in rural areas. These places provided factory space, electricity, warehousing facilities, telecommunications facilities, and other conditions to help reduce the initial investment hurdles. They represented a commitment embodied in a sunk cost that government would have to absorb if SMEs failed to emerge.

Indirect signals were also provided, as illustrated by the government's tolerance of counterfeited products. In 1985 *Business Week* indicated that 60 percent of the world's pirated manufactured goods came from Taiwan.[22] "In a late 1970s case, several factories were found to be manufacturing circuit fuse breakers with forged Westinghouse and Mitsubishi labels. When Mitsubishi complained to the authorities, the firms were fined all of U.S.$600."[23] SMEs were more likely than large firms to engage in counterfeiting.

Facilitating the Flow of Information

Facilitating the flow of information between the private and public sector is another important aspect of coordination. As part of its strategy, the KMT compelled all businesses to join state-sponsored trade associations. These associations became a convenient vehicle for the informal exchange of ideas and information with the KMT.[24] But because industry was dominated by many independent small- and medium-sized enterprises, these associations could not be as tightly knit

21. In the language of the new industrial organization, the government effectively "signaled its type." As Rodrik (1989) suggests, if a government is unable to signal its true type then its efforts to pursue a particular policy will be wasted. The reason is that economic agents will adjust their behavior to the uncertainty and in the process derail the policy. For example, a government may announce its intentions to withdraw quantitative restrictions on imports and eliminate tariffs. For various reasons, economic agents may not believe it and so assume that the current move is only a temporary phenomenon and that next year the status quo will be restored. If so, they will tend to import more than normal. This in turn would cause unforeseen problems, which would likely force the government to reimpose some restrictions.

22. Thomas C. O'Donnell and others, "Counterfeit Goods," *Business Week*, December 16, 1985, pp. 64–72.

23. Wade (1990, p. 268).

24. Chu (1992).

as their counterparts in Japan and Korea.[25] Hence, a council-type system would have been an inadequate means of harnessing information.[26] Other mechanisms therefore were needed to facilitate the flow of information.

To monitor the rural economy, the KMT revived the agricultural associations established by the Japanese under colonial rule. The associations had disseminated farm technology and served as a surveillance mechanism—the Japanese stationed personnel in each of the villages to "assist" the village association.[27] The KMT basically adopted the same arrangement: to disseminate new ideas through the associations and to monitor local developments by stationing party members in each of the villages.[28]

The KMT used a similar approach in the industrial sector, organizing the party into departments that ran parallel to the bureaucracy (though by no means as extensively staffed). The main function of each department was to monitor the activities and performance of its parallel bureau or agency. To facilitate this monitoring task, the KMT uncharacteristically allowed the newspapers (which were owned by the party or by senior party officials) to print complaints from businesses about policies that the bureaucracy planned or implemented. Hence, a bureau's failings were quickly communicated to the KMT. Moreover, when such developments arose within the economic bureaucracy, the KMT created a task force led and managed by the private sector to perform the functions of the ailing agency or bureau and in some cases to replace it altogether.[29] This arrangement essentially facilitated the flow of information between leadership and the private sector.

Participation at the Local Level

Although the KMT was anxious to prevent Taiwanese elites from acquiring substantial political power, the party nonetheless permitted

25. In Korea, industry is dominated by the chaebols (very large conglomerates) and in Japan, SMEs are linked tightly through a supplier network to large firms. Itoh and Urata (1993).

26. Wade (1990) observes that communication between the government and the business community is much more informal in Taiwan than in Japan and Korea. Implicit in his observation is the stark fact that SMEs pervade industry.

27. See Amsden (1979); Gold (1986).

28. The rice-for-fertilizer barter scheme was conducted through the associations. Amsden (1979).

29. The task force is discussed in more detail in chapter 6.

villages to hold regular local elections in which native Taiwanese were selected as town officials.[30] This limited devolution of authority to local officials is the political analogue of the SME thrust: both granted native Taiwanese a limited voice in local affairs, either political or economic.

The two arrangements may be more closely linked than is initially apparent. Given sufficient authority, mayors could introduce policies to make their jurisdictions attractive to small-scale, and sometimes medium-scale, enterprises. This would have encouraged local entrepreneurs to remain in the towns and villages rather than to move to Taipei and would have fostered competition among the localities, since entrepreneurs could compare conditions in several localities. Taken together, these two arrangements would have had the effect of granting native Taiwanese significant influence over local economic policies, since local officials had to consult with local entrepreneurs to devise an incentive package that would prevent firms from defecting to other localities.

The KMT's solution to the coordination problem grew out of its military and political defeat on the mainland, resulting in a strategy structured around public enterprises and private small- to medium-sized enterprises. All aspects of this strategy—rent allocation, commitment, information exchange, and legitimation of policy—were conditioned by political imperatives. As with the KMT, the New Order government in Indonesia confronted historical circumstances that led it to pursue a non-council-based strategy for addressing the coordination problem. But its strategy was radically different.

Indonesia

The Indonesian business environment is the least transparent of the HPAEs, and property rights receive the weakest protection. An annual

---

30. "A fifty-five person Provisional Provincial Assembly was elected by county and municipal assemblies at the end of 1951. Subsequent assemblies were elected by direct vote of the electorate. . . . Beneath the provincial level are elected county and municipal assemblies and governments, which have a great degree of say over local affairs. Magistrates and mayors are elected except for the mayor of any city run directly by the national government, *e.g. Taipei*. . . . Though continuing its dominance over government at all levels, with the introduction of direct suffrage and self-government, the KMT's proportion of local elected representatives fell below that at the national level. To compete effectively, the party *has had* to field Taiwanese candidates." Gold (1986, pp. 61–62).

survey of business executives conducted by the World Economic Forum, for example, ranks Indonesia's business environment consistently below the fiftieth percentile among a group of fourteen newly industrializing countries (table 5-3). Along several categories (that pertain to the business environment) in the forum's 1992 study, Indonesia almost always falls among the bottom seven. In contrast, the other HPAEs (excluding Japan) take the top six slots.[31] One would thus expect private investment as a share of GDP to be lower in Indonesia relative to the other high performers. This is borne out by the evidence. As discussed in chapter 1, the share is systematically lower than in the other high performers with the possible exception of Taiwan.[32] Moreover, as shown in table 5-4 this observation remains unchanged even when one controls for the level of development.

But there is a puzzle. When compared with two similarly large, oil-producing developing countries, Indonesia's ratio of private investment to GDP compares favorably. Nigeria, which like Indonesia has a military regime and about the same real per capita GDP, has a much lower ratio; to a lesser extent the same is true for Venezuela, which is largely democratic and has a much higher per capita GDP, conditions that would tend to suggest a higher private investment ratio (table 5-5).[33] Given the level of development and nature of government, Indonesia would be expected to have a ratio closer to Nigeria's and significantly lower than Venezuela's.[34]

We believe Indonesia's reliance on informal social networks, instead of on predictable rules and procedures, has resulted in private investment trends lagging behind those of its East Asian neighbors. These

31. Japan is generally ranked in the middle, at par with the United States, among developed countries. Rankings that cut across the developed and the newly industrializing countries do not exist.

32. Gross domestic investment as a proportion of GDP however is higher in Taiwan owing to the predominance of investment through public enterprises.

33. To be more precise, one must control for real interest rates. Evidence suggests that real interest rates have on average been positive and higher in the high performers than in other parts of the developing world. World Bank (1993a). Higher rates would imply lower investment ratios given the same level of income. But Indonesia and the other high performers have in fact higher private investment ratios.

34. It is widely recognized that secure property rights are critical for sustaining long-term private investment. Of course, authoritarian governments are more likely than democratically elected governments to violate property rights, a situation that discourages private investment. North (1981, 1985); Weingast (1993).

TABLE 5-3. *Legal and Regulatory Environment, Ranking Based on Selected Criteria*

Region and country	Criteria[a]					Sum of ranks	Borda index
	Transparency	Antitrust laws	Security	Justice	Bribery and corruption		
High-performing Asian economies							
Singapore	1	1	1	1	1	5	1
Hong Kong	6	3	3	3	2	17	2
Taiwan	4	6	5	9	5	29	3
Korea	7	2	7	8	7	31	4
Malaysia	2	5	2	2	6	17	2
Thailand	5	10	4	6	9	34	5
Indonesia	9	12	8	11	14	54	10
Others							
Mexico	3	8	9	10	8	38	7
India	8	4	6	7	11	36	6
Pakistan	10	9	10	12	10	51	9
Venezuela	11	13	14	14	12	64	11
South Africa	12	7	11	5	3	38	7
Brazil	13	14	13	13	13	66	12
Hungary	14	11	12	4	4	45	8

Source: World Bank (1992). Similar results are noted in *Investor's Country Risk Guide* (Syracuse, N.Y.: Political Risk Services).

a. The relevant questions were (i) Is the government transparent toward its citizens? (transparency); (ii) Do antitrust laws prevent unfair competition? (antitrust); (iii) Is there full confidence among the people that their person and property are adequately protected? (security); (iv) Is there full confidence in the administration of justice? (justice); and (v) Do improper practices such as bribery and corruption prevail in the public sphere? (bribery and corruption).

TABLE 5-4. *Average Private Investment to GDP Ratios: Indonesia, Thailand, Malaysia, and Korea*

Country	Years	GNP/Cap $	Priv. Inv./GDP %
Indonesia	1975–80	$342	10.5
	1981–89	$548	11.9
Thailand	1973–77	$356	17.9
	1977–81	$600	17.3
Malaysia	1970–72	$416	14.5
	1972–74	$567	17
Korea	n.a.	n.a.	n.a.
	1972–76	$504	18.1

Sources: Miller and Sumlinski (1994); World Bank, *World Tables* (Washington, 1994); World Bank, East Asia Miracle database, 1993.

n.a. Not available

TABLE 5-5. *Real Gross Domestic Product per Capita and Ratio of Private Investment to GDP in Three Oil-Producing Countries, 1980–92*

Year	Indonesia GDP/Cap $	Indonesia Priv. Inv./GDP %	Nigeria GDP/Cap $	Nigeria Priv. Inv./GDP %	Venezuela GDP/Cap $	Venezuela Priv. Inv./GDP %
1980	361	11.6	426	6.90	3,067	12.82
1981	380	13.7	375	6.50	2,971	9.67
1982	372	13.6	361	6.10	2,827	7.59
1983	397	13.2	326	4.30	2,647	4.33
1984	416	12.3	303	2.30	2,613	10.50
1985	420	10.4	321	2.00	2,549	11.00
1986	436	12.1	317	3.30	2,646	10.90
1987	449	11.6	307	3.90	2,672	12.20
1988	467	11.6	328	4.00	2,759	12.37
1989	493	12.6	340	4.40	2,453	7.95
1990	518	13.3	348	6.10	2,560	4.91
1991	543	13.4	356	6.00	2,760	8.19
1992	568	12.4	360	NA	2,894	9.98

Source: Miller and Sumlinski (1994); World Bank, *World Tables*; World Bank, East Asia Miracle database, 1993.

same networks, however, have helped sustain private investment at levels above those of similarly situated developing countries. These networks emerged because of leadership's need to nurture political support from the military, which was then the only institution capable of governing the country.

The Armed Forces and the Rise of the New Order

The state machinery left behind by the Dutch was very weak: the government lacked the capacity to exercise the standard attributes of statehood. It could not collect taxes, so it could not pay its officials; it could not provide an adequate legal system, as the laws were out of date and the judicial system was dysfunctional; and most of all, it could not provide order. The only effective organization with roots throughout the nascent nation-state was the armed forces. Its role in Indonesian politics was greatly strengthened during the restructuring that followed the collapse of parliamentary democracy in 1957.

With the backing of the military, President Sukarno declared martial law and restored the 1945 Constitution, using it as the basis for legitimizing his rule. The military's "growing political strength was reflected in the formal institutions set up under 'Guided Democracy.' In the cabinet appointed in July 1959, immediately after the restoration of the 1945 Constitution, nearly one-third of the ministers were drawn from the armed forces in contrast with only three in the previous cabinet and none before 1958."[35] Since then army officers have been appointed to the cabinet and the bureaucracy and have served as regional governors. In 1984 a study found that fourteen of the thirty-seven cabinet ministers had military backgrounds, and that nearly half of the 106 subcabinet positions (secretaries-general, directors-general, and inspectors-general) were held by seconded officers. The same study found that the armed forces provided about three-quarters of the twenty-seven governorships and a small majority of district headships.[36]

As discussed earlier, Sukarno, concerned that the increasing power of the military might threaten his position, supported the rise of the PKI, Indonesia's Communist Party, as a counterweight to the military. This led to a power struggle between the army, other elements of the armed forces, and the PKI, which eventually spun out of control. From

35. Crouch (1978, p. 47).
36. Liddle (1985, p. 72).

the resulting confusion and violence arose the New Order government, with General Soeharto as the head of state and the army as the glue that held together an ethnically diverse, highly populated, and geographically dispersed country.

The Technocrats and Regime Credibility

Upon seizing power, Soeharto and the army faced the daunting task of rebuilding a rapidly decaying economy. Inflation was at an all-time high of 1,000 percent, and foreign exchange reserves were at an all-time low; foreign debt service had become unmanageable; the agriculture/rural sector was failing, food shortages threatened; infrastructure had deteriorated; the economy was contracting.[37] To contend with the economic crisis, Soeharto recruited a team of U.S.-educated technocrats.[38] As a colonel, Soeharto had been exposed to Western economics in lectures at the Army Staff and Command School. The lectures were conducted by a group of civilian economists whose most senior members were educated in the University of California at Berkeley.

Although the crisis presented a serious problem for Soeharto's New Order regime, it also offered an opportunity to establish legitimacy. By resolving the immediate problem of inflation and thereafter addressing problems of agriculture, infrastructure, poverty, and growth, the regime sought to compare favorably with the previous government.[39] Soeharto hoped that these achievements would cause Indonesians to prefer the New Order regime's continuance in power over the risks involved in any change.[40] For these reasons, Soeharto and the army accepted the technocrats' counsel.[41]

The policies they designed produced results. Responsible macroeconomic management—including stringent controls on the budget, depreciation, and convertibility of the currency—reduced inflation to

37. Bhattacharya and Pangestu (1992).

38. "In 1966, he asked one of them, Professor Widjojo Nitisastro, . . . to form a team of economic advisers, beginning a close association that continues to this day." Liddle (1991, p. 408).

39. Interviews with Professor Sadli and Professor Wardhana, both long-standing technocrats, indicated that this was the strategy pursued by the technocrats and supported by Soeharto.

40. A number of scholars have made this argument (in different ways), for example, Crouch (1978); Glassburner (1978); Liddle (1985); Schlossstein (1991); Robison (1985).

41. Liddle (1991).

manageable levels in the late 1960s and early 1970s and eventually to single-digit levels in the 1980s. This in turn opened the way for foreign assistance from multilateral and bilateral sources.[42] Foreign loans and grants increased the financial resources available for agriculture and infrastructure, the focus of the first three five-year development plans, Repelita I, II, and III.[43] Economic growth proceeded at an unprecedented pace. Each success helped to prepare the way for the next. Had the technocrats' initial policy prescription failed to produce results, the New Order regime might have abandoned them early in the game.

The technocrats' influence has waxed and waned with the state of the economy. In particular, the technocrats appear to be most influential during times of crisis—times when the flow of financial resources has been threatened. Since the economic debacle of the early to mid-1960s, two crises have occurred, one in 1975 and another in 1982, both related to oil. In 1975 the state-owned oil company, Pertamina, failed to meet some of its foreign debt obligations. Because Pertamina was one of the largest borrowers of foreign exchange in the country, its failure would have jeopardized the inflow of foreign loans. An investigation revealed that Pertamina had greatly overextended itself and that senior management officials had abused their power.[44] Soeharto called upon the technocrats to devise a plan to hold Pertamina accountable for its actions and dismissed an old ally, General Ibnu Sutowo, as head of Pertamina.[45]

42. "The flow of large amounts of foreign assistance—given annually by the Intergovernmental Group on Indonesia, a consortium of Western countries plus Japan—and of smaller amounts of foreign investment is attributable directly to the *economists'* policies and the trust that foreign lenders, governments, and investors have in them." See Liddle (1991, p. 418).

It is also worth noting that in 1965 Indonesia was one of the poorest nations in the developing world, with a real per capita income of $60. World Bank (1993a). Moreover, at that time, the Organization of Petroleum Exporting Countries had not been formed so that the country could not benefit from its vast oil reserves. Hence, foreign loans, grants, and investment were the only sources of funding that could be tapped to stimulate growth. This was probably important in giving the technocrats their initial leverage. Success of the early policies then sealed their influence.

43. World Bank (1990b).

44. Schlossstein (1991, p. 84) reveals that "Sutowo, the head of Pertamina, and other senior officers affected lifestyles that emulated those of private industry executives in New York or Houston. One celebrated his birthday in Geneva. Another took a safari vacation in Africa. Others had their pick of Jakarta's most beautiful fashion models as mistresses."

45. "Pertamina was prohibited from further independent borrowing and was brought more closely under the supervision of the Minister of Mines. Bank Indonesia, the state

The second crisis broke out in the early 1980s, when oil prices collapsed, plunging from about $35 a barrel in 1982 to a low of $12 in 1986.[46] From 1981 to 1985, export earnings from oil and gas fell by almost 70 percent.[47] Alarmed, Soeharto again called on the technocrats for advice. The government began a wide-ranging program of reform and deregulation that the technocrats had long advocated without success. Measures included tax reform, trade and financial market liberalization, and contracting the assessment and collection of import duties to a Swiss firm. Each contributed to the objective of stabilizing the flow of financial resources.[48] Tax reform increased revenue. Trade liberalization and substitution of a highly regarded foreign firm for the corrupt and inefficient customs bureau lowered the cost of doing business, which encouraged the development of non-oil-manufactured exports. These in turn brought in foreign exchange. Banking deregulation lured foreign banks, increasing access to financial resources. In both instances, the technocrats' advice not only facilitated economic development directly, it also made the country attractive to the international lending community. The technocrats' value to the government, then, has come directly from the professional expertise they possess, and indirectly, through access to foreign funds that their reputation facilitates.

The Chinese Cukong—Rent Allocation and Credible Commitments

The technocrats' policies—good macroeconomic management, stable prices, and exchange rates—attracted private investment and increased the likelihood of continued economic growth. This is evident when comparing Indonesia's experience with private investment with Venezuela's. Venezuela, also a large oil exporter, has always been much richer than Indonesia, with its real per capita income more than five times higher. And yet, since the early 1980s, the ratio of private invest-

---

bank, accepted responsibility for Pertamina's outstanding loans, half of which were then canceled or reduced through renegotiation. . . . Pertamina's non-petroleum-related projects were either axed or put under the *economists'* control. In early 1976, Sutowo was himself replaced by an army general respected by the economists." Liddle (1991, p. 420).

46. The price had fallen to $9 a barrel in August 1986.

47. MacIntyre (1990, p. 57).

48. Liddle (1991).

TABLE 5-6. *Change in the Consumer Price Index in Indonesia and Venezuela, 1981–92*

	Percent change in index	
Year	Venezuela	Indonesia
1981	16.2	12.2
1982	9.6	9.5
1983	6.7	11.8
1984	12.3	10.5
1985	11.4	4.7
1986	12	6
1987	27.7	9.4
1988	29.4	7.8
1989	84.3	6.4
1990	40.8	7.5
1991	34.2	9.1
1992	31.5	7.7
Average	26.3	8.6
Variance	421.9	4.8

Source: World Bank, East Asia Miracle database, 1993.

ment to GDP has been considerably lower on average in Venezuela (table 5-5). This difference can be attributed, at least in part, to much better macroeconomic management in Indonesia. Table 5-6 shows inflation rates in the two countries (based on the consumer price index) between 1981 and 1992. Clearly, inflation was much higher and variable in Venezuela, which suggests that the macropolicy environment there was much less stable.

But a stable macroeconomic environment may not be sufficient in itself to attract the high levels of private investment needed for rapid, sustained growth. This requires a business environment in which investors can feel reasonably secure from expropriation.

The importance of a secure business environment with credible assurances against expropriation over and above good macroeconomic management is evident in a comparison of Indonesia and Ghana, which has stabilized its macroenvironment and is sometimes considered a minor 'miracle' in Africa. Annual inflation in Ghana is down to about 26 percent, a fall of 40 percentage points from the previous decade, and the current real per capita income of $390 is about the same as

TABLE 5-7. *Private Investment Ratios, Ghana and Indonesia*

	Ghana			Indonesia	
Year	GDP/Cap ($)	Priv. Inv./GDP (%)	Year	GDP/Cap ($)	Priv. Inv./GDP (%)
1986	371	2.27	1980	361	11.6
1987	375	2.57	1981	380	13.7
1988	383	3.26	1982	372	13.6
1989	390	6.08	1983	397	13.2
1990	389	5.43	1984	416	12.3
1991	398	4.94	1985	420	10.4
1992	400	4.08	1986	436	12.1
Average 1986–92	387	4.09	Average 1980–86	398	12.41

Source: World Bank, *World Tables.*

Indonesia's in the early 1980s.[49] Yet Ghana's ratio of private investment to GDP is much lower than the ratio in Indonesia during that period (table 5-7). The main problem in Ghana is the highly uncertain business environment, especially weak property rights.[50]

How has the New Order government in Indonesia differed from Rawling's government in Ghana? Although both derive their power from the military and both have stabilized the macroeconomy, the fear of expropriation has not undermined business confidence in Indonesia. Instead the business environment has been widely perceived as (relatively) sound, and a relatively higher level of private investment has occurred.[51]

This paradox is explained by relations between the military and the business sector, which is largely dominated by ethnic Chinese. Chinese dominance dates from the Dutch colonial era, when the Dutch leased monopoly rights to Chinese traders in such things as salt, tobacco, road

49. World Bank (1993). Indonesia's inflation rate during the period was approximately 10 percent.

50. Campos and Esfahani (forthcoming); World Bank (1993a).

51. One might argue that Indonesia has oil. First of all, much of the investment in the oil industry in Indonesia has been undertaken by a public enterpise, Pertamina. But second, even when compared with oil-rich Nigeria whose macroeconomic management has been fair relative to other countries in Sub-Saharan Africa and certainly better than the management in many Latin American countries, Indonesia still attracts much higher levels of private investment. World Bank (1994).

tolls, and, most important, bazaar leases. It was through these leases that the Chinese acquired practically all of Indonesia's local market trade.[52] In 1985 Chinese enterprises owned 93 percent of all spindles found in domestic private spinning enterprises and in 1987, 61 percent of the assets of privately owned general insurance firms.[53] The Chinese have also dominated the pharmaceutical industry.[54]

The Chinese seem better suited to economic activities than native Indonesians not for any genetic reason but because, as an ethnic minority, they can impose a code of ethics on their members. They can sanction deviations by ostracizing those who violate the moral code. If a member of a persecuted ethnic minority is ostracized from the kin group, not being able to join the mainstream, the individual will have nowhere to turn. The native majority does not have the same sanctioning capacity and has to depend instead on the authority of formal laws. In short, the ethnic subgroup and its internal "rules of the game" have been a surrogate for effective contract law: kinship-based trade depends on social institutions that economize on information costs when public institutions are weak.[55]

Although the Chinese dominate business, they have been excluded from a direct political role. Since the colonial era, they have depended on personal connections with officialdom. This tradition was particularly useful for the New Order regime.[56]

52. "By the 1970s it was estimated that the Chinese ethnic minority was about 4 million in total—only about 3 percent of Indonesia's total population at the time—but they controlled more than a third of the Indonesian GNP and comprised 90 percent of the managerial class." Schlossstein (1991, p. 68). The Chinese according to Mackie (1990) made their economic ascension during the period 1957–66 because they "were able to adjust to the difficult conditions of inflation and shortages of key materials, foreign exchange and capital with a much greater degree of flexibility than the ponderously bureaucratic state enterprises which took over the former Dutch investments." Mackie (1988, p. 237).

53. See MacIntyre (1990) for evidence of Chinese ownership in the spinning and insurance industries. In 1985 total assets in the general insurance industry amounted to 512 billion rupiah of which 38.9 percent accrued to state owned firms; in 1987, 47 percent of all spindles belonged to private locally owned firms.

54. "Of all the pharmaceutical companies in Indonesia, only one is pribumi (native Indonesia). . . . The industry is overwhelmingly Chinese in character." MacIntyre (1990, p. 153).

55. Landa (1994).

56. One of the regime's principal concerns was the contentment of the armed forces. "Inheriting a chaotic administration and a declining economy, the new government felt

Seconding military officers to the central and local bureaucracy was among the first actions taken by the New Order. The military gained control over licensing, the awarding of contracts, and regulation, providing leverage over private business.[57] It therefore became convenient for any business enterprise to have a military officer to deal with fellow military officers in the bureaucracy. Ethnic Chinese business owners, known as *cukong*, responded by taking on military officers as partners, granting them shares in Chinese enterprises. Under this arrangement, which continues today, the Chinese provide the bulk of the capital investment and the organizational and management expertise, while their military partners facilitate the granting of licenses and contracts and provide protection from harassment by regulatory bodies.[58]

Similar arrangements have governed foreign investment. Between 1971 and 1973 foreign investment rose from $222 million to $1 billion. Japanese investment surpassed that of the United States, and again most arrangements were joint ventures of the military and Chinese businessmen.[59] The Chinese are especially desirable as partners to the

---

that it had little prospect of raising adequate funds for the armed forces by conventional means, but it was very aware that the failure of earlier governments to provide for the economic well-being of military personnel had led to discontent and contributed to open rebellion." Crouch (1978, p. 274).

57. Liddle (1985); Crouch (1978).

58. Because of the secrecy surrounding such arrangements, it was not possible to obtain detailed information about these links. The authors tried to contract with an Indonesian think tank to conduct a survey of firms that could have revealed formal connections between the military and Chinese enterprises. But the institute declined. Interviews with private enterprises conducted by the authors did indicate that such arrangement do exist. In fact, in interviews with two different enterprises, one of the authors was introduced by the Chinese general managers in each firm to two different military officers who held high-ranking managerial positions with the firms. It should also be mentioned that a similar phenomenon has been observed in Thailand during the late 1950s and early 1960s. Riggs (1966) has documented this phenomenon, which he has called "pariah entrepreneurship." The JPPCC (discussed in chapter 4) was established in the 1980s in part to transform under-the-table deal making, which this system encouraged, with more transparent over-the-table arrangements.

59. "The new foreign investment law of 1967 opened the way for a rapid inflow of foreign capital in the late 1960s which turned into a flood in the 1970s. By 1971 only $222 million had been invested (apart from investment in oil), but by 1973 this figure jumped to almost $1 billion, and Japanese investment overtook that of Americans. The typical arrangement was for the investment to take the form of a joint venture in which the Indonesian side consisted of a partnership between senior military officers and Chinese businessmen." Crouch (1978, p. 287).

military because on their own they lack political clout. In a society in which ethnic cleavages are the most salient ones, the marginal status of the Chinese enhances their appeal as business partners with the military because despite their wealth the Chinese do not pose a political threat to the military.[60]

As partners of powerful regime insiders who nonetheless lack political power of their own, ethnic Chinese industrialists and traders have security, but they are not capable of capturing the state or challenging the New Order's rule or policies. Their arrangements with the military are simply a surrogate for the consistent application of rules. This joining of the interests of the ethnic Chinese, with their capital and business experience, and the interests of the military, with their political and coercive authority, has been critical to Indonesia's success.[61]

The *cukong* system is a personalized and informal resolution of the rent allocation and the commitment problem; it allows the Chinese to

---

60. "For all the talk we have heard since the early years of the New Order about the close connections between wealthy Chinese *cukong* and powerful Indonesian generals, there is little evidence that any of them have been able to carry much weight in the general decision-making processes that determine the broader outlines of national economic or social policy formation." See Mackie (1990, p. 83).

61. Robison (1986), analyzing the Indonesian experience from the perspective of a class conflict, similarly concludes. "The military has become a corporate owner of capital and as such has developed a vested political interest in the perpetuation of conditions conducive to the accumulation of capital and the generation of profits. . . . But there is a much more concrete relationship between the military and the capitalist class. Through the mechanism of the company and the joint venture, Chinese and international capital effectively operate as the financiers of the military in that they provide the capital and organizational resources to turn the license, the contract or whatever concession into profits and, ultimately, income for the military. It is natural, therefore, that the military has become committed not merely to abstract ideologies of capitalism but to the social dominance of the capitalist class, even to the fortunes of particular companies. This is given another dimension of emphasis by the fact that increasing numbers of military men are moving into private business on their own behalf [(Robison 1986, p. 258)]. . . . A politico-economic alliance between the military and major Chinese and international business groups affords Chinese and foreign capital in general a significant degree of political protection" (1986, p. 267). Robison documents the connections between military officers, Chinese businessmen, and foreign companies as partners in specific enterprises (see his chapters seven and eight). Other scholars of varied intellectual persuasions ranging from left to right who have studied Indonesia with some depth have all come to the same conclusion (Liddle, Crouch, Schlossstein, Mackie, MacIntyre, Glassburner). They all agree that a tight business relationship exists between the military and the minority Chinese.

dominate the economy in collaboration with the power elite, that is, the military.[62] The military gains rents in exchange for supporting the nation's economic mobilization, while the Chinese, and the foreigners who invest in joint ventures with them, acquire assurances against expropriation. In the absence of formal institutions to enforce contracts, this arrangement provides relatively secure property rights, and these in turn have encouraged investor confidence. Because military officers have shares in Chinese enterprises and foreign joint ventures, the government is keenly aware that expropriating these firms—or indeed any others—would undermine the military support that provides the foundation of the New Order.

But the cukong system has had its drawbacks as suggested by the fact that the ratio of private investment to GDP in Indonesia has been lower on average than the ratio in the other high performers even after adjusting for level of development (table 5-4). This stems from the fact that the system depends and in fact thrives on the lack of predictability of and transparency in the regulatory environment. Bureaucratic delay, a measure of the transparency and predictability of the regulatory regime, was significantly worse than in the other high performers in the 1970s. And as table 5-3 shows, this feature does not seem to have changed much in the 1980s.[63]

Putting Oil to "Good" Use

Indonesia is a major oil exporter and, for most of the 1970s until the mid-1980s, the government relied heavily on the oil sector for revenues. From 1979 to 1984, more than half of annual government revenue was attributable to oil and gas activities.[64] Hence, much of the New Order's development programs have been financed by oil.

62. See De Long (1991) and Ramirez (1992).

63. However, deregulation, which began in 1985, seems to have had some positive effect on private investment perhaps because it has loosened the noose somewhat on the private sector. The average of the ratio of total investment to GDP fell by approximately 10 percent between 1981 and 1985, the period immediately preceding deregulation, and the period 1986–92 when various deregulatory measures were introduced. Miller and Sumlinski (1994, p. 46). Between these same periods, the average ratio of private investment to GDP fell by only 4 percent. And not surprisingly, the ratio of private investment to total investment rose between these two periods, from 53.5 in 1981–85 to 58.8 in 1986–92. IFC (1994). The differential could be interpreted loosely as a measure of the impact of deregulation on private investment.

64. MacIntyre (1990).

Oil earnings were not used strictly to finance development projects. To the contrary, some, most likely a substantial portion, were rents allocated mostly to the military, especially from Pertamina, the state oil corporation.[65] This suggests rather strongly that oil money was used partly to combat potential dissidence among military personnel during the early years of the New Order. Until the economy had stabilized and began to grow robustly, it was necessary to find some means to improve the material well-being of military personnel. The regime's viability was at stake. Oil then may have helped saved the day for the New Order at least until the cukong system became firmly established and the technocrats' policies began to bear fruit.[66] Oil helped make it possible for the New Order to satisfy the material interests of military personnel, its key backers, and lay the foundation for sustainable growth.

How Resilient Is the System?

The Indonesian model deviates from the patterns of public–private interaction characteristic of the other high performers. In Indonesia a credible bureaucracy and deliberation councils were not the mechanisms used to coordinate the contact between state and society.[67] Con-

65. "The most important source of funds for the army during the early phase of the New Order was the state oil corporation, Pertamina. . . . Pertamina's financial affairs have been clouded in secrecy. Balance sheets were never published and profits were unannounced. Although its taxation payments to the government rose from 15 percent of the government's domestic revenues in 1967 to more than 50 percent after the 1973 price rise, it was clear that a large part of Pertamina's profits, especially in the early phase, was not transferred to the government. The secrecy surrounding the financial affairs of Pertamina was intended to disguise its role as a major source of funds at the disposal of the military leadership." Crouch (1978, p. 278).

66. It would be interesting to compare the New Order's history with those of military regimes in Nigeria and Venezuela, both also oil exporters and members of OPEC. De Silva (1993) compares Nigeria with Indonesia and concludes that the New Order's vigilance in pursuing the policies recommended by the technocrats enabled it to avoid the fate that has befallen Nigeria. By choosing to establish the basic foundations for sustainable growth, the New Order has managed to survive even the drastic drop in oil prices in the mid-1980s.

67. The dragooning of all civil servants into a monolithic government organization that is the key support of the party, Golkar, means that political loyalty and patronage determine career paths in the bureaucracy. Party strength and support in the rural areas determine the fortunes of bureaucratic careers. Therefore the bureaucracy outside of the technocrats has been unreliable. For example, despite tax reform the bureaucracy has yet to demonstrate its capacity to collect taxes. Vatikiotis (1989).

strained by the need to staff its bureaucracy with military personnel, the New Order leadership developed an alternative coordination system that depended on personal assurances of performance.

The strength of the system was tested in the mid-1980s during the drastic decline in oil prices. Before 1985, the Indonesian economy had been heavily regulated. As mentioned earlier, the government responded to the drop in revenues by introducing far-reaching deregulatory measures despite opposition from the private interests of military personnel, including senior officers and their Chinese partners. Profits of the cukong enterprises had been based in large part on rents created by grants of monopoly, controlled licensing, and in general protection through the regulatory regime.

Political tranquility remained despite deregulation. When the government announced that the Customs Bureau would be closed and its functions subcontracted to a Swiss firm, the army's commander-in-chief also announced the army's support for the new policy and hinted that any challenge to it would be an affront to the New Order regime.[68] This is somewhat puzzling given that deregulation would almost surely mean increased competition and lower profits for the joint military-Chinese enterprises. Two explanations exist. First, as mentioned earlier, the flow of financial resources was likely to contract with the drop in oil revenues. Consequently, the regime would have fewer resources to allocate to development and to rents. A smaller pie would be inevitable unless new revenue-increasing measures were introduced. Deregulation promised to deliver a larger pie after a short period of contraction, and given the past successes of the technocrats the promise was credible to leadership and the military. Further, deregulation would lead to increased support from multilateral lending agencies, providing a buffer during the period of contraction. In fact, foreign aid as a source of government revenue increased significantly during the critical period between 1985 and 1987.[69] Second, owing to the cukong system, military officials would share in the burden of the contraction. Hence, a sense of fairness existed in the allocation of the burden, which eliminated a potential source of discontent.[70]

Bureaucratic clientilism has triumphed in Indonesia because im-

68. Interview with Dr. Hadi Soesastro, executive director, Center for Strategic and International Studies.

69. See Macintyre (1990, p. 253, fig. 7.1).

70. Liddle (1991) makes a similar argument.

portant real or potential constituencies feel that they are getting a fair deal. The perception that everyone gets a piece of the action is as important as the reality, because it suggests that the New Order has accomplished much of what it promised. The lack of strong institutional foundations, however, raises doubts about the sustainability of the political deals on which much investment has depended. Regime leaders have stayed in power by securing sweetheart deals for military officials, friends, and relations while spreading growth throughout the lower strata of society. The regime welcomed the advice of the economic technocrats because political patrimonialism and economic success were closely related. Staying in power has required the regime to have at its disposal large quantities of wealth to disburse as patronage: the policies of the economists have helped produce the goods on which the regime's political support rests.

Today grumbling about the Chinese tycoons is matched by complaints about the president's family.[71] When the president boasts of the growth of indigenous entrepreneurs, Indonesians look to Bimantara and Humpuss—two conglomerates that have grown rapidly since the deregulation process began. Both are run by his children.[72]

Part of the family's fortune comes from the role of family members as intermediaries.[73] A firm seeking to invest in Indonesia will seek out members of Soeharto's family as shareholders of a project not only to seek protection from the insecure legal environment but also to reduce the costs of gathering, organizing, and communicating information. As a result, family members are represented on the boards of many firms

71. By 1986 Liddle reports, "The president's children had become the major beneficiaries of the protectionist policies of the nationalists and patrimonialists." Liddle (1991, p. 421).

72. Soeharto touts the role of family members as a way to build the role of indigenous Indonesians in an economy dominated by Chinese Indonesians. The hope is that once full-scale liberalization is introduced, Indonesia will have native capitalists who can reduce the nation's dependence on international capital.

73. "A good indicator of the families' growing share is the number of multinationals which line up to court the Soeharto's sons or well connected Chinese Indonesian groups in efforts to win major contracts . . . Wining control of license and supply and service contracts, and letting others execute them, is the mainstay of the family's businesses." Handley (1986, p. 40). One reason the businesses appear to be mainly tollgates is that the Soeharto children do not actively manage their investments. "You cannot get involved in an important deal any more if you don't bring in at least one of the children." Adam Schwarz, "All Is Relative: Suharto Family's Businesses Face Mounting Criticism in Indonesia," *Far Eastern Economic Review*, April 30, 1992, p. 54.

and hold shares in a wide range of companies. Family members are chosen because their position in the political hierarchy offers information about conditions in the economy or industry that outsiders may not possess, and their participation serves as a stamp of approval and plays a monitoring and signaling role, giving confidence to investors. In the absence of a competent bureaucracy and an efficient legal system, bringing the family into a deal creates value for shareholders. Investors can assume that those companies will perform better than others similarly situated.[74]

Nevertheless, the growth of the "Soeharto" business empire presents a difficult problem for the system, which heretofore has worked rather well. When the president departs, the wealth his children have accumulated will be questioned. Although the wealth could be moved outside to safer havens, two factors will constrain this step. First, it would weaken the legitimacy of the president's rule since he has criticized domestic capital flight. Second, and perhaps more important, much of this wealth is based on fixed investments in the country and so cannot be disposed of without substantial loss. Hence, the great "Father of Development" (and more generally the regime) finds himself in a quandary. How this issue is resolved is likely to spell the difference between continued success for Indonesia and the beginning of turmoil that may interrupt what the president has fostered.

74. *Economist*, "A Survey of Indonesia: Wealth in Its Grasp," April 17, 1993. "Family businesses [are not] simple 'tollgate operations,' extracting a fee for providing access to contracts and markets. That ignores their entrepreneurial role in initiating projects. 'They don't just set up a toll booth,' argues one diplomat, 'they actively go out and round up the cars.' " A telecom project with NEC and another with Mitsui are cited as examples.

Six

Leadership and the Economic Bureaucracy

THE ASIAN MIRACLE was fostered by politicians who identified the long-term viability of their regimes with the attainment of shared growth. East Asian leaders recognized that shared growth depended on the standards of public performance maintained by the economic bureaucracy, and therefore they devised rules so that bureaucrats' incentives were consonant with promoting shared growth.

Bureaucrats have two types of information. The first is technical knowledge of the economic consequences of policies—knowledge that can be put to work for the public good. The second is detailed knowledge of the regulatory environment and the relative position of firms—knowledge that can be put to work for short-term gain, by selling favors. They choose which type of information to use according to their calculation of risks and rewards. If they choose the first, then they may forgo higher income from private sector employment or the potential returns of using their position to make enormous profits quickly. If they choose the second, then they give up the relative security and prestige (where this exists) of public employment and risk dismissal, disgrace, and punishment. To structure an effective economic bureaucracy, leaders must find ways to adjust the risk-reward calculation so that bureaucrats will use their knowledge of the economic consequences of policies to promote shared growth.

This is precisely what leaders in East Asia managed to do. The segment of the bureaucracy that was offered a mix of incentives ranged from a small core of experts in Indonesia to the entire civil service in Singapore. In each case, however, a competent, powerful but accountable group of bureaucrats was created. The creation of this economic bureaucracy stands out as one of the most original and successful of the

138

institutional innovations that distinguish the high-performing Asian economies (HPAEs) from the patterns characteristic of Latin America and Africa.[1] How was this done?

To minimize bureaucrats' temptation to use knowledge of regulations and firms for a large, quick payoff, leaders provided incentives for bureaucrats to identify their own interests with the country's long-term economic expansion. This was done by promising an attractive lifetime stream of benefits in exchange for responsible, restrained, and disciplined performance. This required several steps.

First, leaders had to convince officials already in office and those subsequently recruited that economic growth was indeed the overriding objective. Officials not persuaded of this aim would be less likely to perform their functions properly and efficiently: without growth, there could be no long-term returns; short-term profiteering would thus be more attractive. Second, to attract competent individuals to the economic bureaucracy, leaders established merit-based rules and procedures for the recruitment and promotion of personnel and offered relatively attractive compensation schemes. Third, to ensure that technical questions were resolved on strictly technical criteria, leaders had to grant the economic bureaucracy some independence and establish mechanisms to help the bureaucrats resist demands of interest groups at odds with national economic objectives. And finally, given the economic bureaucracy's independence, an oversight mechanism was necessary to ensure that the economic bureaucracy would be accountable to leadership for its performance.

Expectations and Credibility

The willingness of bureaucrats to believe promises of a long-term stream of benefits and thus forgo short-term opportunism depends on the persuasiveness of leadership's commitment to growth. As discussed in earlier chapters, leadership signaled its commitment to shared growth to the general population—and, not so incidentally, to the bureaucrats as well—through mechanisms ranging from land reform to universal education. And in most of the high-performing economies, leaders also took steps to demonstrate to the bureaucrats that officials who undermined this objective would be dealt with severely.

1. See Wade (1994) for a concrete example of HPAE solutions to this agency problem.

In Singapore, Lee Kuan Yew removed corrupt officials after publicly shaming them, thus signaling his determination to cut ties to the past—and putting officials on notice that the risks of seeking short-term gains were substantial. With the old boys out of the way, government had to offer a new way that worked. The new bureaucracy was small, so responsibilities were unambiguously assigned and Lee could closely supervise performance. Adopting sometimes draconian measures for acquiring evidence and meting out justice, he established a Corruption Control Committee to find and penalize wrongdoers. The message was that leadership expects nothing but the best.

In Indonesia, Soeharto manifested his commitment to growth by following the advice of his technocrats during times of economic crisis. Upon assuming power, to cut the runaway inflation of the Sukarno years, he accepted the advice of his technocrats lock, stock, and barrel. In a further signal of his acceptance of the technocrats—and his determination to provide a sound macroeconomic framework for shared growth—he had a balanced budget requirement inserted into the constitution in 1967. When it became apparent in 1975 that close associates had mismanaged the state oil company, he dismissed the associates and, with the advice of the technocrats, put the firm's management in the hands of more reputable individuals. When oil prices collapsed in 1983 he again followed the difficult advice of the technocrats: open the economy, deregulate, and encourage export investment to bring in foreign exchange. He did so, although the liberalization jeopardized the rents of powerful regime supporters.

General Park reorganized Korea's economic bureaucracy around the newly created Economic Planning Board and gave that body extensive powers over economic affairs. He then imprisoned a number of chaebol leaders so they would understand business was going to be done differently. Moreover, when his first five-year plan did not produce results he began his famous New Year visits—visits to each of his ministers to discuss goals and strategies to implement those goals. Park returned the following year to each minister and went through the promises sentence by sentence. Those ministers who achieved less than 80 percent of what they promised were fired. After two or three years the ministers understood the drill. Each department had to define its performance objectives in terms that were clear to all. Ministers learned to communicate the need for precise targets to their subordinates. Only those managers who fulfilled the plans survived.[2] Park made it clear that what mattered most was sustainable economic growth.

In Taiwan, the need for a reputable economic bureaucracy to monitor and guide economic development was foremost in the minds of the KMT leaders. They had learned some important lessons from their debacle in the mainland. Integrity was instilled in the civil service by examples set early in the regime's history. When Wang Zeng-Yi, Chiang Kai-Shek's brother-in-law, was successfully impeached by the Control Yuan, a clear signal was sent about the regime's commitment to accountability. Even the premier's closest relations were not protected from the standards that applied to all public servants. The use of insider advantages by officials was actively and purposely resisted by the creation of an independent examination board to monitor recruitment into the civil service. The Control Yuan had complete powers of impeachment and investigation over all members of the government.[3]

In each case, to induce public officials to contribute to creating a greater social product, leadership made its promise to promote growth credible. Bureaucrats' expectations were thus attuned to the possibility of obtaining long-term rewards for good performance.

The Route to Competency

In the HPAEs, the implementation of a merit-based recruitment or promotion system was an essential step toward sustaining competent performance. Of the three broad types of merit-based systems that have appeared among the HPAEs, the first, exemplified by the Japanese and Korean systems, is more formally institutionalized: recruitment is based on tough civil service examinations; promotions are based on proven ability.[4] Applicants need not have a college degree (although

2. Interview with Young Whun Hahn, January 1995.
3. Interviews with exgovernment officials, January 1995.
4. Although seniority bears heavily on promotion decisions, performance does count. The pyramidlike structure of the bureaucracy guarantees competition. In Japan, "An entering class works together to ensure that its members prosper. . . . Who becomes a bureau chief, a director-general, or ultimately the one (administrative) vice minister is a source of intense competition among the classes in a ministry." Johnson (1982, p. 62). In Korea, promotion decisions are based on seniority and various performance criteria with predetermined weights assigned to each element. See Wade (1994).

in practice it is extremely difficult to pass the exams without training in a well-established university). The second, which is also highly institutionalized, is exemplified by Singapore's system. There, recruitment is based on high standards of academic performance (at the undergraduate level) and rigorous personal interviews.[5] Promotions are based on performance rather than seniority. Reaching the highest level of service, that of permanent secretary, can occur at a relatively young age as exemplified by cases of individuals' being appointed permanent secretary in their thirties. In Indonesia and Thailand a third system exists in which exams are largely perfunctory and are thus an ineffective filtering device. There the filters tend to be the successful completion of graduate degrees, especially a Ph.D. from a foreign institution. Not surprisingly, the bureaucracies in these countries are also the weakest among the HPAEs.[6]

The Taiwanese and Malaysian systems fall into the first category. In Taiwan, civil service exams are not so stringent, but their relative weakness is offset by the constant recruitment of academics from major universities, usually for fixed periods ranging from three to six years.[7] The foreign graduate degree filter therefore supplements the exams. In Malaysia, the results of the civil service exams are subject to affirmative action requirements introduced under the New Economic Policy. Although the exams are difficult, quotas allocate a certain percentage of slots to the Bumiputras.

The Korean system features strong filters in the form of exams, performance criteria, and graduate degrees. The research institutes attached to various ministries emphasize graduate degrees.[8]

5. Personal interviews with current and ex–government officials indicate the following process of recruitment. Each year the top 200 college graduates (based on academic performance and interviews) are identified and given an offer to join government service. Those who elect to do so are then put through a rigorous one-year training program. Thereafter, each is sent abroad for further studies, usually to England or the United States. They are then assigned to different branches of government upon their return. This system has worked well in Singapore because of its small size.

6. The problem is more severe in Indonesia. In Thailand, the economic/finance-related agencies are highly regarded and command respect among the general population. Interviews with officials in Thai agencies indicated that these agencies are more stringent in their recruitment and promotion policies.

7. See Wade (1990).

8. For example, the Korean Development Institute (KDI) was established in 1971 to assist the Economic Planning Board (EPB) in developing medium- and long-term plans.

Whichever system has been adopted, some mechanism to identify the more competent individuals has been employed to recruit the economic bureaucracy. Tough exams, academic performance, and doctoral degrees determine the selection from among a given crop of applicants.

The overall competency of the economic bureaucracy reflects the qualifications of those who aspire to government jobs. This potential pool of applicants is in turn influenced by the compensation that government offers. Comparisons between public sector and private sector salaries are complex. In general, however, although civil servants nearly everywhere (Singapore is the remarkable exception) are less well paid than their private sector counterparts, the differential between civil servants' salaries and private sector salaries is smaller in the HPAEs than in other developing countries. Moreover, there are frequently other advantages of public sector employment in the high-performing East Asian countries that attract competent candidates who might otherwise choose private employment.

For basic salary comparisons, estimates are available for most of the HPAEs and a few other low- and middle-income countries. Indexes of the public sector-private sector differentials in five of the HPAEs and several other developing countries are shown in table 6-1. Singapore is an obvious standout—even by East Asian standards—with public sector salaries that are higher on average than private sector salaries and are even better than salaries of equivalent senior officials in the United States—where per capita GNP is about one and a half times higher.[9]

In Japan salary differentials between the public and private sector

---

"The Korea Educational Development Institute (KEDI), founded by the Ministry of Education in 1972, the Korea Rural Economic Development Institute (KERI), founded by the Ministry of Agriculture and Fishery in 1978, and the Korea Land Development Institute (KLDI), established in 1978 by the Ministry of Construction, are other cases." See Leipziger and Kim (1992, p. 15). Researchers in these institutes generally possess a Ph.D., many from highly reputable Western academic institutions.

9. As of 1993, the base salary of a (full) minister ranges from S$22,100 to S$27,825 a month, which under the current exchange rate is equivalent to U.S.$13,812 to U.S.$17,390. A minister of state is paid the equivalent of U.S.$5,625 to U.S.$7,688. Recently, the government announced that it would once again raise public sector salaries to keep up with increases in the private sector. The annual salary of a minister is to be set at S$776,000, which is approximately U.S.$500,000. "Competitive Salaries for Competent and Honest Government," White Paper, Government of Singapore, October 1994.

TABLE 6-1. *Estimates of per Capita GDP and Ratio of Public to Private Sector Salaries, Developing Countries*

Country or region	Per capita GDP[a]	Senior level (%) A	B	Mid-level[b] (%) A	B	Entry-level (%)
High-performing Asian economies (HPAEs)						
Singapore	14,920	114[b]	114	115[3]	115	107
South Korea[c]	7,190	69.3	69.3	57.1	57.7	58.7
Taiwan, China	7,954	65.2	60.3	63.5	65.8	60
Malaysia	5,900	40	33.3	34.3	50	n.a.
Thailand	4,610	47.1	46	37.2	34.9	78.9
Other Asia						
Philippines	2,320	27.7	24.3	25	32.5	62.5
Latin America						
Chile	6,190	70.36	63.2	n.a.	n.a.	n.a.
Trinidad and Tobago	8,510	63.53[b]	63.53	76.88	77.92	n.a.
Venezuela	6,740	29.54	42.38	53.4[b]	53.4	n.a.
Uruguay	6,000	n.a.	n.a.	37.1[b]	37.1	n.a.
Argentina	4,680	24.11[b]	24.11	28.57[b]	28.57	n.a.

Sources: World Bank, *World Development Report* (Washington, 1992); Taiwan, *Statistical Yearbook* (1992). Salaries for the HPAEs and the Philippines were provided by local consultants and are based on latest available information. Salary data on Latin American countries were extracted from Reid (1992).

n.a. Not available.

a. In 1992 international dollars, according to United Nations International Program.

b. Average is used for both sublevels A and B.

c. Estimates of private sector salaries include allowances and bonuses so that the ratios are actually higher. Data are from a survey of companies with 500 or more employees.

are deliberately kept small. The government undertakes an extensive annual survey of pay rates (including allowances) in both sectors and adjusts civil servant salaries accordingly so that public employees do not fall behind those in the private sector. In 1992, for example, the survey covered 7,425 establishments, 653,046 individuals, and 91 job classifications.[10] Results showed monthly remuneration in the private sector is only slightly higher on average than that in the public sector (this excludes public enterprises).[11]

In Taiwan, Korea, Malaysia, and Thailand, public sector salaries are systematically lower across the board.[12] A recent study of the public sector in Indonesia indicates that the differential is widest in Indonesia.[13] In Indonesia, the differential across rank categories, already large at the junior manager level, increases dramatically with rank.[14]

In some HPAEs, government salaries are supplemented with substantial allowances and bonuses not unlike those offered by the private sector.[15] In Singapore, public sector wages are supplemented by an end-of-year thirteenth-month annual allowance equivalent to the Christmas bonus in many private firms, an annual variable component (AVC) tied to the performance of the economy akin to the profit-sharing schemes in private industry; and for superscale officers, special performance bonuses that roughly mimic performance bonuses of corporate executives.[16]

In Japan public servants benefit from "an elaborate system of ten

10. National Personnel Authority (NPA), *Annual Report, 1992.*

11. In making comparisons, the NPA controls for job, rank, academic background, location, and age. The average differential for each service level is calculated by using a Laspeyres formula. See Hirose (1993, p. 48).

12. The finance-related agencies in Thailand, for example, the Bank of Thailand and the Budget Bureau, have their own personnel and recruitment programs. There, salaries are said to be about 30 percent higher across the board than in the rest of the public sector.

13. Steedman (1993).

14. Interviews with some government officials and Indonesian academics also suggest that a fresh graduate from an Indonesian university gets a base salary of about Rp 170,000 in a government department and Rp 250,000 in a state enterprise. The graduate can earn between Rp 350,000 and Rp 500,000 at entry level in a private enterprise.

15. Information on public sector allowances was not available for Malaysia, Taiwan, and Thailand.

16. The AVC is awarded in the form of end-of-the-year monthly bonuses. Depending on the performance of the economy, public sector employees could get a bonus from one to several months' salary.

kinds of allowances, from 'family allowance' and 'adjustment allowance' to 'commuter allowance' and 'diligence allowance.'"[17]

In Korea, public employees are eligible for fifty-nine different types of allowances, and almost half of a public sector employee's compensation comes from these allowance.[18] With the allowances included, average total compensation in the public sector is still significantly lower than the average in large, private companies. Nonetheless, when total compensation is adjusted for all bonuses and allowances earned by public sector employees, the gap between public sector and private sector total compensation narrows.[19]

If compensation in the private sector exceeds that in the public sector, as suggested by the available data, one would expect the public sector to have difficulty attracting and keeping talented individuals. Thus, without compensating factors, talented individuals will migrate to the private sector. Yet except for Indonesia and to a lesser extent Thailand, in the HPAEs graduates from the top universities compete intensely for public sector slots.[20]

In the HPAEs with solid and extensive economic bureaucracies, competent individuals join the public sector and remain there despite lower compensation for many reasons. First, employment is usually secure.

17. "Perhaps the most remarkable of these allowances is the 'end-of-the-term-allowance,' which is paid to public employees serving on March 1, June 1, and December 1 of each year. On March 1, the employee is paid 50 percent of the basic amount (the total of his monthly salary, family allowance, and adjustment allowance); on June 30, 140 percent of the basic amount; and on December 10, 190 percent of the basic amount. Thus a Japanese public employee receives 380 percent of the basic amount each year in addition to his regular salary. This generous allowance is comparable to the bonuses paid in American industry." See Kim (1988, p. 9).

18. Ministry of Government Administration, Seoul, Korea, April 1991.

19. Estimates of allowances are very rough. Personal interviews with some former public officials indicate that not all civil servants received the same allowances. When these allowances are incorporated, the ratio of public to private sector compensation improves: approximately 90 percent for senior levels, 80 percent for mid and entry level.

20. Interviews with officials at the Bank of Thailand and researchers at the Thailand Development Research Institute (TDRI) indicate that the competition to get into the four "elite" government agencies in Thailand is also stiff. In Japan graduates scramble each year to enter the public sector. "Despite this relatively short [application] period, the number of applications for the higher civil service entrance examinations is staggering. In each year since 1972, the National Personnel Authority has passed no more than 1,700 applicants at the senior entrance examinations, yet there have been more than 32,000 applicants annually." See Kim (1988, p. 23).

Unless a serious mistake is committed, dismissal is unlikely. Only the very top positions are filled by political appointees (table 6-2). Civil service or other institutionalized procedures govern appointments (including promotions) at all other levels. And in some cases, for example, Malaysia, even the recommendations for the top-level positions come from the civil service. Furthermore, a public employee can look forward to a pension upon retirement which, except in very large corporations, he or she could not generally expect in private industry. Security of tenure translates into lower income variability, which in turn provides incentives for public employees to accept a lower (mean) salary.[21]

Second, a well-defined, competitive career path, with the possibility of substantial rewards at the end, exists in the bureaucracy. Japan has the best-developed civil service system among the HPAEs, but many of the conditions of civil service employment observed there also exist in the other high performers, though usually to a lesser degree. In Japan "promotion to section chief is virtually guaranteed to every career officer who does not make a major mistake . . . Competition over promotion begins beyond the section chief level . . . Those who are promoted are still in the running for the vice-ministership; those who are not are compelled to 'resign'—or, as it is known in the Japanese government, to 'descend from heaven' (*amakudari*) into a lucrative job in a public corporation or private industry" arranged by more senior officials.[22] Table 6-3 gives a sample of retired MITI senior officials and their amakudari patrons.[23] Senior officials are sometimes recruited by the Liberal Democratic Party to run for political office or are retired to a position in local government. Similar arrangements, in which retirement from government occurs at a relatively young age and retirees "descend down" to the private sector also exist in Korea, Taiwan, Singapore, and Malaysia. In each case, these transitions provide an incentive for members of the economic bureaucracy to perform well over the course of their public service career.

21. Because they are risk averse, individuals are generally willing to trade off higher mean salaries for lower variances at some implicit price.

22. Johnson (1982, p. 63). In Singapore, owing to the PAP's penchant for getting the best individuals to serve in government, senior managers in private industry are often invited to serve fixed terms in government agencies. To our knowledge, no systematic data on amakudari exists in Singapore or the other HPAEs. But personal interviews with officials and researchers in these countries indicate that the practice is widespread.

23. See Inoki (1992).

TABLE 6-2. *The Structure of the Bureaucracy in Selected Asian Countries*

Philippines	Thailand	Indonesia	Malaysia	Singapore	Taiwan	Korea	Japan
Secretary	*Minister*	*Minister*	*Minister*	*Senior Minister*	*Minister*	*Minister*	*Minister*
Undersecretary	*Deputy minister*	*Junior minister*		*Deputy minister*	*Political vice minister*	*Vice minister*	*Parlimentary vice minister*
							Administrative vice minister
Assistant secretary	Permanent secretary		Secretary	Permanent secretary	Administrative vice minister	Assistant minister	Deputy vice minister
	Deputy permanent secretary		Undersecretary				
Bureau director	Bureau director	Bureau director		Deputy permanent secretary	Bureau director general	Director general	Director general
Regional director	Agency head	Agency head		Agency head	Department director		
Service director				Assistant head			
Division chief	Division chief	Division chief	Division chief		Division chief	Office director	

Sources: Local consultants, organizational listings, and interviews. Positions that are subject to presidential appointment are indicated in italic.

TABLE 6-3. *MITI Vice Ministers and Their Amakudari Positions*

Name	Vice ministers, dates	Amakudari positions
Yamamoto Takayuki (1929–1952)	5/49–3/52	Vice president, Fuji Iron and Steel; died May 17, 1961
Tamaki Keizo (1930–1953)	3/52–11/53	President, then chairman, Toshiba Electric Co.
Hirai Timisaburo (1931–1955)	11/53–11/55	President, then adviser, New Japan Steel Corp.
Isihara Takeo (1932–1957)	11/55–6/57	Vice president, then auditor, Tokyo Electric Power Co.
Ueno Koshichi (1932–1960)	6/57–5/60	Vice president, then adviser, Kansai Electric Power Co., president, Kansai Oil Co.
Tokunaga Hisatsugu (1933–1961)	5/60–7/61	Vice president, New Japan Steel Corp., then president, Japan Petroleum Development Corp.
Matsuo Kinzo (1934–1963)	7/61–7/63	Chairman, Nippon Kohan Steel Co.
Imai Zen'ei (1937–1964)	7/63–10/64	President, Japan Petrochemical Corp.
Sahashi Shigeru (1937–1966)	10/64–4/66	Sahashi Economic Research Institute; chairman, Japan Leisure Development Center
Yamamoto Shigenobu (1939–1968)	4/66–5/68	Executive director, Toyota Motor Co.
Kumagai Yoshifumi (1940–1969)	5/68–11/69	President, Sumitomo Metals Corp.
Ojimi Yoshihisa (1941–1971)	11/69–6/71	President, Arabian Oil Company
Morozumi Yosihihiko (1941–1973)	6/71–7/73	President, Electric Power Development Company
Yamashita Eimei (1943–1974)	7/73–11/74	Managing director, Mitsui Trading Co.; president, Iran Chemical Development Co.
Komatsu Yugoro (1944–1976)	11/74–7/76	Director, Kobe Steel Corp.

Source: Johnson (1982, p. 72).

Hence, in most HPAE economic bureaucracies, a relatively high degree of upward mobility exists. Like the private sector, the government offers a clear path for advancement. More important, a considerable prize to those who are successful is early retirement, frequently with a substantial pension complemented by a hefty salary from a public or private sector enterprise as a director or senior official.[24] In effect, the price acts like a performance bond: a bureaucrat suffers a large financial loss for nonperformance.

Besides selecting talented individuals, a highly competitive, merit-based recruitment and promotion system performs a signaling function, identifying the talented to the general public. Because of the difficulty of the exams, successful entry is a notable achievement. Hence, the high value attached to public service in the HPAEs. A trait that is sometimes linked to Confucian values or other cultural factors may in fact be the product of a filtering system that could be replicated in other societies.

A merit-based recruitment system creates value for the successful entrant. Being a part of the bureaucracy gives the entrant recognition not available from the private sector.[25] To determine the monetary equivalent of this recognition, consider the traditional granting of awards by the king in Thailand. There, for many centuries, the king granted highly coveted awards to individuals who excelled in the service of the kingdom. Awards came in the form of sashes of different

24. As Aoki (1988, p. 22) comments, "Amakudari positions *in Japan* are provided as the final prize in the competition among bureaucrats in the ranking hierarchy." Emphasis added.

Further, as Inoki (1992) shows, the prize improves the permanent incomes of public sector employees. Inoki (1992) provides evidence supporting the thesis that amakudari is a mechanism designed to increase the lifetime incomes of bureaucrats. He notes that there are social costs to the practice of amakudari such as the potential for collusion on regulation among current and retired bureaucrats. But he argues that these costs should be balanced against the social benefit of attracting competent people and keeping them in public service.

25. There is another largely positive feature that a merit-based system of recruitment and promotion creates. Because such a system attracts the cream of the crop and most of the cream comes from highly selective universities, an esprit de corps is created among bureaucrats. The strong bonds that develop among the workers strengthen the bureaucracy. They create a mutual support system and loyalty to the institution. Thus the bureaucracy can deal with the private sector from a position of strength. Johnson (1982).

colors signifying different degrees of service. This tradition has continued until the present. In the modern context, royal decorations are usually awarded to exemplary public servants. On occasion, however, a businessperson deemed to have contributed to the betterment of the country could qualify for a decoration. But that person must donate a set amount of money, depending on the type of decoration suitable. At the current exchange rate, the donations range from U.S.$12,000 to more than U.S.$1.2 million.[26]

Lemons and Long-Term Dynamics

The importance of a merit-based recruitment system resides in its capacity to distinguish talent. Recruitment rules that are non-merit-based lend themselves easily to favoritism. In turn, the potential for favoritism creates an adverse selection or "lemons" problem.[27] Talented individuals who might aspire to public service decide not to do so because they perceive that the average public employee is likely to be mediocre, that is, there is little status associated with employment in the public sector. This perception unfortunately creates a long-term dynamic in which only mediocre individuals choose to join the bureaucracy. The main consequence of this dynamic is likely to be poor performance.

A comparison of the Philippine and Indonesian bureaucracies with those of four HPAEs illustrates this syndrome. The relative public sector-private sector pay differentials are largest in the Philippines and Indonesia. Furthermore, political appointments are deeper and more extensive in the Philippine bureaucracy, suggesting that recruitment and promotion in the Philippines is less likely to be merit based. Table 6-4 presents a rough measure of bureaucratic performance for the Philippines, Indonesia, and the other HPAEs. The measure—extent of bureaucratic delay—is an index of responses obtained in a survey of business executives conducted by the Business Environmental Risk Intelligence (BERI). The index ranges from a low integer score of 1 to a high of 4. Besides Thailand, the Philippines and Indonesia have the lowest scores in the region. These observations suggest that low pay

26. Importantly, Thai royal decorations are granted for public service and generally are accorded only to those in public employment. See Samudavanija (1992).

27. See Akerlof (1970) for the discussion of the lemons problem.

TABLE 6-4. *Index of Bureaucratic Delay — East Asia, 1972, 1982*

Country	1972[a]	1982[a]
Singapore	3.1	3.1
Japan	2.6	2.7
Taiwan	2.7	2.5
South Korea	2.1	2.5
Malaysia	2.3	1.9
Thailand[b]	1.4	1.6
Philippines	1.5	1.8
Indonesia	1.4	1.2

Source: BERI index from Keefer and Knack (1993).

a. Higher numbers indicate relatively better performance.

b. The performance of the four central ministries is not reflected in the BERI. For the most part, this index reflects only the performance of line agencies.

combined with a non-merit-based recruitment system leads to poor performance.[28]

Because a merit-based promotion system means objective criteria for promotion, it is much less prone to abuse by authorities, particularly politicians. If politicians can interfere with promotion decisions in the bureaucracy, uncertainty is introduced into the career paths of bureaucrats. Public servants will thus have doubts about the usefulness of complying with the rules. If, for instance, bureaucrats can move up by having politicians intercede on their behalf, then they will have an incentive to lobby politicians instead of performing their jobs effectively. In India, despite tough civil service entry exams, performance has been dismal.[29] Bribes become a determinant of promotions and politicians intervene in promotion decisions.[30] The BERI bureaucratic delay index for India is 1.2, lower even than that of the Philippines and Indonesia. Obviously, to inhibit a lemons problem, both the recruitment system and the promotion system must be merit based, sealed from solicitations of powerful individuals and interest groups.

The experience of the advanced HPAEs, and to a lesser extent Malay-

28. The lemons problem is likely to persist even when competitive pay is combined with non-merit-based recruitment. Because the pool of recruits will consist of both talented and mediocre applicants, the prestige factor that could tip the balance among talented individuals in favor of public employment disappears. Hence, the incentive to seek public employment is weakened.

29. See Wade (1985) for a discussion of the Indian bureaucracy.

30. Wade (1985).

sia and Thailand, in building their bureaucracies suggests that objective, merit-based rules and procedures governing public sector employment must be institutionalized. These include a merit-based, highly competitive system of recruitment, rules that establish a well-defined career path open equally to all who wish to compete for advancement (a merit-based promotion system), compensation—salaries, allowances, and bonuses—that closely tracks those in the private sector, and a grand prize of substantial value upon retirement for upper-echelon officials.

Balancing Independence and Accountability

Recruiting and keeping qualified personnel was the second step in the process of building an effective economic bureaucracy. The third involved the complex task of balancing independence of the economic bureaucracy with accountability to leadership. The experience of the HPAEs is instructive, since they suggest different ways of achieving this balance. Ways were found to delegate responsibility and authority over economic affairs to qualified experts while at the same time enhancing accountability to the leadership.[31] For leaders to promote growth, they must obtain the information necessary to choose appropriate policies. To induce experts to divulge this information, leaders must give them proper incentives, including the responsibility and authority to formulate and implement economic policies.[32] This authority increases officials' confidence that proposed policies are likely to be adopted, hence their incentive to use their knowledge to solve problems. However, since delegation of authority is no guarantee that experts will indeed use their information for the public good—they could, for instance, grant favors in exchange for bribes—a low-cost monitoring mechanism is necessary.

Authority through the Merit-based System

Although used mainly to establish competency in the economic bureaucracy, the merit-based system of recruitment and promotion also

31. The logic of this balancing act is explained well by Bates and Krueger (1993). In this section we describe and analyze the balancing of independence and accountability in the HPAEs. We do not cover all possible avenues or methods adopted by each of the economies.

32. See Gilligan and Krehbiel (1987) and Krehbiel (1991) for theoretical discussions and discussions in the context of legislative committees and the legislature.

helped secure for the members of the economic bureaucracy the necessary independence to do their jobs. By establishing objective rules for
appointments, the system gives bureaucrats confidence that they can
not easily be demoted, fired, or blocked from rising simply because
their decisions conflict with those of powerful private sector interests. In many developing countries, such as the Philippines, influential
groups (and even individuals) can ask politicians to pressure a civil
servant to alter a decision that they do not like. Because politicians
may influence the career of a civil servant, the latter must often accede
or leave the bureaucracy. A merit system reduces such politically motivated interventions. In light of the established rules, politicians would
have to justify exerting pressure. The system also gives politicians a
convenient and valid excuse for refusing to intercede on a supporter's
behalf.

Independent Personnel Agencies: Japan

In Japan, the merit system has been supplemented by the institution-
alization of an independent agency that handles all affairs pertaining
to personnel matters. The National Personnel Authority (NPA) is one
of only two executive agencies unattached to any ministry. It is also
independent of the legislature. Its principal function is to formulate
and administer personnel policies that govern recruitment and promotion in the bureaucracy.[33] It administers the highly competitive civil
service examinations and determines the pay scales and pay increases
of bureaucrats. It evaluates and approves recommendations for promotion, and it hears and decides on grievances.[34] Because of its independence from the Diet, the NPA is not easily subjected to political pressures. The prime minister, for instance, has limited power to make
appointments to the bureaucracy. He or she can appoint only a few
individuals to the ministries. In addition to the ministers, the prime
minister can appoint only one of the two vice ministers.[35]

33. For a discussion of the functions of the NPA, see Kim (1988) and (1993).

34. By law, public sector employees are prevented from going on strike. So the NPA
is an outlet, allowing workers to express discontent.

35. Each ministry has two vice ministers, a parliamentary one and an administrative
one. The former is appointed by the prime minister. The latter is always a career bureaucrat promoted from the ranks.

Institutionalizing Hard Budget Constraints:
Thailand, Indonesia, and Japan

Establishing hard budget constraints is one way of giving the economic bureaucracy some independence over macroeconomic policymaking while at the same time introducing a low-cost means of
monitoring its performance. That constrains the influence of politicians
and private parties over government expenditures. Because low inflation results, budget constraints also provide a straightforward indicator
of the bureaucrats' success at managing the macroenvironment—the
inflation rate. Among the HPAEs, Thailand, Indonesia, and Japan have
been the strongest adherents of hard budgets.

Thailand and Indonesia (after Sukarno) have steadfastly maintained
a stable macroeconomic environment and have exerted much effort in
keeping inflation low. This tenacity has historical reasons. In Thailand,
the military government of Field Marshal Sarit Thanarat, which gained
power in a 1958 coup, needed to establish an economic development
strategy that contrasted with the previous regime's nationalist, highly
interventionist approach. This was necessary in order to establish that
the new government was fit to rule because it could better manage the
economy.[36] Macroeconomic management was left almost entirely to
the new economic agencies, the Ministry of Finance and the Bank of
Thailand. Field Marshal Sarit's legacy has continued to the present.
The military, which has essentially ruled the country, rarely intervenes
in fiscal and monetary decisions,[37] allowing the four guardian agencies

36. "Sarit garnered his support base among private entrepreneurs and military elites
hostile to the group that promoted nationalist policy. Leading Chinese firms [who formed
the bulk of industry and finance] favored a more stable macroeconomic environment
and in fact had lobbied, prior to the coup, for a reduction of state economic intervention.
To accomplish this objective, Sarit ordered the creation of new economic agencies and
had them located directly under the Prime Minister. The most critical ones were the
NESDB and the Bureau of Budget. . . . The objective was to curb sectorial interventions
of the line ministries and to provide stricter and more centralized monitoring." Siamwala
and Christensen (1993, pp. 46-47).

37. Part of the reason for this abstention, as Siamwala and Christensen (1993) note, is
that the military learned over time that technocratic management of the budget provided a
more lucrative defense budget. Waste that would result from mismanagement and
extralegal activities could be reduced with part of the gain allotted to defense. However,
since a 1990 constitutional amendment, cabinet members, now elected MPs rather than

to manage the macroeconomy. The officials, known as the "techno-crats," in the National Social and Economic Development Board (NESDB), the Budget Bureau, the Ministry of Finance, and the Bank of Thailand (central bank) have worked in tandem to maintain a stable exchange rate and a low inflation rate. Rigid fiscal and monetary poli-cies are their main lever to attain the conservative macropolicies they advocate. Although legally its mandate only covers management of the expenditure side of the budget, the Budget Bureau dominates the whole process. It takes inputs from the NESDB about public invest-ments proposed in the current five-year development plan (which the NESDB formulates) and estimates of revenues from the Ministry of Finance and consults with the Bank of Thailand about the amount of deficit financing the economy can tolerate. Then it determines how much to allow each government agency to spend, that is, it establishes the aggregate allowable expenditure for the year.

The bureau submits its budget recommendations to the cabinet for approval, presenting the cabinet only with the broad expenditure out-lines for each ministry. The details are obscured. The cabinet may propose changes to these broad expenditure categories. Once cabinet-level changes have been factored in, the final product is sent to Parlia-ment by the bureau. Within Parliament, the Budget Scrutiny Committee is responsible for evaluating the budget proposal. The committee is composed of ordinary members of Parliament (MPs) and ministerial MPs. Influence within the committee is asymmetrically distributed. In particular, parliamentary rules restrict the ordinary MPs to amend-ments that adjust the budget downward. The ordinary MPs cannot propose increases to the overall budget and can only propose minimal changes to components of the budget. Historically, the sectoral (compo-nent) changes have not amounted to more than a few million baht.[38]

The procedures allow the Budget Bureau to tightly control the annual budget. To exercise influence over the agenda, first, it presents a highly

---

technocrats, have made decisions that bureaucrats saw as preemptive and overly political. Agencies like the Central Bank have become the objects of power struggles between ministers and top bureaucrats. Dalpino (1990, p. 211). Nonetheless, it is still true that the positions of head of the Central Bank and the Minister of Finance must be filled by highly qualified and respected individuals. The business sector demands this concession in the interest of maintaining a stable exchange rate and low inflation. (Interview with Poonsup Piya-anant and Thongchai Lumdubwong).

38. See Siamwala and Christensen (1993) for a more extensive discussion.

compressed version of its proposed budget to the cabinet. Second, because ordinary members of Parliament cannot amend the budget upward, budget allocations are partially shielded from political considerations. In countries where the legislature can make upward adjustments, the budget becomes the centerpiece of policymaking and politicking. For instance, in order to get bills passed, the U.S. Congress has developed the mechanisms for distributing pork barrel projects over a fairly large number of congressional districts, which inevitably encourages deficits.[39]

The Thai Budget Bureau also draws support from several *legal mandates* that govern the national budget.[40] A budgetary law passed in 1959 and amended in 1974 essentially limits the government deficit to a maximum of 20 percent of the year's total appropriations plus 80 percent of that part allocated to repayments of the principal on loans. Moreover, throughout the 1960s and 1970s, a cap on the public debt service ratio to export earnings was imposed. In December of 1961, the Council of Ministers established a 5 percent cap on the ratio, increased to 7 percent in 1964, and maintained at this level throughout the 1970s. Presently an absolute cap of $1.5 billion exists. Finally, to further prevent external debt from overburdening the economy, a limit was also imposed on the amount of public debt that could be taken out of the annual budget. No more than 13 percent of the budget could be used to service the debt.[41] These mechanisms, along with the four agencies, and the Budget Bureau as housekeeper, have institutionalized a process that promotes rational macroeconomic policies. Figure 6-1 illustrates their success. Except for the years surrounding the two oil crises, the annual inflation rate has been flat at close to 5 percent. Few developing countries can claim an equivalent achievement. Even the more ad-

39. See, for instance, Shepsle, Weingast, and Johnsen (1981).

40. These laws by themselves need not necessarily be binding. In Thailand, conservative management of the budget results from the fact that governments, beginning with Sarit, have been judged by the business sector partly by their ability to keep debt and, by implication, inflation under control. If high inflation occurs, businesses will take their funds elsewhere. In more recent times, the liberalization of financial markets has exerted an additional discipline on the fiscal behavior of government. Capital markets stand ready to take advantage of inconsistencies resulting from bad macroeconomic management. See Campos and Pradhan (1996). For example, a rising deficit can lead to a crisis in the exchange rate as capital managers shift their funds and assets quickly and en masse to other countries in anticipation of a devaluation.

41. See Siamwala and Christensen (1993).

FIGURE 6-1. *Inflation Rate, Thailand, 1954–90*
CPI 1987 = 100

Percent[a]

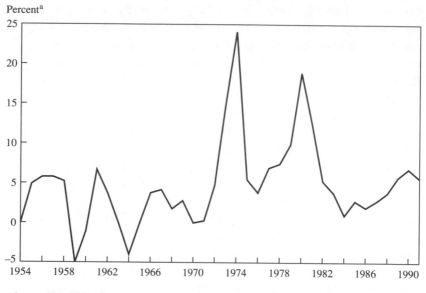

Source: World Bank (1993a).

a. The average inflation rate in other developing countries is about 68.1 percent World Bank (1993).

vanced HPAEs such as Hong Kong and South Korea have had higher rates.

The budget process in Indonesia is also governed by a hard budget constraint. It was introduced by the New Order government in the mid-1960s, which deposed and replaced then-President Sukarno. Under Sukarno, the government ran very high budget deficits partly to finance the struggle to return Irian Jaya from the Dutch and the country's confrontation then with Malaysia. These circumstances led to hyperinflation, a deterioration of infrastructure, and general economic stagnation. General Soeharto made low inflation a basis upon which the legitimacy of the New Order government rested by recruiting a team of technocrats sometimes called the "Berkeley Mafia" to rebuild the economy: stabilizing the macroeconomy was the primary goal. Since then a law was passed institutionalizing a balanced budget and making it the cornerstone of government policy: domestic revenues + foreign assistance (loans and aid) = routine (current) expenditures + development expenditures.[42] Furthermore, the Ministry of Finance acts as housekeeper by institutionalizing a review process requiring each ministry to justify its proposed expenditures on a line-by-line basis. Finally, parliamentary rules restrict parliament to discussions of and debates over budgetary policies. The details and contents of the budget are not subjected to legislative scrutiny.

The balanced budget law, the review process, and the parliamentary rules inhibit politicians and private parties from tinkering with the budget. The law that balances the budget keeps the Indonesian technocrats one step removed from the political demands of legislators and other parties. The only way the latter can override the technocrats is to alter the budget law. Because the balanced budget is a foundation for the legitimacy of the New Order government, signaling competent economic management, it is unlikely to be altered. Hence, the law provides a buffer for the technocrats. The parliamentary rules perform essentially the same function. To gain some control over the budget, Parliament can overturn the current rules. A challenge of this order to the guiding principles set by leadership is unlikely. Armed with these instruments, the Ministry of Finance has, as figure 6-2 shows, brought the inflation rate down since the hyperinflationary years of the mid-1960s and, except for short periods during the two oil crises, inflation has remained low, again even by East Asian standards.

In most developing countries control over the budget is fragmented among different government agencies and legislative tinkering is common.[43] Consequently, it becomes difficult to locate blame when problems arise, in particular, high inflation. Delegating budgetary control to a well-defined and small set of experts and agencies and giving them the necessary instruments to do their jobs offers a low cost way of monitoring performance. In Thailand and Indonesia, leadership has

42. The balanced budget law has an interesting feature that gives the Indonesian technocrats some leverage over foreign borrowing. The law considers foreign borrowing part of the revenue base. Because most of these loans come from international lending institutions and since these institutions impose conditionalities that require countries to contain their budget deficits (domestic revenues less domestic expenditures), technocrats can use the conditionalities and the law to keep foreign borrowing in check. Perhaps because of this restraint also, the technocrats have been persuasive (on issues of macropolicy). To obtain foreign loans, Soeharto may have thought it prudent to follow their advice.

43. See, for instance, UNDP Development Paper 13 (1993).

FIGURE 6-2. *Inflation Rate, Indonesia, 1969–91*
CPI 1987 = 100

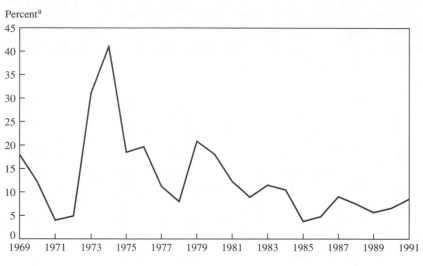

Percent[a]

Source: World Bank (1993a).

a. The average inflation rate in other developing countries is about 68.1 percent World Bank (1993).

managed to do just that. A balanced budget law and related instruments were established and a small group of experts— in Indonesia, the so-called Berkeley Mafia and in Thailand, the four elite agencies[44]—were granted authority and responsibility for maintaining a stable macroeconomic environment.

The Japanese approach to budgetary control bears some similarity to the Thai and Indonesian approach. As in Thailand and Indonesia, Japan's Ministry of Finance acts as housekeeper. But unlike them, it has the discretionary power to "set a finite limit on the expansion, from one year to the next, of any agency's budget."[45] Historically, the limits started out high at 50 percent but have gradually been lowered over the years. That limit has virtually dropped to zero beginning in the early 1980s, and in some instances has been slightly negative, keeping inflation low in Japan (figure 6-3).

44. The four elite agencies are the NESDB, the Ministry of Finance, the Budget Bureau, and the Central Bank. Macroeconomic management has been left almost entirely to these agencies. Christensen and Siamwala (1993).

45. Pempel and Muramatsu (1993a, p. 32).

FIGURE 6-3. *Inflation Rate, Japan, 1961–91*
CPI 1987 = 100

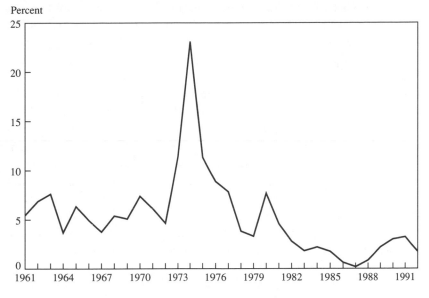

Source: World Bank, East Asia Miracle database (1994).

Institutionalized hard-budget constraints give the Thai and the Indonesian technocrats as well as the MOF bureaucrats in Japan an instrument to inhibit private sector demands from circumventing their mandate—to stabilize the macroeconomy. Like an independent (and competent) central bank, constraints provide a credible signal that high inflation will not be tolerated.[46] They also offer a low-cost mechanism for imposing accountability on the economic bureaucracy.[47]

46. See Cukierman, Webb, and Neptali (1992) on the independence of the central bank.

47. The hard-budget constraint is given more impetus in Japan because of periodic comprehensive reviews of the functions and the size of the bureaucracy. As Pempel and Muramatsu (1993a) show, Japan's bureaucracy is significantly smaller than bureaucracies of other OECD countries—the ratio of government employment to total employment is 7.9 in Japan, the lowest among all OECD countries. Pempel and Muramatsu argue that the institutionalized process of keeping the bureaucracy small has forced ministries to become more efficient since nonperforming programs (with their personnel) get cut off. By losing a program, a ministry's reputation and thus leverage falls in comparison with other ministries. The process induces interministerial competition, which in turn induces efficiency and indirectly enhances accountability.

Policymaking and Statutory Boards: Singapore

Singapore's 620 square kilometers can be traversed in an hour. Being small reduces the challenge of balancing the independence of its bureaucracy with accountability. But small size did not produce a complacent leadership. Indeed officials took several measures to monitor the economic bureaucracy, including establishing statutory boards with well-defined and narrow responsibilities. Sixty-one statutory boards exist, a large number for a country no bigger than Chicago.[48] Each decides whom to hire, promote, and fire, and each is "financially independent in the sense that they are expected to generate their own revenues for their expenditure. . . . Any surplus generated by the statutory boards can be invested and credited to a reserve or capital fund, and deficits may be covered through low-interest government loans and sometimes through government subsidies."[49] Each has been given the authority and flexibility to formulate and implement the policies within its mandate, for example, low-cost housing for the poor or family planning.[50] This approach, delegating responsibility and authority for each element to a single statutory board, helps to identify who is accountable if policies do not work.

The policies that a statutory board recommends are subject to parliamentary approval. However, because a board's management must consult frequently with top leadership and because the PAP has been the dominant party since 1959, approval is presumed. Partly because of this feature, the PAP leadership has often been criticized for autocratic manipulation of the legislature, rendering it a rubber stamp. But the logic set forth above suggests a different story. The lesson, as Robert Bates and Anne Krueger suggest in a different context, is that legislative tinkering with economic policies makes it more difficult to monitor the performance of economic bureaucrats.[51] As long as politically motivated demands are allowed to permeate economic policymaking, the link between economic bureaucrats and outcomes will be blurred.

48. Quah (1987b).
49. Castells and others (1990, p. 220). Statutory boards have to pay back loans from the central government. Moreover, failure to maintain financial viability results in closure. For example, the Housing Development Board (HDB) must recoup its expenses from the rents from public housing units and, as the case may be, the sale of units to tenants.
50. For a detailed discussion of statutory boards see Quah (1987a) and for the Housing Development Board (HDB) see Quah (1987b).
51. Bates and Krueger (1993).

Administrative Guidance: Japan

The bureaucracy in Japan during the 1950s through the 1970s enjoyed wide latitude in policymaking.[52] Laws and regulations were prepared by the bureaucracy in consultation with the private sector and leadership through the deliberation councils and policy committees of the LDP. This structure allowed the bureaucracy to gain authority over policymaking and gave rise to what has been called administrative guidance.[53]

Administrative guidance combines broad mandates with limited enforcement powers that strike a balance between agency independence and agency accountability. The broad mandate includes the authority to plan, adjust, rationalize, inspect, test, and research. Rarely does it include specific regulatory edicts, for example, a law that allows an agency to penalize a firm for pollution. Hence, agencies have few legal levers to enforce policies. Instead a carrot-and-stick approach is used. Government provides generous incentives to private actors, for example, loan subsidies. But because it has no legal levers, it guarantees performance by threatening to indirectly punish failure. Explicit threats are not used since highly specific forms of regulations, for example, antitrust regulations, are weak or may not exist; instead the economic bureaucracy uses other coercive instruments, such as the withdrawal of a license or the reduction in foreign exchange allocation, or the termination of loan subsidies.[54] Administrative guidance thus endows the economic bureaucracy with leverage over economic policymaking, but with a caveat: coercion can only be exercised selectively. It cannot be exercised on a whole industry, as the failed automobile laws proposed by MITI exemplify; it can only be applied to recalcitrant individual firms. If a whole industry rejects a proposed program, the responsible ministry, specifically the responsible bureau, cannot withdraw the license of all the firms in the industry, for this action would freeze

52. MITI and MOF were especially powerful. See Mabuchi (1993) and Johnson (1982).

53. Haley (1993, p. 13) explains administrative guidance: "Typically, a ministry will be granted the authority to intervene and supervise, *i.e. be given a broad mandate* but not to issue binding legal orders subject to sanctions for failure to comply. As a result, the most important levers of power exercised by a ministry are encompassed within its licensing and approval authority." Emphasis added.

54. Administrative guidance is discussed in Yamamura (1986); Haley (1993); Mabuchi (1993).

that industry, thereby compromising growth.[55] Moreover, firms in the industry are likely to register their dissatisfaction through their representatives in the LDP-dominated Diet. Given that shared growth is the foundation for the LDP's continued dominance, this discontent would alarm the LDP leadership, inviting an investigation.[56] Thus, to promote rapid growth, the economic bureaucracy needs to craft a consensus over economic policies among private sector agents in that sector. In this manner administrative guidance indirectly enforces some accountability on the economic bureaucracy.

The deliberation councils have proved useful in this context. As discussed earlier, consent is extracted within councils in which the views of private sector participants are incorporated into a proposed policy. Council agreement is essential to policy approval by the Diet. Councils complement administrative guidance by enhancing the accountability of the economic bureaucracy: private sector agents become the "alarm bells" that help leadership monitor the bureaucracy's performance.

Administrative Guidance: Korea

Shortly after taking power in 1961, South Korean President Park Chung Hee signaled the new direction in Korea's development policies. As part of the reorientation, he ordered the creation of the National Security Council to handle defense issues and the Economic Planning Board (EPB) to manage crucial areas of economic policy. The EPB took over important policy functions from various ministries: planning was moved from the Ministry of Reconstruction; budget preparation and coordination was shifted from the Ministry of Finance; collection and

55. This becomes more credible in light of the fact that the government, and specifically the individual agencies, are liable (legally) for a wide range of negligence. As Haley (1993) argues, "No industrial state provides more extensive relief in the form of monetary compensation for as wide a range of administrative misfeasance. [The National Compensation Law] makes the state liable for all manner of 'negligent' conduct by public authorities, local as well as national, as well as all 'defects' in the 'management of public facilities'. . . . The Law only provides for after-the-fact compensatory damages. . . . Nevertheless, the law does ensure the legal accountability of Japan's civil service (p. 16)."

56. "Diet hearings allow political investigations into the actions of government agencies." Pempel and Muramatsu (1993a, p. 18). Hence, "policies that require extensive direct compulsion tend to be avoided. Voluntary compliance can best be assured by negotiating for consent in the process of formulating policies." Haley (1993, p. 14).

analysis of statistics was moved from the Ministry of Internal Affairs. It was also made responsible for the inflow of foreign capital and technology, a crucial function given the shortage of both.[57]

Park's reorganization gave rise to the EPB and granted that agency extensive authority especially over budgetary matters. Government control over the banking system also gave the economic bureaucracy leverage over big business. Because access to funds was crucial to corporate growth and equity was largely insufficient, private enterprises, the *chaebol* in particular, had to rely on government-backed financing, which enhanced the economic bureaucracy's control over the private sector, especially big business.[58]

But as in Japan, this added leverage was conditional on the promotion of growth and exports. To promote rapid growth and improve export competitiveness, the economic bureaucracy needed private sector acceptance of the proposed economic policies. Although penalties in the form of withheld foreign exchange or temporary withdrawal of a license were effective in persuading recalcitrant firms, they could not be used to coerce all firms in an industry since such broad reprisals could impede growth.[59] Consensus building thus became essential to elicit compliance.

The process of consensus building has been less formal in Korea than in Japan. Policy initiatives can come from the top or the bottom. Sometimes higher-level bureaucrats prepare and submit an agenda to the president. At other times ideas percolate from the bottom up through the system of councils. As already discussed, the process of decisionmaking includes the private sector. Economic ministries often conduct extensive meetings with the private sector. Before a policy becomes law, meetings at different levels have occurred in which officials invite representatives of the private sector to solicit their cooperation.

57. "Since effective coordination among ministries required both power and prestige, the EPB was made a 'Super Ministry.' [It was] the only ministry in the government led by the Deputy Prime Minister." Leipziger and Kim (1992, p. 7).

58. The debt-equity ratio has been inordinately high in Korea. Official statistics indicate ranges of 310 to 380, although the "true" figures are said to be around 160 to 180. Wade (1990). Nevertheless, these figures are still high compared with the ratio in the United States and Great Britain, which ranges from 50 to 90.

59. As in Japan, the government is made liable for decisions that injure an industry's well-being. This constraint, however, may not be an effective one given the weakness of the judiciary in Korea. What made this binding was Park's obsession with growth.

Under Park the link between leadership and bureaucratic account-ability was cemented. Park granted the economic bureaucracy wide-ranging authority while guarding against its capture by the private sector. Viewing bureaucratic competency as essential to economic per-formance, Park introduced features modeled upon the Japanese bu-reaucracy, such as competition in the recruitment and promotion of personnel and control over foreign exchange. He exercised a strong and direct role over the promotion and firing of bureaucrats.[60] His close surveillance of the bureaucracy allegedly included allowing the Korean Central Intelligence Agency to monitor bureaucrats.[61] But he also gave prime importance to the private sector's participation in policymaking. Under him three mechanisms for achieving consensus were introduced. The monthly economic briefing, attended by the president and held at the EPB, involved business leaders and financial organizations. The quarterly trade promotion conference was attended by the president, all the ministers, and virtually all large trading companies. The ministers issued reports on meeting export targets and gave recognition to private sector leaders who made outstanding contributions.[62] The president also attended annual meetings with senior officials of individual minis-tries. The president openly voiced his concerns to prevent ambiguity about where he stood. As did Japan's LDP (though less extensively), Park used the private sector as a means to monitor the performance of the economic bureaucrats.[63]

Although the economic bureaucracy lacked direct or explicit coercive capability, in both Japan and Korea their control of budgetary and financial powers were powerful instruments to gain compliance from industry.[64] One important tool was subsidies to firms that participated in government programs. The subsidies included tax rebates on im-ported raw materials used for exports, low-interest loans, and govern-ment- managed cartels that provided a domestic market cushion for

60. Based on interviews with government officials.

61. See Kang (1994).

62. The annual awards for outstanding export performance were enthusiastically sought after by the big firms.

63. Later, President Chun brought a wider subset of the public into the discussions by launching the Public Economic Education Program to instruct the public on economic priorities such as price stability. Leipziger and Kim (1992).

64. They no longer have this capability. Trade and financial liberalization in the 1980s have effectively eliminated these instruments.

heavy exporters. The bureaucracy also imposed penalties on those firms that failed to meet its objectives or that might refuse to participate in its programs. For instance, it reduced or withheld a firm's foreign exchange allocation or withdrew subsidies to nonperforming firms. Such powers gave the bureaucracy wide discretion over policies that affected the profitability of firms in the private sector. Such discretion could easily have degenerated into bribery and corruption. Consequently, extreme precautions were taken in Korea and Japan to make the process transparent and to monitor bureaucratic performance.

Parallel Bureaucracies and Task Forces: Taiwan

In Taiwan, the locus of decisionmaking over economic planning resides at the very top of the political hierarchy.[65] Although this informal body of top-echelon officials makes the final decisions, they obtain considerable input on macroeconomic issues from the Council for Economic Planning and Development (CEPD—an advisory body), on industrial development from the Industrial Development Bureau (IDB) of the Ministry of Economic Affairs, and on agricultural development from another advisory body, the Council for Agricultural Planning and Development.[66] The responsibility for and authority over implementation resides primarily in the Ministry of Economic Affairs, which is divided into several bureaus and commissions. The IDB is the principal agency that manages the country's industrial development programs, and like MITI in Japan or EPB in Korea, has subtle coercive powers over private industry. But because Taiwan lacked formal deliberation councils, the IDB potentially could have been less accountable for its performance than MITI or the EPB. A different form of accountability had to be established.

The IDB is responsible for both domestic industrial policy and trade and foreign investment policy and has the authority to implement such policies recommended by the CEPD and approved by top leadership. Robert Wade argues that this power has given the agency the capacity

65. "Economic policy making is intensely centripetal. . . . The process is dominated by little more than a dozen individuals. They range from the President, to a number of relevant cabinet ministers, to senior people in several government ministries or commissions, to managers of the largest public enterprises, to a few private businessmen who are well connected to the party." Wade (1990, p. 195).

66. For a thorough discussion of the economic bureaucracy, see Wade (1990), especially chapter 7.

to conduct a limited form of administrative guidance.[67] For instance, the IDB has used the threat of blocking or permitting imports of an intermediate good in order to get the local producers of the domestic substitute and the local users to comply with a policy that is designed to improve the international competitiveness of the producers. Or it can provide domestic market protection to an industry in exchange for an agreement to conform to a timetable for the production of internationally competitive output. The threat of withdrawing protection empowers it to enforce conformity. Although weaker than its counterparts in Japan and Korea, the IDB nevertheless can coerce private industry into complying with mandated policies.

With such powers, the IDB could well overstep its bounds and hinder growth in one or more sectors. Private sector participation in deliberation councils limits such powers in Japan and Korea. Taiwan's industrial structure inhibited such participation, and so another method had to be found. Robert Wade suggests that accountability is probably enforced (at least in part) through a parallel organization created by the KMT to monitor the performance of the different bureaus.[68] The parallel organization's function is to identify agencies that fail to pursue their mandates efficiently and to alert top leadership.

In Japan and Korea, the response to identifying a failing agency is to reorganize—to cut off sick parts, dismissing incompetent personnel. Taiwan's response is to create a task force of private and public sector experts (including foreign consultants) to improve (and sometimes take over) the functions the agency has failed to perform well. A task force employs the expertise and knowledge of the private sector to improve the formulation and implementation of policies that the bureaucracy has failed to accomplish efficiently. It is not governed by civil service rules but functions as a private sector entity: it does not have preallocated funds from the budget and obtains funding from the government

67. Wade (1990).

68. Wade (1990). The KMT inherited an extensive system of agricultural associations from the Japanese, the colonial rulers of Taiwan from the late 1890s to the end of the World War II. The Japanese used this system to "facilitate police surveillance and control over the local population." Amsden (1979, p. 346). As discussed earlier, the KMT reactivated the system, organizing farmers into local associations and handing control over to party supporters. The KMT also established public service centers in each township "staffed by full-time party officials whose job it is to advance party interests and maintain surveillance over the associations and the local government administration." Wade (1990, p. 242).

on a project-to-project basis; it can hire and pay competitive salaries.[69] Its impact has generally been to invigorate "sick portions" of the bureaucracy, compelling agencies to improve their performance or, failing that, to close ailing sections by not replacing employees who leave or retire. Hence, the use of task forces effectively enforces some accountability on the economic bureaucracy.[70]

Anticorruption Agencies: Hong Kong

By virtue of being a colony of the United Kingdom, Hong Kong's bureaucracy enjoys great independence from domestic political pressures.[71] But precisely because it has wide-ranging powers, the bureaucracy had to be prevented from using those powers extralegally, for example, extracting rents from the private sector. In fact, a reputation for corruption handicapped growth in Hong Kong until the 1970s. In February of 1974, in an effort to overcome that reputation, the governor transferred responsibility for detecting and investigating corruption from the police force to an outside organization, the Independent Commission Against Corruption (ICAC). Situating the responsibility for investigating corruption in a department within the police force had created conflicts of interest since the department found it difficult to investigate and prosecute corruption among police.[72] This result weakened the legitimacy and thus the effectiveness of the department.

The commissioner of the ICAC reports directly to the governor and is not subject to the purview of any other branch of the Civil Service. Staff members are paid higher salaries than equivalent civil servants, but they can be dismissed from their jobs without appeal if there is any suspicion of wrongdoing. Opportunity costs to suspected wrongdoers in the ICAC therefore are greater than to members of the civil service. The main instrument of the commission is the extensive powers

69. See Wade (1990), especially chapter 7.

70. An example is the industrial automation task force. "From a professional staff of five at the start of 1983, numbers grew to ninety by early 1984 and are expected to go to near 150. Its core work is to promote the introduction of automative technology by individual firms. One method is by lectures. . . . The more important method is the factory visit. Six hundred and fifty factories were visited in 1983, most of them more than once." Wade (1990, p. 214).

71. Singapore also created an anticorruption agency for similar reasons. But the approach is somewhat different. See Quah (1993) for a comparison.

72. See Quah (1993).

of investigation that it has been granted. It can authorize officers to examine bank accounts and safe deposit boxes; require subjects to verify property acquisition, expenditures, liabilities, or any money sent out of Hong Kong on their behalf; question on oath persons other than suspects; restrict the disposal of a suspect's property during an investigation or apply to a court to restrict its disposal if it is held in the name of a third party; obtain, through order of a magistrate, the surrender of travel documents while an investigation is in progress. Investigating officers may also arrest suspects without a warrant for other offenses disclosed during the investigation of a suspected offense. Suspects may be detained for forty-eight hours for the purpose of further inquiries.

With such extensive powers, the ICAC could easily become a predator, using its powers to extract rents and concessions from innocent victims. To mitigate such possibilities, the commission is subject to annual review by several advisory committees, one for each of the departments within the commission. The committees consist of private citizens who are appointed by the governor and who come from different sectors of the community. They report their findings to an Overall Advisory Committee, which then discusses the findings with the governor. Needless to say, the success of the ICAC implies a high degree of integrity at the level of the governor's office, for such powers improperly used could lead to "negative corruption"—charging political opponents with corruption.[73]

That the ICAC has reduced corruption in the bureaucracy is indicated by survey results. Between 1974 and 1983, 22,391 corruption complaints were received, 10,642 were investigated, and 3,033 prosecutions resulted. The annual report of 1982 indicated a 74.9 percent conviction rate. In a survey conducted in the same year, 59 percent of complainers willingly identified themselves, compared with 33 percent when the commission began work, suggesting that the public had by then developed more confidence in the commission. In that same survey, 95.6 percent of those interviewed considered corruption less prevalent and regarded corruption as a moral and social offense. This response sharply contrasted with the early 1970s, when corruption was regarded

73. The powers of the ICAC are just as extensive as those of the Anti-Corruption Agency in Singapore. And yet, in contrast to Singapore, rarely does one hear Hong Kong lambasted as an autocratic state, with the capacity to infringe upon the population's basic human rights.

as a necessary evil and as normal business practice. Finally, 87 percent feared corruption would recur if the commission disbanded.

Getting the Balance Right

East Asian bureaucratic performance is often attributed to the insulation provided by political leaders. In an extensive literature that implicitly touts a regime's authoritarian character as a virtue, the ability of the technocratic core to pursue rational economic policies is linked to the fact that authoritarian leaders do not have to make concessions to public opinion, that autocrats protect or insulate their officials from interest group pressures.[74] The discussion in this chapter suggests that this interpretation is not entirely accurate. Although leaders in the HPAEs did establish wide-ranging measures to give the economic bureaucracy substantial independence, they also saw to it that the private sector participated in the decisionmaking process in ways that made that bureaucracy accountable for its performance.

Implications for Economic Growth

Philip Keefer and Stephen Knack suggest a possible linkage between a reputable economic bureaucracy and economic growth.[75] Using survey data contained in the International Country Risk Guide (ICRG) and from the Business Environmental Risk Intelligence (BERI), they estimate the effect of bureaucratic quality, bureaucratic delay, corruption, the risk of expropriation, and the risk of contract repudiation on average per capita growth from 1960 to 1989 in a sample of developing and developed countries while controlling for variables normally included in endogenous growth models.[76] The first measure, bureaucratic

74. See, for instance, Johnson (1987); Haggard (1990).

75. Keefer and Knack (1993) present a relatively comprehensive econometric analysis of institutions and their impact on growth. More precisely, they investigate the relationship measures of institutional capacity and the ability of relatively less developed countries to catch up with the more developed. They define institutional capacity broadly as capacity to secure and enforce property rights.

76. Bureaucratic quality refers to "relative autonomy from political pressure, the strength and expertise to govern without drastic changes in policy or interruptions in government services, and the existence of an established mechanism for recruiting and training. . . .*corruption* to high government officials demanding special payments and illegal payments generally expected throughout lower levels of government. . .and *bureaucratic delays* to the speed and efficiency of the civil service including processing of customs clearances, foreign exchange remittances, and similar applications." Emphasis

FIGURE 6-4. *Unexplained Growth Rate and Bureaucratic Effectiveness*

Index of bureaucratic effectiveness[a]

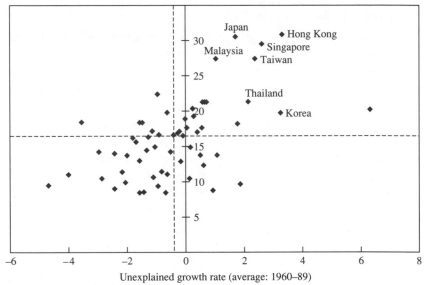

Unexplained growth rate (average: 1960–89)

Source: Keefer and Knack (1993).

a. Data for the index of bureaucratic effectiveness are for 1982, 1984, or 1985, depending on which year the data first became available. For most countries included in the data set, 1982 was the first year for which data were available. The data do not vary much over time (beginning 1982).

quality, reflects the relative power of the bureaucracy. The first and third measures reflect the level of competence and the second and third the degree of integrity and accountability of the bureaucracy. The two risk indexes tend to capture the "pro-growth inclination" of leadership: if leadership were truly interested in promoting growth, then it would commit to nonexpropriation and to upholding contracts in order to attract investment; these commitments would imply a concern by leadership to ensure that bureaucrats adhere to the two principles. Thus the risk indexes are indirect measures of the accountability of the bureaucracy to the leadership.

Keefer and Knack introduce each of the above measures individually into an otherwise standard (econometric) endogenous growth model

added. Keefer and Knack (1993, p. 31). Depending on the availability of the data across countries, sample size was either 46 or 97.

and find that each has a significant and independent effect on per capita growth rates.[77] They show that an increase in the bureaucratic quality index by one integer point increases growth by about .30 percentage point; a decline in the bureaucratic delay index increases growth by about 1 percentage point; a decline in the corruption index increases it by about .30 percentage point; an increase in the index of nonexpropriation by about .14 percentage point; and an increase in the contract enforcement index by 1.4 percentage points.[78] Assuming an annual per capita growth rate of about 2 percent (about the average for all countries), the bureaucracy's effectiveness could account for 7 percent to 70 percent of the growth rate.

Figure 6-4 compares the HPAEs with other developing countries in terms of "unexplained growth"—growth not attributable to factor accumulation, relative price changes, and distance from the world technological frontier—and an index of the overall effectiveness of the bureaucracy (measured along the vertical axis). The index consists of an additive score of four indexes taken from ICRG: bureaucratic quality, corruption, risk of expropriation, and risk of contract repudiation. The figures shows that the index of bureaucratic effectiveness correlates highly with the "unexplained" portion of the growth rate with the HPAEs (excluding Indonesia) exhibiting higher indexes associated with higher "unexplained growth." This suggests that bureaucratic effectiveness (as we have defined it) has made a significant marginal contribution to the economic performance of the HPAEs.

77. Using a different data set, Mauro (1993) also investigates the effect of bureaucratic credibility (with a related but different measure) on growth after controlling for political instability. He finds that it has a significant effect on economic growth.

78. This is derived from their regression estimates in tables 3 through 5 of the paper. The bureaucratic quality and corruption indexes range from a low of 0 to a high of 6 and the bureaucratic delay index from a low of 1 to a high of 4.

Seven

Conclusion:
The Rise of East Asia
in Comparative Perspective

IN THE HISTORY of the modern world, few countries have overcome the barriers to development. Aside from the Western democracies, only the high-performing Asian economies have succeeded so far. Japan and the first-tier high performers—Korea, Taiwan, Hong Kong, and Singapore—followed by the second-tier high performers—Thailand, Malaysia, and Indonesia—have all experienced rapid, relatively broad-based growth in the past twenty to thirty years. Their remarkable performance offers new perspectives on the kinds of political institutions that encourage economic growth. Representative institutions that legitimized the rule and restrained the discretion of monarchs claiming absolute powers were key to the Anglo-American success.[1] In East Asia's high performers, a different set of political institutions emerged to establish regime legitimacy and limit government discretion over economic policies.

The regimes responsible for East Asia's unusual success are widely perceived as authoritarian, even dictatorial. This perception occurs largely because of the failure of Western observers to recognize in East Asia systems for ensuring accountability and consensus building that differ from Western-style institutions. But the mechanisms that Westerners expect to see—written constitutions, elected legislators, a formal system of checks and balances—are but one set of solutions to establishing regime legitimacy and guaranteeing limits on government action. These mechanisms are not the only ones for obtaining public support

1. Root (1989, 1994; Weingast and North (1989).

or that can be effective in restraining ruling cliques from overriding the economic rights of others. Our analysis of the institutions governing economic policymaking in Japan, South Korea, Taiwan, Singapore, Hong Kong, Thailand, Malaysia, and Indonesia has shown that there are indeed other ways of achieving the same outcomes, especially at the early stages of economic development. Despite substantial variations, these countries share enough common elements to suggest a developmental model that differs from the trajectory of the Western democracies and from the autocracies of the past and present.

Developing countries often fail to achieve rapid sustained growth because their governments fail to establish legitimacy and their political systems do not adequately protect the property rights of economic actors in the emerging private sector. Many developing country governments, past and present, are largely authoritarian. And many have assumed power through coercive means. Possessing wide discretionary powers over civil society, they can confiscate property just as easily as they can confer ownership. Their coercive powers allow them to selectively enforce property rights.[2] Weak property rights in turn discourage investment in human and physical capital.[3] With limited investment, conflicts over access to resources escalate, weakening already fragile political support. Without a popular mandate, prospects of the regime's being overthrown increase. Investment then further contracts. Conflict intensifies until a new regime arises. The cycle repeats itself. The low-level equilibrium trap is sealed.

By contrast, a secure political foundation for economic rights underlies the Asian miracle. Regimes in East Asia's high performers recognized the importance of courting the business community. By giving bargaining power to constituent groups in exchange for information needed to formulate and implement rational economic policies, East Asian rulers overcame private sector reservations about their intentions. Communication mechanisms such as deliberation councils help nurture investor confidence in the ability of the government to restrain itself from highly discretionary and arbitrary policymaking. Leadership fortified this commitment to growth through the creation of a reputable economic technocracy, if not bureaucracy, that could enforce rules

2. Weingast (1993).
3. North (1981); North and Thomas (1973).

impartially. The risk of confiscation or ex post expropriation of private sector assets was reduced. Firms became more willing to invest in productive activities. Growth ensued.

The process was solidified by leadership's commitment to shared growth. Wealth sharing insured broad social support, thereby reducing the threat that the regime would fall to destructive rent seeking or insurgency. It encouraged the belief that the government was acting on behalf of citizen interests, so that unpopular decisions could be made more easily acceptable. The increased likelihood of regime survival meant that development could be sustained over time and that profits were not likely to be confiscated by an incoming coalition. Reducing the danger of massive political change expanded the investment horizons of the private sector.[4] In turn, long-term investment created greater wealth, further increasing support. Thus, through shared growth, firms kept economic profits while leadership reaped political benefits—stability and the right to rule.

In sum, the inconsistencies that usually plague autocracies have not occurred in the successful East Asian economies. There, governments have not discounted the future; they have not acted like roving bandits taking as much as they can in a single raid. They have considered the future output of society and have offered incentives to productive investment (physical and human) that are typically found only in the Western democracies. These governments have created what Thomas Metzger and Ramon Meyers have called an "inhibited center" that ensured economic rights of the citizens for the indefinite future.[5]

The Asian miracle was built upon a broad consensus that the need for rapid economic growth was so urgent that it justified mobilizing the entire society as if for war. China had just witnessed the greatest peasant revolution in world history, and no country in the region felt safe from the threat of similar political upheaval. Despite the absence of multiparty elections in the high performers, political contestability was among the highest in the developing world. In fact, South Korea, Taiwan, and Singapore were sufficiently vulnerable to political risk to warrant the reputation of being among the least likely of developing nations to succeed. But leaders in these countries as well as in the other high performers

4. "Assured political stability [in Korea] tended to lengthen time horizons and made manufacturing a much more feasible alternative to commerce as a field of entrepreneurial activity." Mason and others (1980, p. 143).

5. Metzger and Meyers (1991).

understood that failing to deliver economic development meant more than just losing an election. A consensus emerged in each country on the appropriateness of shared growth as a legitimating principle.

The political institutions developed by the high performers reflected this commitment to shared growth: governments established narrow, highly controlled channels for representation and dialogue between state and society. Increasingly, however, these countries are facing rising demands for representation from previously unrepresented groups. Significant opposition parties have sprouted in Thailand, Korea, Taiwan, and Japan. A long-time opposition leader is now president of Korea. The LDP in Japan has lost its majority in the Diet. In Indonesia, some key members of Parliament have publicly voiced concern over the ever-growing monopolies of individuals closely associated with the regime's leadership. And even in Singapore, the presidential candidate of the dominant People's Action Party won the most recent elections by a much smaller margin than in the past.

The next challenge for Asia's high performers, like the last, will be political. As the early conditions that produced a consensus for growth give way to a more affluent, complex, and diverse body politic, can new procedures for the aggregation of social choice be found? Can they be as effective as the old in forging consensus about rational economic policies? Increasingly, governments in the high-performing countries will have to take into account the divergent ambitions of a society that has achieved a fairly high level of affluence. Political forms will have to accommodate a policy dialogue in which fundamental issues are no longer at issue and in which small differences are likely to be deeply contested. Success will depend on finding political institutions that can resolve the clashes of tastes and preferences that inevitably arise from the creation of wealth. How to consume wealth can prove more controversial than how to produce it.

Whatever the future holds for East Asia's high performers, their past has implications for countries that continue to struggle to get on the path of rapid, sustained growth. Although the geopolitical motivation for the kinds of policies undertaken by the high performers cannot be reproduced, the systems they adopted illustrate possibilities for getting on this path. And as governments in other developing countries address their own unique challenges, they can study these systems to gain a better understanding of how and why they worked and ultimately to discover their own best starting points.

References

Adelman, Irma, and Sherman Robinson. 1978. *Income Distribution Policy in Developing Countries: A Case Study of Korea*. Oxford University Press.

Akerlof, George. 1970. "The Market for 'Lemons': Quality Uncertainty and the Market Mechanism." *Quarterly Journal of Economics* 84 (August): 488–500.

Alam, Shahid. 1989. *Governments and Markets in Economic Development Strategies: Lessons From Korea, Taiwan, and Japan*. Praeger Publishers.

Alesina, Alberto, and Roberto Perotti. 1992. "Income Distribution, Political Instability, and Investment." Working Paper 53. Washington: Institute for Policy Reform.

Amsden, Alice. 1979. "Taiwan's Economic History: A Case of *Etatisme* and a Challenge to Dependency Theory." *Modern China* 5 (July): 341–80.

———. 1989. *Asia's Next Giant: South Korea and Late Industrialization*. Oxford University Press.

Aoki, Masahiko. 1988. *Information, Incentives, and Bargaining in the Japanese Economy*. Cambridge University Press.

Balassa, Bela. 1988. "Lessons of East Asian Development: An Overview." *Economic Development and Cultural Change* 36 (Supplement): S273–S290.

Barro, Robert. 1991. "Economic Growth in a Cross Section of Countries." *Quarterly Journal of Economics* (May): 407–43.

Bates, Robert, and Anne Krueger. 1993. *Political and Economic Interactions in Economic Policy Reform*. Oxford: Blackwell Publishing Company.

Bhagwati, Jagdish, and T. Srinivasan. 1982. "The Welfare Consequences of Directly-Unproductive Profit-Seeking (DUP) Activities." *Journal of International Economics* 13 (August): 33–44.

Bhattacharya, Amar, and Mari Pangestu. 1992. "Indonesia: Development Transformation since 1965 and the Role of Public Policy." In *Lessons of East Asia: A Country Studies Approach*. World Bank, forthcoming.

Birdsall, Nancy, and Richard Sabot. 1993. "Virtuous Circles: Human Capital, Growth, and Equity in East Asia." Washington: World Bank, Policy Research Department.

Boyce, James. 1992. "The Revolving Door? External Debt and Capital Flight: A Philippine Case Study." *World Development* 20 (March): 335–49.

Brunetti, Aymo, and Beatrice Weder. 1994. "Political Credibility and Economic Growth in Less Developed Countries." *Constitutional Political Economy* 5: 23–43.

179

Campos, Jose Edgardo, and Donald Lien. 1994. "Asymmetric Information, Rent-Seeking, and the Deliberation Council." Working Paper 1321. Washington: World Bank, Policy Research Department.

Campos, Jose Edgardo, and Hadi Esfahani. Forthcoming. "To Initiate Public Enterprise Reform or Not: What Drives the Decision?" *World Bank Economic Review.*

———. and Hadi Esfahani. 1995. "Credible Commitment and Success with Public Enterprise Reform." Washington: World Bank, Policy Research Department.

Campos, J. E., and Sanjay Pradhan. 1996. "The Impact of Budgetary Institutions on Expenditure Outcomes: Binding Governments to Fiscal Performance." Washington: World Bank, Policy Research Department.

Castells, Manuel, L. Goh, and R. Y-W Kwok. 1990. *The Shek Kip Mei Syndrome,* London: Pion Limited.

Chang, Oh-Hyun. 1992. "The Role of Non-Market Institutions in Korean Economic Development during the 1960s and 1970s." Washington: World Bank, Policy Research Department.

———. 1993. "The Role of Non-Market Institutions in Korean Economic Development." Washington: World Bank, Policy Research Department, Finance and Private Sector Development.

Cho, Yoon Je, and Thomas Hellman. 1993. "Government Intervention in Credit Markets: An Alternative Interpretation of Japanese and Korean Experiences from the New Institutional Economics Perspective." Washington: World Bank, Policy Research Department, Financial Sector Development Department.

Choi, Young Back. 1984. "Industrial Policy as the Engine of Economic Growth in South Korea: Myths and Reality." In *The Collapse of Development Planning,* edited by Peter Boettke, 231–55. New York University Press.

Chu, Yun-han. 1992. *Crafting Democracy in Taiwan,* National Policy Research Series 2.T. Taipei, Taiwan: Institute for National Policy Research.

Crone, Donald. 1993. "States, Elites, and Social Welfare in Southeast Asia." *World Development* 21 (January): 55–66.

Crouch, Harold. 1978. *The Army and Politics in Indonesia.* Cornell University Press.

Cukierman, A., S. Webb, and J. Neptali. 1992. "Measuring the Independence of the Central Banks and Their Effect on Policy Outcomes." *World Bank Economic Review* 6 (September): 353–98.

Cumings, Bruce. 1987. "The Origins and Development of the Northeast Asian Political Economy." In *The Political Economy of the New Asian Industrialism,* edited by F. Deyo, 44–83. Cornell University Press.

Dalpino, Catharin. 1990. "Thailand's Search for Accountability." *Journal of Democracy* 2 (Fall): 61–72.

David, Paul. 1985. "Clio and the Economics of QWERT." *American Economic Review* 75 (May): 332–37.

De Long, J. Bradford. 1991. "Did J. P. Morgan's Men Add Value?" In *Inside the Business Enterprise*, edited by Peter Temin, 205–36. University of Chicago Press.

De Silva, Migara. 1993. "The Political Economy of Macroeconomic Changes in a Revenue/Commodity Windfall: Performance of the Nigerian and Indonesian Economies in the 1970s." Ph. D. dissertation, Washington University.

Deyo, Frederic. 1987. "State and Labor: Modes of Political Exclusion in East sian Development." In *The Political Economy of the New Asian Industrialism*, edited by Frederic Deyo, 182–202. Cornell University Press.

Dollar, David. 1991. *Decision and Change in Thailand: Three Studies and Support of the Seventh Plan*. Washington: World Bank.

Dollar, David, and Peter Brimble. 1990. *Technology Strategy and Policy for Industrial Competitiveness: A Case Study in Thailand*. Washington: World Bank.

Esfahani, Hadi. 1992. "Reputation, Product Quality, and Production Technology in LDC Markets." University of Illinois at Urbana-Champaign, Department of Economics.

Fei, J., G. Ranis, and S. Kuo. 1979. *Growth with Equity: The Taiwan Case*. Oxford University Press.

Fields, Gary. 1992. "Changing Labor Market Conditions and Economic Development in Hongkong, Korea, Singapore, and Taiwan." Washington: World Bank, Policy Research Department.

Gelb, Alan. 1985. *Oil Windfalls: Blessing or Curse?* Research Publication. Washington: World Bank.

Gershenkron, Alexander. 1962. *Economic Backwardness in Historical Perspective*. Harvard University Press.

Gilligan, Thomas, and Keith Krehbiel. 1987. "Collective Decisionmaking and Standing Committees: An Informational Rationale for Restrictive Amendment Procedures." *Journal of Law, Economics, and Organization* 3 (Fall): 287–336.

Glassburner, Bruce. 1978. "Political Economy and the Soeharto Regime." *Bulletin of Indonesian Economic Studies* 14 (November): 24–51.

Gold, Thomas. 1986. *State and Society in the Taiwan Miracle*. M. E. Sharpe.

Grief, Avner, Paul Milgrom, and Barry Weingast. 1994. "Coordination, Commitment, and Enforcement: The Case of the Merchant Guild." *Journal of Political Economy* 102 (August): 745–76.

Gupta, Dipak. 1990. *The Economics of Political Violence*. Praeger.

Haggard, Stephan. 1990. *Pathways from the Periphery: The Politics of Growth in the Newly Industrializing Countries*. Cornell University Press.

Haggard, Stephan, Byung Kook-Kim, and Chung In-Moon. 1990. "The Transition to Export-Led Growth in South Korea, 1954–1966." WPS 546. Washington: World Bank, Policy Research Department.

Haley, John. 1993. "Japan's Post War Civil Service: The Legal Framework." Working Paper 93–27. Washington: World Bank, Studies and Training Division.

Hamilton, Gary C., M. Orru, and N. Biggart. 1987. "Enterprise Groups in East Asia: An Organizational Analysis." *Financial Economic Review* 161: 78–106.

Handley, Paul. 1986. "Coming to the Defense of the Family Business." *Far Eastern Economic Review.* May 22: 40–43.

Harris, T., and M. Todaro. 1970. "Migration, Unemployment, and Development: A Two Sector Analysis." *American Economic Review* 60 (March): 126–42.

Hawes, Gary. 1987. *The Philippine State and the Marcos Regime: The Politics of Export.* Cornell University Press.

Hirose, Haruko. 1993. "The Civil Service System and Personnel Administration." In *The Management and Reform of Japanese Government,* edited by Toshiyuki Maujima and Minoru O'uchi. Tokyo: Institute of Administrative Management.

Hughes, Helen, ed. 1988. *Achieving Industrialization in East Asia.* Cambridge University Press.

Husken, Frans, and Benjamin White. 1989. "Java: Social Differentiation, Food Production, and Agrarian Control." In *Agrarian Transformations: Local Processes and the State in Southeast Asia,* edited by Gilliam Hart, Andrew Turton, and Benjamin White, 235–65. University of California Press.

Hutchcroft, Paul. 1991. "Oligarchs and Cronies in the Philippine State: The Politics of Patrimonial Plunder." *World Politics* 43 (April): 414–50.

International Monetary Fund. 1993. *World Economic Outlook.* (May) Washington.

Inoki, Takenori. 1992. "Japanese Bureaucrats at Retirement: The Mobility of Human Resources from Central Government to Public Corporations." Working Paper 93–32. Washington: World Bank.

International Road Federation. Various years. *World Road Statistics.* Washington.

International Telecommunication Union. 1993. *Yearbook of Common Carrier Telecommunication Statistics.* Geneva.

Itoh, M., and S. Urata. 1993. "Small and Medium Enterprise Support Policy of Japan." Working Paper 1403. Washington: World Bank, Policy Research Department.

Japan Development Bank and Japan Economic Research Institute. 1993. "Policy-Based Finance: The Experience of Postwar Japan." Tokyo.

Jazairy, I., M. Alamgir, and T. Panuccio. 1992. *The State of World Rural Poverty: An Inquiry into Its Causes and Consequences.* Published for the International Fund for Agricultural Development, New York University Press.

Johnson, Chalmers. 1982. *MITI and the Japanese Miracle.* Stanford University Press.

———. 1987. "Political Institutions and Economic Performance: The Government-Business Relationship in Japan, South Korea, and Taiwan." In *The Political Economy of the New Asian Industrialism,* edited by Frederic Deyo, 136–64. Cornell University Press.

Kang, David. 1994. "Defense, Development, and Transactions Costs: The Case of South Korea." Ph.D. Dissertation. University of California, Berkeley.

Karnow, Stanley. 1989. *In Our Image: America's Empire in the Philippines.* Random House.

Keefer, Philip, and Stephen Knack. 1993. "Why Don't Poor Countries Catch

Up? A Cross National Test of an Institutional Explanation." Working Paper 60. IRIS, College Park, University of Maryland.

Kim Kihwan, and Danny M. Leipziger. 1994. *Korea: A Case of Government-Led Development*. In *Lessons of East Asia: A Country Studies Approach*, edited by Danny Leipziger. World Bank, forthcoming.

Kim, Paul. 1988. *Japan's Civil Service System: Its Structure, Personnel, and Politics*. Greenwood Press.

———. 1993. "Recruitment of Higher Civil Servants in Modern Japan." Working Paper 93–54. Washington: World Bank.

Kim, L., and J. Nugent. 1993. "Korean SMEs and their Support Mechanisms: An Empirical Analysis of the Role of Government and Other Non-Profit Organizations." Washington: World Bank, Policy Research Department.

Krehbiel, Keith. 1991. *Information and Legislative Organization*. University of Michigan Press.

Kuo, Wan-Yong. 1976. "Income Distribution by Size in Taiwan Area—Changes and Causes." *Industry of Free China* 45.

Kuznets, Simon. 1955. "Economic Growth and Income Inequality." *American Economic Review* 45 (March): 1–28.

Landa, Janet Tai. 1994. *Trust, Ethnicity, and Identity: Beyond the New Institutional Economics of Ethnic Trading Networks, Contract Law, and Gift-Exchange*. University of Michigan Press.

Laothamatas, Anek. 1988. "Business and Politics in Thailand: New Patterns of Influence." *Asian Survey* 28 (April): 451–70.

———. 1992. *Business Associations and the New Political Economy of Thailand*. Westview.

Lau, Lawrence, and Jong-Il Kim. 1992. "The Sources of Economic Growth of the Newly Industrializing Countries on the Pacific Rim." Stanford University.

Lee, Chung. 1992. "The Government, Financial System, and Large Private Enterprises in the Economic Development of South Korea. *World Development* 20: 187–97.

Lee, T. H., and T. H. Shen. 1974. "Agriculture: Dynamic Force for Industrialization." In *Agriculture's Place in the Strategy of Development*, edited by T.H. Shen, 66–70. Taipei: JCRR.

Leipziger, Danny, and Kim Kihwan. 1992. "Korea: A Case of Effective Government-Led Growth." Paper presented at the World Bank Workshop on the Role of Government and East Asian Success, East-West Center, Honolulu.

Levine, Ross, and David Renelt. 1992. "A Sensitivity Analysis of Cross-Country Growth Regressions." *American Economic Review* 82 (September): 942–63.

Levy, Brian. 1994. "Technical and Marketing Support Systems for Successful Small and Medium Size Enterprises in Four Countries." PRD Working Paper 1400. Washington: World Bank.

Lichbach, Mark. 1989. "An Evaluation of 'Does Economic Inequality Breed Political Conflicts?' Studies." *World Politics* 41: 431–70.

Liddle, William. 1985. "Soeharto's Indonesia: Personal Rule and Political Institutions." *Pacific Affairs* 58 (December): 68–90.

————. 1991. "The Relative Autonomy of the Third World Politician: Soeharto and Indonesian Economic Development in Comparative Perspective." *International Studies Quarterly* 35 (Spring): 403–27.

Lim, Youngil. 1981. "Government Policy and Private Enterprise: Korean Experience in Industrialization." Research Monograph 6. Berkeley: Center for Korean Studies.

Mabuchi, Masaru. 1993. "Financing Japanese Industry: The Interplay between the Financial and Industrial Bureaucracies." Working Paper 93–35. Washington: World Bank.

MacIntyre, Andrew. 1990. *Business and Politics in Indonesia*, Southeast Asian Publication Series 21. Asian Studies Association of Australia and Allen and Unwin Ltd.

Mackie, James. 1988. *The Chinese in Indonesia: Five Essays*. Melbourne: Thomas Nelson for Australian Institute of Economic Affairs.

————. 1990. "Property and Power in Indonesia." In *The Politics of the Middle Class in Indonesia*, edited by K. Young and R. Tonter, 71–95. Melbourne: Center for Southeast Asian Studies, Monash University.

Manning, Chris. 1987. "Public Policy, Rice Production, and Income Distribution: A Review of Indonesia's Rice Self-Sufficiency Program." *Southeast Asian Journal of Social Science* 15 (1): 66–82.

Mason, Edwin, and others. 1980. *The Economic and Social Modernization of the Republic of Korea*. Harvard University Press.

Mauro, Paolo. 1993. "Corruption, Country Risk, and Growth." Harvard University.

McCoy, Alfred. 1993. "The Rent-seeking Families and the Philippine State: A History of the Lopez Family." University of Wisconsin, Center for Southeast Asian Studies.

Metzger, Thomas, M., and Ramon H. Myers. 1991. "Introduction, Two Diverging Societies." In *Two Societies in Opposition: The Republic of China and the People's Republic of China after Forty Years*, edited by Ramon H. Myers. Stanford, Calif.: Hoover Institution Press.

Milgrom, Paul, and John Roberts. 1991. *Economics, Organization, and Management*. Prentice Hall.

Miller, Robert, and Mariusz Sulinski. 1994. "Trends in Private Investment in Developing Countries." International Finance Corporation Discussion Paper 20. Washington: World Bank.

Morell, David, and Chai-anan Samudavanija. 1981. *Political Conflict in Thailand: Reform, Reaction, and Revolution*. Oelgeschlager, Gunn, and Hain Publishers.

Munasinghe, Mohan. 1987. *Rural Electrification for Development: Policy Analysis and Applications*. Westview.

Muscat, Robert. 1994. *The Fifth Tiger: A Study of Thai Development Policy*. Helsinki: United Nations University Press.

National Personnel Authority. 1992. *Annual Report, Government of Japan*. Tokyo.

Nishio, Akihiko. 1993. "Land Administration Project in Indonesia: Executive Project Summary." Washington: World Bank.

North, Douglas. 1981. *Structure and Change in Economic History*. W. W. Norton.

————. 1985. "Institutions, Transactions Costs, and Economic Growth." Political Economy Working Paper. Washington University, Center for Political Economy.

North, Douglas, and Robert Thomas. 1973. *The Rise of the Western World: A New Economic History*. Cambridge: The University Press.

O'Donnell, Guillermo. 1973. *Modernization and Bureaucratic Authoritarianism*. University of California Press.

Okimoto, Daniel. 1989. *Between MITI and the Market: Japanese Industrial Policy for High Technology*. Stanford University Press.

Olson, Mansur. 1965. *The Logic of Collective Action*. Harvard University Press.

————. 1982. *The Rise and Decline of Nations*. Yale University Press.

Ono. 1992. *Jissenteki Sangyo Seisakuron*, in Japanese, Tsusho Sangyo Chosakai.

Oshima, Harry. 1993. *Strategic Processes in Monsoon Asia's Economic Development*. Johns Hopkins University Press.

Parker, Noel. 1983. "Classic Conceptions of the State: Introduction." In *State and Societies*, edited by David Held and others. New York University Press.

Pempel, T. J., and Michio Muramatsu. 1993a. "The Japanese Bureaucracy and Economic Development: Structuring a Proactive Civil Service." Working Paper 93–26. Washington: World Bank.

————. 1993b. "The Evolution of the Civil Service before World War II." Working Paper 93–30. Washington: World Bank.

Psacharopoulos, George, and others. 1992. *Poverty and Income Distribution in Latin America: The Story of the 1980s*. Washington: World Bank.

————. 1987a. "Statutory Boards." In *Government and Politics of Singapore*, edited by J. Quah, Chan Heng Chee, and Seah Chee Meow, 120–45. Singapore: Oxford University Press.

————. 1987b. "Public Housing." In J. Quah, Chan Heng Chee, and Seah Chee Meow, eds. *Government and Politics of Singapore*, 233–58. Singapore: Oxford University Press.

Quah, Jon. 1993. "Controlling Corruption in City States: A Comparative Study of Hongkong and Singapore." Paper presented at the Conference on 'The East Asian Miracle.' Center for Economic Policy Research and the Asia-Pacific Research Center, Stanford University.

Raisuddin, Ahmed, and Narendi Rustagi. 1987. "Marketing and Price Incentives in African and Asian Countries: A Comparison." In *Agricultural Marketing Strategy and Pricing Policy*, edited by Dieter Elz, 104–18. Washington: World Bank.

Ramirez, Carlos. 1992. "Did J. P. Morgan's Men Add Liquidity?" Harvard University.

Ranis, Gustav. 1989. "The Role of Institutions in Transition Growth: The East Asian Newly Industrializing Countries." *World Development* 17 (September): 1443–53.

Reid, Gary. 1992. "Civil Service Reform in the Latin American: Lessons of Experience." LATPS Occasional Paper 6. Washington: World Bank.

Reidel, James. 1988. "Economic Development in East Asia: Doing What Comes

Naturally?" In *Achieving Industrialization in East Asia*, edited by H. Hughes. Cambridge University Press.

Rhee, Yung Whee, Bruce Ross-Larson, and Gary Pursell. 1984. *Korea's Competitive Edge: Managing the Entry into World Markets*. Johns Hopkins University Press for the World Bank.

Riggs, Fred. 1966. *Thailand: The Modernization of a Bureaucratic Polity*. Honolulu: East-West Center.

Robison, R. 1985. "Class, Capital, and the State in New Order Indonesia." In *Southeast Asia: Essays in the Political Economy of Structural Change*, edited by R. Higgott and R. Robison, 239–335. London: Routledge and Kegan Paul.

Robison, Richard. 1986. *Indonesia: The Rise of Capital*, Asian Studies Association of Australia and Allen and Unwin Ltd., Southeast Asian Publication Series 13. Melbourne.

Rodrik, Dani. 1989. "Promises, Promises: Credible Policy Reform via Signalling." *Economic Journal* 99: 756–72.

———. 1993. "Industrial Organization and Product Quality: Evidence from South Korean and Taiwanese Exports." In *Empirical Studies of Strategic Trade Policy*, edited by P. Krugman and A. Smith. University of Chicago Press.

Root, Hilton. 1989. "Tying the King's Hands: Credible Commitments and Royal Fiscal Policy during the Old Regime." *Rationality and Society* 1: 240–58.

———. 1994. "Private Sector Development in Africa: Institutional Foundations for a Market Economy in Tropical Africa." Hoover Institution.

Rotwein, E. 1964. "Economic Concentration and Monopoly in Japan." *Journal of Political Economy* 72 (June): 262–77.

Salleh, Ismael, and Sahathevan Meyanathan. 1992. "Growth, Equity, and Structural Transformation in Malaysia: Role of the Public Sector." In *Lessons of East Asia: A Country Studies Approach*. World Bank, forthcoming.

Samudavanija, Chaianan. 1992. "High Speed Growth and High Performance in a Technocratic Polity: The Thai Case." Washington: World Bank, Policy Research Department.

Schlossstein, Steven. 1991. *Asia's New Little Dragons: The Dynamic Emergence of Indonesia, Thailand, and Malaysia*. Chicago: Contemporary Books.

Sen, Amartya. 1973. *On Economic Inequality*. Oxford: Clarendon Press.

———. 1981. "Public Action and the Quality of Life in Developing Countries." *Oxford Bulletin of Economics and Statistics* 43: 287–319.

Shepsle, Kenneth, and Barry Weingast. 1994. "Positive Theories of Congressional Institutions." *Legislative Studies Quarterly* 29: 149–319.

Shepsle, Kenneth, Barry Weingast, and Christopher Johnsen. 1981. "The Political Economy of Benefits and Costs: A Neoclassical Approach to Distributive Politics." *Journal of Political Economy* 89: 642–64.

Siamwala, Amar, and Scott Christensen. 1993. "Institutional and Political Bases of Growth-Inducing Policies in Thailand." In *Lessons of East Asia: A Country Studies Approach*. World Bank, forthcoming.

Staniland, Martin. 1985. *What is Political Economy? A Study of Social Theory and Underdevelopment*. Yale University Press.

Steedman, David. 1993. "Indonesia: Civil Service Issues," Discussion Paper EA3PH. Washington: World Bank.

Taiwan, China. Various years. *Statistical Yearbook*.

Taiwan, China. Various years. *Statistical Yearbook of the Republic of China*. Taipei: Directorate General of Budget, Accounting, and Statistics.

Taiwan, China. 1990. *Statistics for Small and Medium Enterprises*. Ministry of Finance.

Todaro, Michael. 1969. "A Model of Labor Migration and Urban Unemployment in Less Developed Countries." *American Economic Review* 59 (September): 138–48.

Tullock, Gordon. 1987. *Autocracy*. Dordrecht, The Netherlands: Kluwer Academic Publishers.

Turnbull, C. Mary. 1977. *A History of Singapore: 1819–1975*. Kuala Lumpur: Oxford University Press.

Turnham, David. 1993. *Employment and Development: A New Review of Evidence*. Paris: OECD.

United Nations. 1990. *Economic and Social Survey of Asia and the Pacific*. New York.

United Nations Development Program. 1992. *Human Development Report*. New York.

United Nations Development Program. 1993. *The Control and Management of Government Expenditure: Issues and Experience in Asian Countries*. Development Papers 13. United Nations. New York.

Vatikiotis, Michael. 1993. *Indonesia under Suharto: Order, Development, and Pressure for Change*. London and New York: Routledge Press.

Wade, Robert. 1985. "The Market for Public Office: Why the Indian State Is Not Better at Development." *World Development* 13 (April): 467–97.

———. 1990. *Governing the Market: Economic Theory and the Role of Government in East Asian Industrialization*. Princeton University Press.

———. 1994. "Public Bureaucracy and the Incentive Problem: Organizational Determinants of a 'High Quality Civil Service': India and Korea." Washington: World Bank.

Weingast, Barry. 1993. "The Economic Role of Political Institutions." Working Paper IPRS46. Washington: Institute for Policy Reform.

Weingast, Barry, and Douglas North. 1989. "The Evolution of Institutions Governing Public Choice in 17th Century England." *Journal of Economic History* 49 (December): 803–32.

Williamson, Oliver. 1985. *The Economic Institutions of Capitalism*, New York: Free Press.

Wintrobe, Ronald. 1994. "The Dictator's Dilemma." University of Western Ontario, Department of Economics.

Woo, Jung-en. 1991. *Race to the Swift: State and Finance in Korean Industrialization*, New York: Studies of the East Asian Institute, Columbia University.

World Bank. Forthcoming. *The Changing Role of the State: Public Enterprise Reform in Developing Countries.* Policy Research Report. Washington.

World Bank. 1990a. *Growth, Poverty Alleviation, and Improved Income Distribution in Malaysia: Changing Focus of Government Policy Intervention.* Washington.

World Bank. 1990b. *Indonesia: Poverty Assessment and Strategy Report.* Washington.

World Bank. 1993a. *The East Asian Miracle: Public Policy and Economic Growth.* Policy Research Report. Washington: World Bank and Oxford University Press.

World Bank. 1993b. *Thailand: Poverty Assessment Report.* Washington.

World Bank. 1992. *World Competitiveness Report.* Lausanne, Switzerland: IMD and World Economic Forum.

World Bank. Various years. *World Development Report.* Washington.

Wurfel, David. 1988. *Filipino Politics: Development and Decay.* Cornell University Press.

Wyatt, David. 1982. *Thailand: A Short History.* Yale University Press.

Yamamura, Kozo. 1982. *Policy and Trade Issues of the Japanese Economy.* University of Washington Press.

———. 1986. "Caveat Emptor: The Industrial Policy of Japan." In *Strategic Trade Policy and the New International Economics*, edited by Paul Krugman, 169–209. MIT Press.

Yeung, Yue-man. 1973. "National Development Policy and Urban Transformation in Singapore: A Study of Public Housing and the Marketing System." Research Paper 149. Department of Geography, University of Chicago.

Index